Contents: Preface •
Changing Patterns o[...]
from Mexican States [...]
Bustamante; Macro-Pat[...]
gration between Mexico [...] U.S., *Richard C.
Jones*; Origins in Mexico: Illegal Mexican Immigra-
tion to California from Western Mexico, *W. Tim
Dagodag*; Agricultural Development and Labor
Mobility: A Study of Four Mexican Subregions,
Kenneth D. Roberts; Patterns of U.S. Migration
from a Mexican Town, *Joshua S. Reichert and
Douglas S. Massey*; External Dependency and the
Perpetuation of Temporary Migration to the United
States, *Raymond E. Wiest*; Network Migration and
Mexican Rural Development: A Case Study, *Rich-
ard Mines*: Destinations in the United States: Occu-
pational and Spatial Mobility of Undocumented
Migrants from Dolores Hidalgo, Guanajuato, *Rich-
ard C. Jones, Richard J. Harris, and Avelardo
Valdez*; The Channelization of Mexican Nationals to
the San Luis Valley of Colorado, *Phillip R. Guttier-
rez*; Illegal Mexican Aliens in Los Angeles; Locational Characteristics, *W. Tim Dagodag*; Geographical Patterns of Undocumented Mexicans and
Chicanos in San Antonio, Texas: 1970 and 1980,
Avelardo Valdez and Richard C. Jones.

About the Editor: Richard C. Jones is Associate
Professor of Geography in the College of Social
and Behavioral Sciences at the University of Texas
at San Antonio.

Patterns of
Undocumented Migration

Patterns of
Undocumented Migration

Mexico and the United States

edited by
R I C H A R D   C. J O N E S

ROWMAN & ALLANHELD
PUBLISHERS

JV 6493 .P37 1984

Patterns of undocumented migration

ROWMAN & ALLANHELD

Published in the United States of America in 1984
by Rowman & Allanheld, Publishers
(A division of Littlefield, Adams & Company)
81 Adams Drive, Totowa, New Jersey 07512

Library of Congress Cataloging in Publication Data
Main entry under title:

Patterns of undocumented migration.

Includes index.
    1. Aliens, Illegal—United States—Addresses, essays,
lectures.   2. Alien labor, Mexican—United States—Ad-
dresses, essays, lectures.   3. United States—Emigration
and immigration—Addresses, essays, lectures.   4. Mexico—
Emigration and immigration—Addresses, essays, lectures.
I. Jones, Richard C., 1942–   .
JV6493.S67   1984   325′.272′0973   83-27233
ISBN 0-86598-130-2

84 85 86 / 10 8 9 7 6 5 4 3 2 1

Printed in the United States of America

Contents

Tables

Figures

Preface

The idea for this book originated in my reading of the pioneering studies of undocumented migration by Samora, Bustamante, Cornelius, and North and Houstoun. Specifically, the brief but tantalizing presentation of the areal breakdowns of migrant origins and destinations, given with little commentary, piqued my geographic curiosity. Conversations with both Bustamante and Cornelius encouraged me to pursue the topic in depth. This book is the result.

This book is the culmination of two years of effort on the part of the editor, a board of editorial reviewers, and a number of typists. I am indebted to several institutions and people who provided financial, moral, and mechanical support when the road seemed endless. Boris Graizbord, my friend and geographic *compadre* at the Universidad Nacional Autonoma de Mexico (now at the Colegio de Mexico), invited me to give a series of lectures at the UNAM in Mexico City in early 1979. This provided me with an opportunity to become acquainted with Mexican researchers and research. I made follow-up visits there during 1980 and 1981. The Association of American Geographers provided me with a small research grant to collect data from the Mexican Center for Labor Information and Statistics in Mexico City in March 1980. Finally, in December 1981, the Trull Foundation of Palacios, Texas, provided two UTSA sociology colleagues (Harris and Valdez) and me with funds for a pilot study of undocumented mobility in the United States (carried out during late December 1981 and early January 1982 in central Guanajuato state). These funds were important in providing the incentive and means for my early research on undocumenteds, the results of which appear in four chapters of this volume (1, 3, 9, and 12).

Early in the process, I set up an editorial review board composed of specialists in population geography and regional development. Ole Gade, Barry Lentnek, Curtis Roseman, and Stephen White all put in considerable work on the manuscripts I sent them. I greatly appreciate their efforts.

My division director in Social and Policy Sciences, Dr. Thomas Bellows, has provided both encouragement and vital secretarial help in the latter stages of the project. I wish to give special thanks to Karen Bodai, who typed the final draft of the chapters and most supporting materials, and supervised the rest. In catching stylistic inconsistencies and grammatical or logical errors, Karen is without equal. Other valuable typing assistance was provided by Henry Alvarado, Victoria Cross, Alice Jimenez, and Rose Nelson.

Of the twelve chapters in the book, six (1, 7, 9, 10, 11, and 12) were prepared for this volume, and the other six (2, 3, 4, 5, 6, and 8) are revisions of earlier work, two of these (3 and 6) having been extensively revised.

I would like to dedicate this book to my two children, Ricky and Katrina Jones, whose love provided continual replenishment throughout the whole process.

Richard C. Jones

1
Introduction

RICHARD C. JONES

More than a hundred articles and over twenty books have emerged since 1970 on the topic of undocumented (illegal alien) migration to the United States from Mexico. The topic has been researched by anthropologists, economists, sociologists, historians, political scientists, and geographers. Still, the issues involved in this topic are as current, controversial, and unresolved as ever. There are several reasons for this. First, the crucial "impact" questions—whether undocumenteds exacerbate or ameliorate conditions of employment and social well-being at the destination, and whether their remittances and experiences aid or hinder village development in Mexico—remain unanswered. Second, the issue has become politicized by the popular media, with the result that the public has become polarized into groups who either support all possible sanctions and controls, or object to any controls at all. Third, recent research has shown that the phenomenon has roots that are decades old, which cannot be eliminated as one would prune the superfluous branches of a tree. Finally, the issue continues to be viewed—by both popular media and many scholars alike—in aggregate, macro terms. In such terms one can neither adequately understand the place-specific push and pull forces that motivate different migrant subpopulations, nor the differential impacts they have on their destinations.

This book addresses the final point—the absence of a concern in the literature for spatial patterning and its explanation. The principal focus is on patterns of migrant origins, destinations, and pathways, and the factors that explain these patterns.

This approach offers a detailed view of the migration process, one which addresses questions that are unanswerable in other studies. For example, (a) What are the distinguishing structural characteristics of areas which send few migrants as opposed to those which send many?

(see chapters by Bustamante; Jones; and Roberts). (b) How prevalent is stepwise migration in Mexico prior to migration to the United States? (see Bustamante; Dagodag, chap. 4; and Guttierrez). (c) Does migration behavior differ for migrants with different personal characteristics and experiences? Specifically, if we separate illegal and legal migrants, or migrants who have "succeeded" (experienced occupational, social, or spatial mobility in the U.S.) from those who haven't, do we find certain systematic underlying characteristics (age, educational background, number of trips, economic status in Mexico)? (see Reichert and Massey; Mines; Jones, Harris, and Valdez). (d) How do repatriated migrants' earnings flow within and outside the village and what impacts do these flows have on the village? (see Wiest; Mines). (e) In what parts of destination cities do undocumented migrants tend to concentrate, and what is the process of residential succession vis-à-vis other groups? (see Dagodag, Chap. 11; Valdez and Jones). (f) What places make up the macro-migration field for Mexico-U.S. undocumented migration? This latter question is important enough to the theme of this book that it will be answered now. A single map (Figure 1.1) synthesizes the research conclusions of many spatial studies. It also identifies specific origin areas in the United States and destination areas in Mexico which are investigated in this volume.

This book thus represents an emerging subset of research concerned with spatial questions. The subset can be shown on a graph in which both *spatial scale* and the *degree of spatial pattern analysis* are represented (Figure 1.2). The studies plotted on the graph are illustrative rather than exhaustive. Also, the location of these studies is schematic rather than quantitative. In particular, the locations of studies involving more than one spatial scale and including both spatial and aspatial analyses have to be approximated. The result, nevertheless, is a useful organizing framework.

"Traditional" research has been carried out at spatial scales from the village or town to the country level, both in Mexico and in the United States. Despite this areal variety, little in the way of spatial analysis has taken place. Traditional studies are able to outline broad push and pull forces, but cannot tell us whether these forces differ among origins and destinations (for example, whether border states in Mexico send migrants with different qualities and motivations from those originating in interior states). In some cases (e.g. Samora, 1971; Cornelius, 1981a; Cardenas, 1976) distributions of migrants by origin and destination states are given, but they are not analyzed in depth. These studies do suggest important questions—for example, why southern Mexico sends so few migrants and why better-off as well as

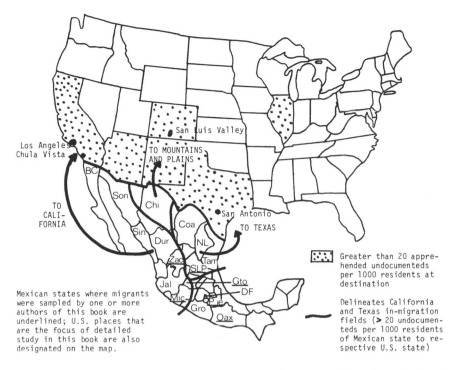

Figure 1.1 In-migration fields for Mexican undocumenteds to the U.S., Mid-1970s (State abbreviations: BC = Baja California; Chi = Chihuahua; Coa = Coahuila; DF = Distrito Federal; Dur = Durango; Gro = Guerrero; Gto = Guanajuato; Jal = Jalisco; Mic = Michoacan; NL = Nuevo Leon; Oax = Oaxaca; Pue = Puebla; Sin = Sinaloa; SLP = San Luis Potosí; Son = Sonora; Tam = Tamaulipas; Zac = Zacatecas.)

poor states send large numbers of migrants (see Jones; Roberts; and Dagodag, Chap. 4, for answers to these questions).

Research on spatial patterns is a relatively recent addition to the literature, the pioneering work of Gamio (1930) and Hancock (1959) notwithstanding. As the motives, characteristics, and numbers of migrants have become better known, research has shifted to questions of impact, policy, and changing locational trends in light of economic and policy changes. The chapters of this book provide illustrations of the full range of spatial studies. One type of study focuses upon the characteristics of migrants from different Mexican states and regions (Bustamante; Dagodag, Chap. 4; Roberts). Another type analyzes social and economic interactions at the village level, and flows between the village and the outside world (Wiest; Mines). These types are both predominantly origin-related. Other studies go into con-

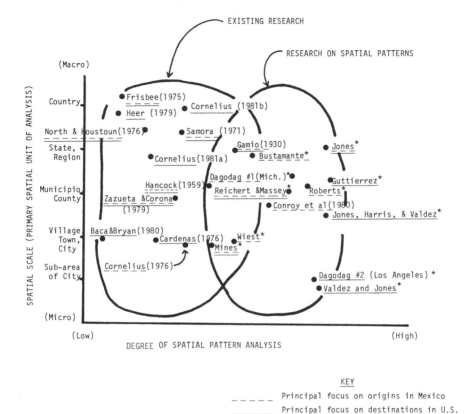

Figure 1.2 Spatial pattern research versus existing research on Mexican undocumenteds

siderable detail, mapping out the paths of individual migrants and groups of migrants at both the regional and interurban scales (Reichert and Massey; Jones, Harris, and Valdez; Guttierrez). Still others show how migrant patterns at national scale (Jones) and intraurban scale (Dagodag, Chap. 11; Valdez and Jones) change across time. Such studies are primarily concerned with U.S. destinations. They engage in a somewhat "higher" form of spatial analysis than the former set, but the conclusions of both sets are equally valuable. The analysis of intraurban undocumented patterns (Dagodag, Chap. 11; Valdez and Jones) is a topic not previously investigated. The two intraurban chapters on undocumenteds are unique to this volume.

What follows is a synopsis of the remaining eleven chapters of the book. The first section (two chapters) is a macro-scale overview of areal migration patterns, with emphasis both on Mexican origins (Bustamante) and on U.S. destinations (Jones). The second section (five chapters) includes studies of particular Mexican origins. Three of these are towns and cities of Michoacán state (Dagodag, Chap. 4; Wiest; and Reichert and Massey); one is a village in Zacatecas state (Mines); and four others are agricultural subareas of four Mexican states—Guanajuato, Oaxaca, San Luis Potosí, and Puebla (Roberts). The third and final section (four chapters) includes studies of movement into subregions of Texas (Jones, Harris, and Valdez) and Colorado (Guittierrez); as well as studies of intraurban movement in Los Angeles (Dagodag, Chap. 11) and San Antonio (Valdez and Jones).

The chapter by Bustamante (Chapter 2) presents a number of penetrating insights from interviews conducted by the Mexican government in the mid-1970s with undocumented migrants recently deported by U.S. immigration authorities. Bustamante finds that interior states in Mexico contribute more migrants than do border states, and that this trend was clearly on the increase during the early 1970s. This finding parallels that of Jones (1984, forthcoming). The increase in interior migration may indicate that agriculture in interior states suffered serious setbacks over this period, a conclusion also verified in other research (Cross and Sandos 1981, pp. 62–73). Bustamante's data reveal only slight incidence of stepwise migration at state scale; migrants tended to travel directly from their states of birth to the United States, without intervening residences in other states. It is interesting that the author finds a high percentage of his sample to be unemployed in the U.S. at the time of capture; that most had been in the U.S. less than two months; and that a higher percentage worked in agriculture in the U.S. than they did in Mexico. These conclusions appear to reflect the low-status, transient nature of the group reflected in his sample, rather than the nature of the undocumented population as a whole. Bustamante makes a convincing argument that undocumenteds are a net benefit to the U.S. He does not, however, endorse a continuation of the status quo because this would perpetuate the "underclass" status of Mexican citizens in the United States. Instead of the status quo, Bustamante suggests an innovative spatial trade policy in which the U.S. allocates some of its "foreign aid" food production to production units in Mexico. These units would be located in undocumented emigrant zones of the country; thus, their development should alleviate push factors in Mexico. Other authors in this book might question whether such a strategy would lessen or increase U.S. labor migration from such zones. Nevertheless, the policy is an interesting and constructive alternative to the restrictionist measures frequently suggested in other studies.

The chapter by Jones (Chapter 3) is based upon recent INS (Immigration and Naturalization Service) data and data from other studies (North and Houstoun 1976; Zazueta and Corona 1979). It shows how concentrated the destinations are in the United States, yet how dispersed the origins are within Mexico. In both countries, however, the phenomenon is spreading to involve states farther from the border. In the U.S., this is attributable both to immigration policy (concentration of personnel along the border) and to the attractions of higher wages away from the border. In Mexico, spread is attributable to worsening interior agricultural conditions, as we noted in the discussion of Bustamante's work. These conclusions should hardly be taken with alarm, because impact questions are as yet unresolved. Finally, Jones uncovers channels of migration between specific Mexican and U.S. states, often over long distances and ignoring intervening opportunities. This suggests not only present-day kinship and village networks, but also historic migration pathways forged during the *bracero* period, the period of the Mexican Revolution, and the railroad-building era in the U.S. Southwest.

The first chapter to focus on a specific Mexican origin is Dagodag's (Chapter 4) on Michoacán. The author uses I-213 form apprehension data from the Chula Vista Border Patrol sector for the early 1970s. Michoacán represents a state with more than 20 percent of the Chula Vista apprehensions, and one with a long history of migration to the United States. Dagodag's sample, like those of the two previous chapters, is of a highly transient subpopulation. It is therefore not surprising to find high unemployment rates and short residence times in the U.S. Dagodag's study *is* surprising in its locational detail. He maps out individual towns and villages, graduated in size in proportion to numbers of migrants, and analyzes the pattern. As in a few other studies (Jones 1983; Cornelius 1976), he finds the sending areas concentrated in a few parts of the state. These are the rural highland basins and plains, where the population is *mestizo* as opposed to *indio*, and where conditions are not the poorest or the best, but somewhere in between. This latter finding needs to be considered more seriously by scholars and policy-makers alike, because it suggests that programs directed to the poorest subregions in Mexico will have little impact on undocumented migration to the U.S. In fact, they may accelerate such migration by giving potential migrants the desire and the means to travel to the U.S.

The chapter by Roberts (Chapter 5) begins with this same point, placing undocumented migration within the context of Lewis's dual economy model. Is it correct, Roberts asks, to view undocumented migration as a permanent flow of labor from low-productivity Mexican agriculture into urban-oriented jobs in the U.S.? Based on extensive farm survey data collected by the author and by the Mexican Centro de Investigaciones Agrarias in the mid-1970s, he argues not. His reasons are enlightening: (a) undocumented migration tends to be temporary or circular, not permanent; (b) it originates in regions undergoing agricultural change and development, not in the poorest agricultural regions; and (c) migrants from agricultural areas have other significant income sources in addition to farming. Thus, U.S. migration is a function of lessened demand for local labor among people with above-average means and expectations. The four areas investigated represent four different points on an agricultural development continuum, only the last (highest) of which exhibits migration to the U.S. The Mixteca Baja (Oaxaca) sends no migrants because of distance, ethnic mix (large numbers of Indians), and low income demands; while Las Huastecas (San Luis Potosí) and Valsequillo (Puebla), although better off than the Mixteca Baja, still have incomes too low to undertake the risk of sending migrants to the U.S., and they rely instead on income from local and regional off-farm sources to meet household needs. The Bajio (Guanajuato) exhibits high U.S. migration levels precisely because it is more technologically advanced, because this technology has displaced farm labor, and because farm families are large enough and well-off enough to afford the risk. Roberts's important conclusions suggest the family-linked or network nature of U.S. migration (as do those of Mines), and the structural determinants of migration (as do those of Wiest).

Reichert and Massey (Chapter 6) focus upon the characteristics of migrants from a small community in Michoacán state (Guadalupe), based upon data they gathered indirectly from knowledgeable informants in the village. This community, like others mentioned in this section, is highly dependent upon U.S. migration (88 percent of the households interviewed in 1977–78 had at least one individual who had been there, and 54 percent of all 15–64-year olds were active U.S. migrants!) Typical of such communities, Guadalupe has a long tradition of migration (going back to 1900 or so); atypical is the fact that almost 80 percent of the active migrants are legal as opposed to illegal. The main thrust of the chapter is a comparison of legal and illegal migrants; illegals are found to send fewer family members (despite larger family sizes than legals), including significantly fewer women. Furthermore, illegal migrants are much more constrained in their spatial movement; the great majority moved either to southern California or to central Florida, and stayed there for the duration of their visits. Only about one-fifth moved from Florida to North Carolina, Pennsylvania, or Michigan, after reaching the United States. In contrast, legal migrants not only moved about among the Pacific states and among states in the East, but also moved readily between Florida and the West Coast. Reichert and Massey's analysis offers valuable insights on how legalizing illegal Mexican migration to the U.S., through amnesty provisions such as those in the Simpson-Mazzoli Bill, could change the character of the streams. Their results imply that such a legitimation process would result in more women, in their dispersion of migrants to more northerly areas, and in greater overall mobility of migrants. Although they would stay shorter periods, they would be settler migrants as opposed to sojourners.

Wiest's chapter (Chapter 7) is the first of two dealing with social and economic impacts of U.S. wage-labor migration on the village of origin. Wiest is critical of standard interpretations such as "economic refugee" theory or the concept of undocumented migration as a form of foreign aid to Mexico. His research in Acuitzio, Michoacán, over a period of seventeen years, has convinced him that U.S. migration (both legal and illegal) has polarized the villagers and made them more dependent both on migration to the U.S. and on goods and services originating outside the village. Although, he notes, it is true that overall levels of living and health standards have greatly improved, the village has had to pay a rather high price for these, in the form of (a) a retrenchment of the role of women as subservient to men; (b) the appearance of a migrant "elite" class who have become the landowners, money-lenders, merchants, and conspicuous consumers; (c) the tendency for a greater percentage of villager earnings to be spent *outside* the village, on goods and services from the United States, Mexico City, and regional cities such as Morelia; (d) the inflation of land values and increase of absentee ownership; and (e) a decline of traditional jobs in the city, due especially to mechanization and to the externalization of input purchases. Wiest's discussion of point (c) is accompanied by a most useful flow diagram tracing migrant expenditures to all levels of the Mexican urban hierarchy and to the U.S. His conclusions remind us that what may benefit individuals in a system may not necessarily benefit the system overall. He forces us to rethink traditional migration theory, and to consider the long-run negative externalities associated with a form of internal colonialism that disturbs and reshapes the traditional, egalatarian way of life in the village.

Mines's chapter (Chapter 8) is a convenient bridge between origin and destination studies. Its focus is on migrant family networks and their role in shaping migration flows. He argues that push and pull forces are inextricably bound together within such networks. The incentives provided by a pool of relatives at origin and destination both compel a given move, and determine whether it is successful or not. His study site is Las Animas, a poor village in the state of Zacatecas which he surveyed in 1979; almost two-thirds of its U.S. migrants are undocumented. Mines finds, just as Reichert and Massey, that the legal migrants are more permanent in the United States; he also finds them to be younger and more occupationally integrated at the destination. Regarding impacts on the origin, legal migrants become a local social elite who are better off than the undocumented group, who in turn are better off than the nonmigrant group. Neither the legals nor the undocumenteds make any substantial productive investments in the village. Land is purchased but production stagnates; an absentee landholder class is created; consumption increases but with few benefits to the village; etc. These arguments coincide with those of Wiest and Reichert (1981). They underline the conclusion that despite higher overall levels of living, the village suffers from an increasing maldistribution of wealth and an increasing dependence on outside jobs and purchases. This trend is accelerating in Las Animas, as young first-time migrants strive for permanent U.S. residence, and do not seem to care if ties with the village are lost.

The chapter by Jones, Harris, and Valdez (Chapter 9) introduces the last section of the book, dealing with destinations in the United States. It contributes, indirectly, to an understanding of destination impacts, by following the spatial and occupational mobility of individual migrants from a town in central Guanajuato state (Dolores Hidalgo), surveyed by the authors during December 1981 and January 1982. The town was chosen on the basis of its frequency of migration to Texas. Sampled migrants are found to be temporary, all male, and equally distributed between the rural and urban sectors by the time of their latest jobs. The authors find a substantial incidence of upward mobility between agricultural jobs in south Texas and urban jobs in San Antonio, Houston, or Dallas. After the first urban job is attained, however, it is more difficult for migrants to improve their job status, even though they continue to move about spatially. Dolores Hidalgo migrants exhibit considerably more spatial mobility than undocumented migrants from Guadalupe in Michoacán (Reichert and Massey), but this is mainly due to the fact that Jones, Harris, and Valdez considered mobility over many trips to the U.S., whereas Reichert and Massey considered mobility only on the latest visit. The most notable conclusion in the Jones, Harris, and Valdez study is that migrants do not progress occupationally beyond a certain level of urban job. Rather than displacing resident workers, they are filling urban jobs not commonly held by such workers.

Guttierrez's chapter (Chapter 10) is interesting because it analyzes undocumented migration to a rural destination—the San Luis Valley of Colorado. Respondents were contacted by chain referral methods and interviewed in the summers of 1979 and 1980. Guttierrez's study population is more established and spatially stable than others analyzed in this volume. Average time in the United States is 3.2 years, mean age is 28.4 years, and the sample includes significant numbers of women (21 percent). Most migrants (some four-fifths) are rural-based. The migrants originate predominantly (79 percent) in Chihuahua state, in major urban areas such as Chihuahua City, Juarez, and Riva Palacio. Although most of them stop for a few days in some southwestern U.S. city before continuing to the Valley, they do not work in these cities. Thus, migration is highly channelized between certain Mexican cities and the Valley. It has a long tradition as a settlement area for Mexican migrants, not just as a "zone of transition" as in south Texas (see Jones, Harris, and Valdez).

Dagodag's study of illegal aliens in Los Angeles (Chapter 11) takes us, finally, to the intraurban scale in the U.S., to the processes of initial settlement and dispersion that have typified other immigrant groups in this country. Dagodag's estimate of the locations of illegal Mexican aliens (IMAs) in Los Angeles is derived from interviews with school officials, and from school district data showing phenomenally-large increases in Hispanic pupils. These increases he attributes to the influx of illegal aliens' children into the district. Several trends emerge from the author's analysis of the resultant spatial patterns: (a) The densest areas of settlement are found in the central business district and adjacent areas. (b) Jobs in heavy industry and warehousing often held by illegals are available in such locations. (c) The poorest residential areas are chosen, although a few IMAs are found in high-rent zones. (d) A form of residential succession has occurred, in which both whites and blacks have moved out to suburban and exurban zones, while Hispanics have filled in the near-CBD areas. It is noteworthy that the bulk of the IMAs are found in the southeastern parts of Los Angeles, in a relatively homogeneous Hispanic zone. In this area, schools are highly segregated ethnically. Other areas with white or black minorities (the San Fernando Valley and the southwestern areas, respectively) and more-integrated populations have fewer IMAs. This suggests that Mexican illegals are associated with the densest cores of Hispanic settlement in a city.

The final chapter, by Valdez and Jones (Chapter 12), is based upon analysis of INS records (I-213 forms); a sample was taken of deported aliens apprehended in the San Antonio District, for whom street address in San Antonio was recorded. The authors draw many of the same conclusions for San Antonio as Dagodag does for Los Angeles. In San Antonio, the densest settlement areas are near the CBD (just to the west and southwest). These are, as in Los Angeles, the traditional manufacturing and wholesaling areas of the city, where food-processing firms, warehouses, stockyards, produce markets, small restaurants, repair shops, etc., provide jobs for undocumenteds. Residential segregation typifies undocumented areas as in Los Angeles, although this segregation is less in San Antonio. Finally, undocumenteds have penetrated Hispanic areas on the near westside of San Antonio. At the same time Hispanics have dispersed farther out, along Loop 410, and whites have moved even farther out, into the far reaches of Bexar County. This trend recalls that of Los Angeles. The authors uncover a strengthening tie between the residential location of undocumenteds, and low-status housing locations in the city, suggesting that undocumenteds may be restricted, or may be restricting themselves, by their legal and economic status. Thus, undocumenteds remain at the bottom of the social ladder, reinforced by both spatial and economic segregation. Their initial locations may be tailored to their economic means and needs for security; in the long run, entrenchment in such areas and jobs maintains their disenfranchised minority status.

In summary, this book brings together spatial analyses of undocumented Mexican migration at different geographic scales, for both origins in Mexico and destinations in the United States. It treats the areal patterns of this phenomenon, the place-specific forces that motivate it, and some of the impacts upon both origins and destinations. In both subject matter and point of view, it stands apart from prior edited volumes on Mexican immigration, which have been more concerned with such topics as historical trends, U.S. legislation, overall economic and social impacts on the U.S., the political economy of migration (particularly Mexico's view), and implications of the migration for governmental policy in the U.S. and Mexico. After reading these chapters, one cannot help but acknowledge the complexity of the phenomenon, and the degree to which it permeates all aspects of life in parts of Mexico and in the U.S. Southwest. One must recognize that there are many benefits from the phenomenon, in both Mexico and the U.S., and that some of the problems which arise stem from this "success." Finally, one cannot help but admire the migrants themselves, who risk and endure so much in coming to the U.S. to sew our garments, build our homes, repair our roads, and serve our meals. Whatever their legal status and their ultimate impacts, they are worthy of our respect.

References

Baca, Reynaldo, and Dexter Bryan. 1980. "Citizenship aspirations and residency rights preferences: The Mexican undocumented worker in the binational community." Report for Sepa-Option, Los Angeles, California.

Cárdenas, Gilberto. 1976. "Manpower Impact and Problems of Mexican Illegal Aliens in an Urban Labor Market." Ph.D. dissertation, University of Illinois.

Conroy, Michael E., Mario Coria Salas, and Felipe Vila-Gonzalez. 1980. "Socioeconomic incentives for migration from Mexico to the U.S.: Magnitude, recent changes, and policy implications." Austin: Institute of Latin American Studies, Mexico-U.S. Migration Research Report #1.

Cornelius, Wayne. 1981a. "The future of Mexican immigrants in California: A new perspective for public policy." Program in U.S.–Mexican Studies, Working Paper #6. La Jolla: University of California, San Diego.

————. 1981b. "Immigration, Mexican development policy, and the future of U.S.–Mexican relations." Program in U.S.–Mexican Studies, Working Paper #8. La Jolla: University of California, San Diego.

————. 1976. *Mexican Migration to the United States: The View from Rural Sending Communities.* Cambridge: Center for International Studies, Massachusetts Institute of Technology.

Cross, Harry E., and James A. Sandos. 1981. *Across the Border: Rural Development in Mexico and Recent Migration to the United States.* Berkeley: Institute of Governmental Studies, University of California.

Frisbee, Parker. 1975. "Illegal migration from Mexico to the United States: A longitudinal analysis." *International Migration Review* 9:3–13.

Gamio, Manuel. 1930. *Mexican Immigration to the United States: A Study of Human Migration and Adjustment.* Chicago: The University of Chicago Press.

Hancock, Richard H. 1959. *The Role of the Bracero in the Economic and Cultural Dynamics of Mexico.* Stanford, California: Hispanic American Society, Stanford University.

Heer, David M. 1979. "What is the annual net flow of undocumented Mexican immigrants to the United States?" *Demography* 16:417–23.

Jones, Richard C. 1983. "Explaining origin patterns of undocumented migration to south Texas in recent years." Paper presented at the Second Conference, Regional Impacts of U.S.–Mexico Economic Relations, Tucson, Arizona, May 25.

————. 1984. "Changing patterns of undocumented Mexican migration to south Texas." *Social Science Quarterly* (in press).

North, David S., and Marion F. Houstoun. 1976. *The Characteristics and Role of Illegal Aliens in the U.S. Labor Market: An Exploratory Study.* Washington, D.C.: Linton & Co., for the Employment and Training Administration, U.S. Department of Labor.

Reichert, Joshua S. 1981. "The migrant syndrome: Seasonal U.S. wage labor and rural development in central Mexico." *Human Organization,* 40:56–76.

Samora, Julian. 1971. *Los Mojados: The Wetback Story.* Notre Dame, Indiana: University of Notre Dame Press.

Zazueta, Carlos H., and Rodolfo Corona. 1979. *Los Trabajadores Mexicanos en los Estados Unidos: Primeros Resultados de la Encuesta Nacional de Emigración a la Frontera Norte del País y a los Estados Unidos* (ENEFNEU), Mexico, D.F.: Centro Nacional de Información y Estadísticas del Trabajo (CENIET).

PART ONE
Overview

2

Changing Patterns of Undocumented Migration from Mexican States in Recent Years

JORGE A. BUSTAMANTE

This paper reviews what is known of the characteristics of undocumented migration from Mexico. It is based upon a presentation of the findings of a survey conducted by the author in nine Mexican border cities, utilizing interviews with Mexican undocumented emigrants recently deported from the United States. A discussion of costs and benefits of the migration, and some suggestions for solutions, are also made.

Socioeconomic Characteristics by State of Origin

Some progress has been made in defining the socioeconomic characteristics of undocumented immigrants from Mexico. There are four major sources of data based on research of a comprehensive scope in this field: The Samora study (1971); the series of reports of the Comisión Intersecretarial (1972; 1974; and 1975); the North and Houstoun report (1976) released by the U.S. Department of Labor; and the CENIET studies (see Zazueta and Corona, 1979).

This is an abbreviated and revised version of "Undocumented immigration from Mexico: Research report." *International Migration Review* 2 (1977):149–77. By permission of the publisher.

This section will describe some of the socioeconomic characteristics, making comparisons among these sources where possible. In addition, some preliminary findings will be presented of a survey conducted by the author in nine Mexican border cities during November and December of 1975. This survey was carried out under the auspices of the Research Program on the Bi-national Border Region (Mexico-U.S.), Centro de Estudios Sociológicos, El Colegio de Mexico; with the cooperation of US immigration authorities. The survey built upon three earlier questionnaire surveys carried out by the Interdepartmental Commission on Mexican Workers in the U.S. (1972; 1974; and 1975). A total of 919 interviews were conducted with undocumented Mexican emigrants upon their return (by U.S. border patrol officials) to eight Mexican border towns. The cities (with sample sizes in parentheses) were Reynosa (32), Matamoros (401), Cd. Acuña (159), Quevedo (99), Piedras Negras (38), Juarez (45), Nogales (84), and Tijuana (60). Given Matamoros's large sample size, the results from migrants returned to that city will be treated more extensively in the following analyses.

CHARACTERISTICS OF DEPARTURE

It may be inferred from Figure 2.1 that the local conditions associated with emigration have not been static. The Mexican states included in this graph represent approximately 80 percent of the total outmigration detected each year by the sources indicated. Data shown in this graph suggest the necessity of studying the differing conditions among the states of origin. The considerable heterogeneity shown among the graphs underscores the fact that emigration is an uneven process. The nation cannot be treated as an homogeneous whole.

It is interesting to note the changes shown in the percentages for the states of Chihuahua, Michoacán, Sonora, and Sinaloa (see Fig. 2.2) from 1971 to 1975. These contrast sharply with the downward trends of the rest of the states during the same period. The increases shown by Sonora and Sinaloa coincide with decreases in agricultural production in the same states for this period. It is possible that these decreases affect the availability of jobs sought not only by people in Sinaloa and Sonora but by the migrants from Michoacán. If it is true that internal migration from Michoacán to Sinaloa and Sonora is associated with emigration from Michoacán to the United States, the trends of these three states could be related to an economic situation derived from agricultural production in Sinaloa and Sonora. The easier access to the United States from Michoacán via Sinaloa and Sonora, along with the highly rural composition of the migrants from

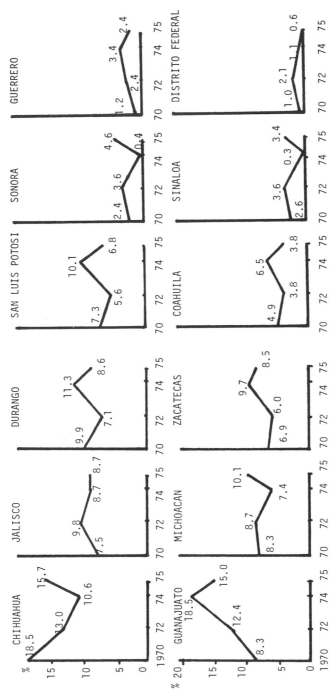

Figure 2.1 Apprehended undocumented Mexican immigration to the U.S. by states of origin [Percentage of total undocumented immigration originating in the state. Source: for 1970, Samora (1971); for 1972, 1974, and 1975, Mexican Government.]

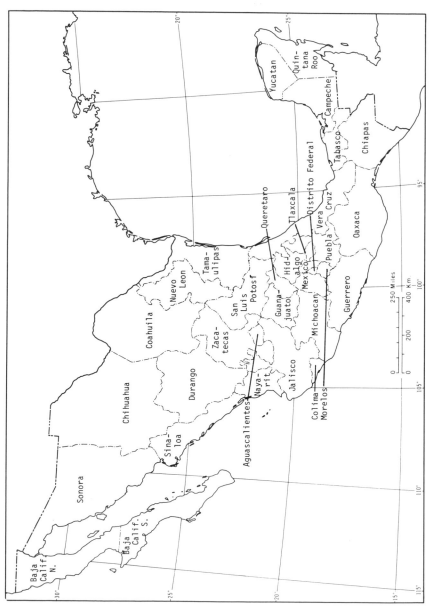

Figure 2.2 States and territories of Mexico

Table 2.1   Employment and Origin Characteristics for Sample of Mexican
            Undocumented Immigrants by State of Origin (November 1975)

State of origin		Number of interviews	%	% employed in Mexico at time of departure	% employed in the US last year	Community of origin: urban %
Guanajuato	b.s.[a]	103	26.5	29.1	70.9	44.7
	r.s.[b]	104	26.3	25.9	52.2	42.3
San Luís Potosí	b.s.	69	17.8	33.3	79.7	29.0
	r.s.	67	16.9	38.8	79.1	28.4
Jalisco	b.s.	43	11.0	27.9	81.4	27.9
	r.s.	39	9.9	20.5	89.7	25.6
Michoacán	b.s.	40	10.3	52.5	52.5	27.5
	r.s.	35	8.9	48.6	54.3	22.9
Zacatecas	b.s.	39	10.1	30.8	79.5	33.3
	r.s.	36	9.1	41.7	80.6	27.8
Durango	b.s.	24	6.2	33.3	79.2	37.5
	r.s.	18	4.6	27.8	72.2	22.2
Chihuahua	b.s.	11	2.8	36.4	63.6	63.6
	r.s.	15	3.8	33.3	66.7	66.7
Mexico D.F.	b.s.	8	2.1	62.5	87.5	100.0
	r.s.	12	3.0	58.3	91.7	100.0
Querétaro	b.s.	8	2.1	50.0	75.0	37.5
	r.s.	8	2.0	37.5	75.0	37.5
Coahuila	b.s.	7	1.8	42.9	71.4	85.7
	r.s.	9	2.3	33.3	66.7	77.8
Aguascalientes	b.s.	7	1.8	57.1	85.7	57.1
	r.s.	9	2.3	44.4	66.7	66.7
Guerrero	b.s.	6	1.5		100.0	
	r.s.	8	1.8	14.3	100.0	
Tamaulipas	b.s.	5	1.3	60.0	60.0	100.0
	r.s.	11	2.8	27.3	63.6	81.8
Veracruz	b.s.	4	1.0	50.0	100.0	50.0
	r.s.			50.0	100.0	50.0
Sinaloa	b.s.	5	1.3		100.0	
	r.s.			20.0	100.0	40.0
Nuevo León	b.s.	6	1.5		33.3	100.0
	r.s.			16.7	66.7	100.0
Other states	b.s.	4	1.0			
	r.s.	10	2.5			

Notes: [a]b.s. - born in state [b]r.s.- resident in state.

Source: Research Program on the Bi-national Border Region, Mexico-US, Centro de Estudios
         Sociólogicos, El Colegio de Mexico. Data obtained from the application of ques-
         tionnaires in Matamoros, Tamaulipas (November 1975) to undocumented migrant
         workers recently deported from the US.

Michoacán (see Table 2.1), could be associated with the impact of
agricultural production upon job opportunities and the volume of
emigration to the United States from these states.

Figure 2.1 also shows that there are five states that invariably
appear in the statistics as sharing the largest proportion of the totals
of undocumented emigration to the United States. With small variations
in the order of predominance, these states are Guanajuato, Chihuahua,

Michoacán, Zacatecas, and Jalisco) They appear to have provided more than one half of the total of INS detected undocumented immigration from Mexico ever since 1969. Table 2.1 shows that the majority of the migrants of four of these states were born and have their actual residence in rural communities; Chihuahua is the only exception.

We looked for some variations in the data controlling for state of birth and state of actual residence. Table 2.1 shows variations in the rural-urban origin, not exceeding 5 percent on the average, for the seven Mexican states with the highest proportion of undocumented immigrants to the United States. This is an interesting indication of a consistent pattern of urban to rural migration. Some statistical tests conducted found that at the 90 percent level of confidence, the differences are just barely significant. We cannot draw any consistent conclusions from this. Based on our data, however, it is tenable to hypothesize that a small proportion of Mexican undocumented immigrants migrated, either before or after entering the United States, from an urban to a rural location in Mexico. These apparent patterns are more intriguing since one would assume the opposite pattern, a loss in the number of rural emigrants when controlled by place of birth and place of residence, to be more likely.

Table 2.1 confirms the notion that the majority of undocumented emigrants are of rural origin. Out of the seven states with the largest emigration, Chihuahua appears as an exception in its rural-urban composition. This is probably influenced by the size of the Ciudad Juarez population, which is rapidly approaching one million.

EMPLOYMENT—UNEMPLOYMENT

The column on unemployment in Mexico (Table 2.1) suggests two concurrent situations: (a) the high unemployment rate among emigrants (reaching as high as 79.5 percent among those who reside in the state of Jalisco), and (b) that approximately one-third of the emigrants from the seven states with the largest emigration had a job at the time of departure. This reflects the effect of not only unemployment but of other factors upon the decision to emigrate. Low wages and low standards of living are obviously notable among these factors.

If our interviews in nine Mexican border cities (N = 919) reflect the unemployment situations of those cities, the figures of Table 2.2 would suggest that unemployment at the Mexican border among undocumented immigrants is among the worst in the largest border cities, Ciudad Juarez and Tijuana. Only Piedras Negras had a higher unemployment rate.

Table 2.2 Employment Characteristics for Sample of Undocumented Immigrants by Community of Origin (November 1975)

Cities where interviews were conducted	Employed in Mexico at time of departure to US	Employed in US last year	Number of interviews	% of N
Cd. Reynosa				
absolute	14	17	32	
percentage	43.8	53.1		3.5
Matamoros				
absolute	137	297	401	
percentage	34.2	74.1		43.7
Cd. Acuña				
absolute	57	59	159	
percentage	35.8	37.1		17.4
Gral. Rodrigo Ma. de Quevedo				
absolute	30	39	99	
percentage	30.3	39.4		10.8
Piedras Negras				
absolute	7	9	38	
percentage	18.4	23.7		4.1
Cd. Juarez				
absolute	9	17	45	
percentage	20.0	37.8		4.9
Nogales				
absolute	41	38	84	
percentage	48.8	45.2		9.1
Tijuana				
absolute	13	33	60	
percentage	21.7	55.0		6.5
Totals				
absolute	308	509	918	
percentage	33.5	55.4		100.0

Source: Interviews with undocumented emigrants detected by U.S. immigration authorities, conducted upon their return to eight Mexican border towns (November 1975).

The same reasoning applies to our data on the questions: Were you employed in the United States last year? This is a better question than: Did you have a job when caught? This is the question we have asked in previous studies (Samora, 1971). Both INS data on apprehensions and our previous studies have shown that approximately 55 percent of those caught did not have jobs. This factor is commonly overlooked by those who leave jobs in Mexico to illegally enter the United States. This percentage appears reduced in general terms when the question refers to last year's experiences, as shown in Table 2.1.

Table 2.3   Type of Job Held in Mexico by Undocumented Immigrants Recently
            Deported by US Immigration Authorities

Type of Job	1972	1974	1975
Employer or business owner	1.7	2.2	2.7
Self-employed	5.5	6.1	7.1
Landholder (ejidatario)	4.4	12.9	4.3
Landless agri-worker	43.0	35.1	35.6
Industrial worker	15.8	17.5	21.5
Services worker	17.8	18.0	18.6
Wageless family worker	5.7	4.0	3.9
Never employed	6.1	4.2	6.3
Total	100.0	100.0	100.0
N =	2,794	1,316	1,658

Source: Questionnaires applied in 1972, 1974 and 1975 respectively, in eight
border cities by the Interdepartmental Commission on problems derived from
migratory currents of Mexican workers to the US (Mexican Government).

The situation appears different when looking at the emigrants in the
Mexican border towns (Table 2.2). The data by state of origin (Table
2.1) refer only to interviews conducted in Matamoros. This is precisely
where the employment experience in the U.S. last year has been the
best among the emigrants interviewed in the nine Mexican border
cities. Table 2.2 also shows that contrary to the common association
of unemployment and emigration, a sizeable proportion of undocumented immigrants had jobs in Mexico at the time of departure to
the United States.

Table 2.3 is a compilation of data from the Comisión Intersecretarial
reports on the employment background of undocumented immigrants.
These data show changes occurring over the years in the occupational
composition of the migrants. Notwithstanding that farmworking oc-

cupations still represent the majority of undocumented emigrants' employment backgrounds, the proportion of farmworkers in the total of emigrants has been generally declining. When the occupational background is broken down into the large categories of agriculture, industry, and services, the Comisión Intersecretarial's data indicate that 57.4 percent of the total of interviewees in 1972 (N = 2,794) worked in agriculture in Mexico. By 1974, the percentage in the same category had decreased to 53.6 percent (N = 1,316). In 1975 it had decreased further to 46.9 percent (N = 1,658).

Comparing the findings of the Comisión Intersecretarial with those of the North and Houstoun study, we find that in the area of employment, no correspondence appears between the occupational background in Mexico and the type of job found in the United States among the undocumented immigrants. Even in the cases where the immigrant lists other than agricultural skills, he or she is found to have been absorbed by the farmworking activities in his or her occupational experience in the United States (Comisión Intersecretarial, 1972, Table 9; North and Houstoun, 1976, Table V-5). An apparent selectivity in the U.S. demand for undocumented immigrant labor is indicated, as well as the negligible effect that his or her occupational background has on this selectivity. Nevertheless, percentages in the occupational categories of industry and services have been rising.

TIME SPENT IN THE UNITED STATES

Our preliminary findings on this variable might have an undetermined although simple bias derived from the place in which the interviews were taken. Mexican undocumented immigrants apprehended by the INS are not sent back to Mexico on a random basis. Place of origin, as stated by the individual who is apprehended, is used by INS as a criterion for the destination of the undocumented immigrant released. He or she who states that he or she is from the interior of Mexico is sent back non-stop by bus or by plane to a city of the interior, with the rationale that this will make his or her return to the United States more difficult. This practice, parenthetically, is in flagrant violation of the Mexican constitution, which establishes the basic right of free transit of individuals within the country.[1]

The practice usually involves the INS and a Mexican busline or airline contracted for the compulsive transportation of the undocu-

---

[1]The practice of transporting undocumenteds to the interior was terminated in 1979.

mented immigrant from the Mexican border. The INS delivers the immigrant to the Mexican busline, and thence to the interior of Mexico as previously agreed upon between the INS and the Mexican busline or airline. This practice has been in existence since the last years of the Ordaz administration. It is a different practice, however, than the current and allegedly experimental airlift program by which INS sends undocumented immigrants back to Mexico on regular flights of commercial airlines. The basic difference between the two practices is that the older program involved the payment of the ticket by the immigrant when caught with enough money. The newer practice involves what has been called, with a peculiar sense of humor, a champagne flight on the INS account. Neither program has had any apparent impact upon the undocumented immigration flow.

Those undocumented migrants who, upon capture, note their residence to be in the Mexican border cities, are released by the INS across the border. This is the group to which our 919 interviewees belonged. Because of this residence factor, (the validity of which we did not determine), the group which stayed fewer than 30 days tended to be larger than those in other studies (Samora, 1971; North and Houstoun, 1976). Some of the interviews in these other studies had taken place in areas other than the Mexican border.

An additional finding of our study derives from the question on the duration of stay of the undocumented migrants in the United States in 1975. Although Table 2.4 shows the average number of days spent in the U.S. during that year, we were unable to determine with a minimum of reliability how many returns to Mexico, voluntary or otherwise, were involved with what duration in the number of days spent in the U.S. during the same year. Note that immigrants from border states such as Coahuila, Tamaulipas, and Nuevo León exhibit low durations, while interior states such as Mexico, D.F., Guerrero, and Zacatecas exhibit longer durations. This partially reflects the attempt to maximize time in the U.S., for those incurring high transportation costs.

Some Aspects of the Costs and Benefits
of the Undocumented Emigration

The income obtained in the United States by the undocumented immigrant comes only from labor. Therefore, focus is placed first on the benefit defined as income. Table 2.5 shows the average amount received by Mexican undocumented immigrants by state of origin. The data corresponding to resident in state (r.s.) in Table 2.5 would suggest that the states with higher rural emigration (see Table 2.1)

Table 2.4 Duration of Stay for Sample of Mexican Undocumented Immigrants by
State of Origin (November 1975)

State of Origin		N = 401	%	Average duration of first stay in US during 1975 (in days)
Guanajuato	b.s.[a]	103	26.5	138
	r.s.[b]	104	26.3	137
San Luís Potosí	b.s.	69	17.8	177
	r.s.	67	16.9	181
Jalisco	b.s.	43	11.0	136
	r.s.	39	9.9	138
Michoacan	b.s.	40	10.3	111
	r.s.	35	8.9	238
Zacatecas	b.s.	39	10.1	225
	r.s.	36	9.1	223
Durango	b.s.	24	6.2	129
	r.s.	18	4.6	83
Chihuahua	b.s.	11	2.8	189
	r.s.	15	3.8	195
Mexico, D.F.	b.s.	8	2.1	377
	r.s.	12	3.0	352
Querétaro	b.s.	8	2.1	123
	r.s.	8	2.0	123
Coahuila	b.s.	7	1.8	83
	r.s.	9	2.3	142
Aguascalientes	b.s.	7	1.8	234
	r.s.	9	2.3	184
Guerrero	b.s.	6	1.5	288
	r.s.	8	1.8	270
Tamaulipas	b.s.	5	1.3	20
	r.s.	11	2.8	128
Veracruz	b.s.	4	1.0	311
	r.s.			311
Sinaloa	b.s.	5	1.3	245
	r.s.			238
Nuevo León	b.s.	6	1.5	40
	r.s.			111
Other States	b.s.	4	1.0	
	r.s.	10	2.5	

Source: Research Program on the Bi-national Border Region, Mexico-US, Centro
de Estudios Sociológicos, El Colegio de Mexico. Data obtained from the application of questionnaires in Matamoros, Tamaulipas (November 1975) to undocumented migrant workers recently deported from the US.
Notes: [a] b.s. - born in state
       [b] r.s. - resident in state

Table 2.5 Income and Expenditures for a Sample of Mexican Undocumenteds by State of Origin (November 1975)

State of Origin		N=401	% of N	Travel expenses to the US last year[a]	Debts left in Mexico last year[a]	Income in the US last year[a]	Family expenditures per day in Mexico	Respondent's expenditures per day in US
Guanajuato	b.s.[b]	103	26.5	367.09	155.92	748.08	3.52	3.97
	r.s.[c]	104	26.3	352.98	142.62	799.80	3.50	4.06
San Luis Potosí	b.s.	69	17.8	475.79	144.29	757.04	2.73	4.34
	r.s.	67	16.9	386.94	98.75	756.66	3.96	4.30
Jalisco	b.s.	43	11.0	373.45	101.86	658.09	3.37	3.98
	r.s.	39	9.9	377.44	112.00	725.59	3.82	3.89
Michoacán	b.s.	40	10.3	392.31	130.10	554.50	5.87	3.84
	r.s.	35	8.9	271.14	104.69	549.14	3.85	4.03
Zacatecas	b.s.	39	10.1	326.97	140.22	848.82	3.62	4.45
	r.s.	36	9.1	303.44	139.06	873.44	3.70	5.69
Durango	b.s.	24	6.2	528.58	50.50	759.48	3.01	4.48
	r.s.	18	4.6	391.78	64.00	631.56	2.84	2.77
Chihuahua	b.s.	11	2.8	471.64	16.36	452.73	5.07	2.98
	r.s.	15	3.8	550.93	16.00	825.33	4.44	0.80
Mexico, D.F.	b.s.	8	2.1	781.25	0	1,155.00	4.17	6.00
	r.s.	12	3.0	893.83	193.33	1,020.33	4.21	4.63
Querétaro	b.s.	8	2.1	333.50	204.00	887.50	5.29	3.67
	r.s.	8	2.0	339.00	204.00	875.00	5.74	3.79
Coahuila	b.s.	7	1.8	226.29	0	484.57	2.73	3.31
	r.s.	9	2.3	53.11	8.00	544.22	3.08	3.16
Aguascalientes	b.s.	7	1.8	555.43	696.00	1,480.00	3.19	6.39
	r.s.	9	2.3	443.11	548.00	1,151.11	2.86	8.92
Guerrero	b.s.	6	1.5	846.67	386.67	1,233.33	3.60	4.07
	r.s.	8	2.0	751.43	428.57	1,268.57	5.94	4.11
Tamaulipas	b.s.	5	1.3	65.20	24.00	149.20	6.08	1.92
	r.s.	11	2.8	67.64	165.45	489.64	6.87	4.65
Veracruz	b.s.	4	1.0	1,119.00	115.00	1,480.00	2.54	8.44
	r.s.			1,119.00	115.00	1,125.00	2.54	8.44
Sinaloa	b.s.	5	1.3	520.67	93.33	986.67	5.60	4.98
	r.s.			704.40	112.00	1,256.00	4.06	4.83
Nuevo León	b.s.	6	1.5	183.33	97.33	105.33	3.79	11.65
	r.s.			371.00	105.33	589.33	3.09	6.52
Other states	b.s.	4	1.0					
	r.s.	10	2.5					

Notes: [a]Averages converted into US dollars at the January 1976 currency rate of eight cents per peso.

[b]b.s. - born in state

[c]r.s. - resident of state

Source: Questionnaire applied in Matamoros, Tamaulipas to undocumented immigrants recently deported by US Immigration authorities.

display lower income. This suggests a probable effect of urbanization on skills and consequently on the likelihood of obtaining higher wages in the United States. It is important to observe, however, that only in the case of Mexico, D.F. is yearly income in the United States higher than the average income for the nation. This is approximately 1,000 dollars at the previous rate, before September 1975 and subsequent devaluation of the peso. Because of this factor, any income in the United States now represents double what it was at the time the data were gathered. This suggests that the attraction of obtaining

U.S. dollars may similarly double with the more recent rate of exchange for the peso. The effect of this attraction has been seen, beginning with Spring 1978, as each year the seasonal flow of emigration to the United States begins to augment, reaching a peak during the summer. A deterrent, however, has been the accompanying inflationary effect on travel and living expenses. This has resulted in the poorest emigrants being unable to afford the trip to the United States, whereas they had previously been able to.

Table 2.5 shows not only an apparent correspondence between proximity to the U.S.-Mexico border and lower travel expenses; it also shows that emigration costs are higher than our previous studies had suggested (Samora, 1971). One can therefore predict an increasing predominance of Mexican border states among states of emigrant origin. One can also speculate that a changing pattern of internal migration in Mexico will become evident as migration to the United States becomes increasingly expensive for the lowest income emigrants of the interior. Nevertheless, an increase is expected in rural to urban migration. This will be particularly apparent in the movement to Mexican metropolitan areas from Guanajuato, Michoacán, Jalisco, and San Luís Potosí causing a consequent decrease in the emigration from these states to the United States. Regardless of the increased attraction of the dollar, the cost of traveling to the United States will be too high for the most rural emigrant of the interior states of Mexico.

PAYCHECK DEDUCTIONS FOR TAXES AND SOCIAL
SECURITY AND THE BENEFIT DERIVED

Table 2.6 shows a breakdown of a group of undocumented immigrants employed in the United States. Here only 7.7 percent received their wages in cash. Because cash payment often indicates that deductions for tax or Social Security have not been made, check-paid workers only were considered for this analysis. It is easier for workers to remember and to respond on a yes or no basis if they were paid by check. Our findings are consistent with the reports of North and Houstoun (1976) and Villalpando (1975) in that the Mexican undocumented immigrant indeed paid taxes and Social Security. Almost three-quarters of the check-paid workers had deductions for tax purposes and two-thirds for Social Security. However, it is evident from the table that very few migrants use government social services such as schools, free medical care, or welfare.

In theory, a case for an international court of law could be made by the Mexican government, if the accumulated amount paid by Mexican immigrants in the form of income tax and Social Security

Table 2.6 Characteristics of a Sample of Mexican Undocumenteds by City Where Interviewed

City where interviewed	Wage workers: form of payment[a] (N = 521)				Check-paid workers: deductions from wages[b] (N = 434)				Children in schools?			(N = 919) US welfare recipient?			US medical care recipient?		
	Cash	Check	wages uncollected	n.a.	Social Security tax		no	n.a.	yes	no	n.a.	yes	no	n.a.	yes	no	n.a.
					tax	ity											
Reynosa	1	16	2	0	10	8	4	2	0	32	0	0	32	0	1	31	0
Matamoros	18	258	21	10	191	178	48	13	3	388	10	18	369	14	32	359	10
Cd. Acuña	8	46	3	2	29	24	12	5	0	155	4	2	155	2	14	143	0
Cd. R.M. Quevedo	6	30	2	1	21	21	8	1	0	96	3	0	99	0	2	91	3
Piedras Negras	2	7	0	0	2	2	5	0	0	38	0	0	38	0	0	38	0
Cd. Juarez	0	17	0	0	16	12	1	1	0	45	0	0	45	0	3	40	0
Nogales	4	28	4	2	26	19	3	3	0	81	3	2	80	2	9	78	3
Tijuana	0	32	0	1	27	25	5	1	5	53	3	7	51	3	11	49	2
Totals	39	434	32	16	322	289	86	26	8	888	23	29	869	21	72	829	18
Percentages	7.5	83.3	6.1	3.1	74.4	66.7	19.9	6.2	0.9	96.6	2.5	3.2	94.5	2.3	7.8	90.2	1.9

Note: [a] n.a. = no answer.

Source: Interviews with undocumented emigrants detected by US Immigration authorities, conducted upon their return to eight Mexican border cities in November 1975.

to the U.S. Treasury could be determined. Assuming our data are correct, the immigrants generally do not receive a proportional benefit in the form of public services for the monies. It could therefore be argued that the Mexican undocumented immigrants have an uncollected balance in their favor chargeable to the U.S. Treasury.

The representativeness of our data is still undetermined, but they are consistent enough with the evidence from other studies (North and Houstoun 1976; Villalpando 1975) so as to suggest that charges against the Mexican undocumented immigrant for being a burden on U.S. taxpayers for 13 billion dollars are totally unfounded.

I have argued elsewhere (Bustamante 1975, 1976) that one of the dangers of allowing alarming statements regarding Mexican immigration to remain unchallenged by scientific research is that these statements become "definitions of the situation" for the general public. That is, when situations are defined as real, they are real in their consequences. One consequence of unfounded alarming statements on this migratory phenomenon might be a certain kind of behavior with no higher rationality than the burning of witches in the history of western civilization.

Some Suggestions for Partial Solutions

Some solutions to the problem of undocumented workers in the U.S. have been attempted in the past. One was the bracero program. Other less-bilateral moves such as massive deportations have also been tried. Enough has been written on the history of the bracero program, particularly by Ernesto Galarza (1964), to forego a long discussion of its merits here. A bracero program would not be useful as a solution for the undocumented immigration, for the following reasons: (a) It becomes an inducement for emigration from Mexico. In the past, those who were not able to be included in the bracero quotas determined by the United States did not necessarily go home. They came to the United States as undocumented workers. (b) It provokes an oversupply of labor that is conducive to conditions of exploitation, exacerbation of ethnic prejudice, and discrimination. (c) It results in the institutionalization of an underclass consisting of the not-too-temporary workers' children born in the United States.

Restrictive measures, such as reinforcing police actions and/or launching massive deportations, have failed several times in the past. The two structurally determined factors operating on the two sides of the border—namely U.S. demands for cheap labor and unemployment in Mexico—cannot be solved by unilateral measures.

No attempts have been made in this paper or elsewhere to suggest international policy directed at the roots of the problem of undocumented emigration to the U.S. Yet the data at our disposal enable us to locate areas in Mexico with high unemployment among undocumented emigrants prior to their trip to the U.S. This being the case, we can make suggestions for a program of employment in Mexico based on concerted actions from both sides of the border.

1. *Creation of "units of production" of foodstuffs.* Within the existing framework and policies of Mexican federal programs for development of rural areas, a selection of strategic locations will be set up for the establishment of units of production of food products. These will include the organization of systems of production based on labor intensity rather than capital intensity for the processing of farm products.

2. *Sources of capital.* The initial sources of capital for these production units would be either the Mexican government directly, or international agencies financing development programs. The main reasons for this strategy include the traditional Mexican reluctance toward "foreign aid" programs.

3. *U.S. imports as immigration policy.* The production of crop units located in Mexico would be destined for certain U.S. programs for foreign aid in which food products are sent to countries with whom agreements of this nature have been established. The purpose of this is twofold: (a) To provide a source of capitalization that will not be dependent upon the forces of international marketing; and (b) to provide conditions of stability to the production units for the programming of long term patterns of production.

   The importation of this food by U.S. government agencies should not be conceived as a commercial operation. Rather, it should be conceived as a measure to curb Mexican undocumented immigration. The expected volume of production during two years of an exploratory program would not be of a magnitude great enough to affect exports of regular U.S. agricultural production. Channeling U.S. imports of the Mexican units' production to U.S. foreign aid programs in foodstuffs will also serve the purpose of not competing with U.S. farmers in the domestic market. Otherwise, this would require an increase in the complexity of the organizational infrastructure of Mexican production units, or a new structure making them dependent upon brokers.

4. *Mexican production units' management.* Preference in hiring practices would be given to: (a) those with no record of apprehension

in the United States by the INS after a certain date; and (b) those within a certain geographical area. The form of ownership of the units of production would be private but collectively owned by a group of operators. The Mexican government would grant loans to this group upon approval of their proposal for operation. The organization of revenues for the owners would correspond to a corporation format of a *Sociedad Anónima* (Anonymous Association) within the Mexican law. Checkpoints would be established by the Mexican financing agency to control the efficiency of each production unit. A manpower training program would be created to fulfill the management necessities of the production units.

5. *Duration of the U.S. imports program.* After two years of an exploratory phase, U.S. imports will be extended for another three years. The fourth year will be used as a transition period to mix operations both of exports within the regular program and sales into the Mexican national market or regular exports programs.

6. *An additional concerted-action program for adjustment of migratory status of undocumented immigrants in the United States.* This measure would respond to the roots of the problem of undocumented immigrants located in the United States—namely, it acknowledges U.S. low-skill labor demands. One major task of U.S.-Mexican concerted actions in this regard would be to orient those who do not qualify for adjustment of migratory status toward the production units in Mexico.

The main resistance to a program such as this would probably come from United States farmers. One question is, however, what the cost would be for the U.S. economy to establish such a program of food imports from the units in Mexico. Another question is whether this program would curb undocumented immigration at a lower price than massive deportations such as those in the past.

These units of production do not have to necessarily provide full employment in Mexico. They will have to demonstrate, however: (a) that the chance of obtaining a job in, and becoming a shareholder of, a Mexican prodution unit is equal to or better than the actual chance of finding a job in the United States; (b) that emigrating to the U.S. without a visa diminishes one's possibility of gaining access to a Mexican production unit; and (c) that the income derived from the emigration to the United States "sin papeles" is not worth the personal risks involved.

There is no doubt that this idea requires a thorough evaluation before it is taken to international negotiations. It is my contention, however, that any possible solution to the chaotic situation of the undocumented immigrant will have to include a consideration of the basic assumptions which prompted these suggestions. These are: (a) There is a real demand for Mexican immigrant workers in the United States that must be regulated; (b) An employment policy, based on labor intensive production, can be designed to curb outmigration in Mexico by focusing on strategic areas where outmigration is larger; and (c) A concerted action by the two governments in the design of their migratory policies is the realistic way to solve problems related to undocumented immigration.

References

Bustamante, Jorge A. 1975. "Espaldas mojadas; materia prima para la expansión del capital Norteamericano." Cuadernos del CES, Series No. 9. Mexico: El Colegio de Mexico.

————. 1976. "The silent invasion issue." Paper presented at the Annual Meeting of the Population Association of America in Montreal.

Comisión Intersecretarial para el Estudio de los Problemas de la Corriente Migratoria de Trabajadores Mexicanos a Los Estados Unidos. 1972, 1974, 1975. "Informes de la encuesta." Mexico, D.F.: Secretaria de Relaciones Exteriores (in press).

Galarza, Ernesto. 1964. *Merchants of Labor: The American Bracero History*. Santa Barbara, California: McNally and Loftin.

Keely, Charles. 1976. "Analysis of methodology used for the Lesko Associates study on illegal aliens." Paper presented at the American Immigration and Citizenship Conference, January 21.

North, David S. 1970. *The Border Crossers: People Who Live in Mexico and Work in the United States*. Washington: Trans Century Corporation.

North, David S., and Marion F. Houstoun. 1976. *The Characteristics and Role of Illegal Aliens in the U.S. Labor Market: An Exploratory Study*. Washington: Linton & Co., March.

Samora, Julian. 1971. *Los Mojados: The Wetback Story*. Notre Dame: University of Notre Dame Press.

Villalpando, M. Vic. 1975. *A Study of the Impact of Illegal Aliens in the County of San Diego on Specific Socioeconomic Areas*. San Diego, California: San Diego County Human Resources Agency.

Zazueta, Carlos, and Rodolfo Corona. 1979. *Los Trabajadores Mexicanos en los Estados Unidos: Primeros Resultados de la Encuesta Nacional de Emigración a la Frontera Norte del País y a los Estados Unidos (ENEFNEU)*. México, D.F.: Centro Nacional de Información y Estadísticas del Trabajo (CENIET).

3

Macro-Patterns of Undocumented Migration between Mexico and the U.S.

RICHARD C. JONES

In the past thirteen years, beginning with Samora's (1971) work, there have appeared a dozen books and more than a hundred articles and monographs concerning the issue of Mexican migration to the United States. A consensus has emerged from this literature on the characteristics of illegal migrants and migration streams. It is clear that the net flow of undocumented migrants to the U.S. is smaller than originally believed. Approximately 100,000 to 300,000 people annually come to the United States (Cornelius, 1978; Heer, 1979), constituting between 3 and 10 percent of total U.S. population growth. It is also clear that the typical migrant is young, male, and usually unskilled in nonagricultural work (Cárdenas and Flores, 1978; Cornelius, 1976, 1978; North and Houstoun, 1976; Samora, 1971). He is poor, but not among the poorest from his village (Roberts, 1980:214–16). He usually (in 60 percent of the cases) comes from a small town or rural area in Mexico (Bustamante, 1977; Dagodag, 1975), but is usually (in 70 percent of the cases) destined for an urban area in the U.S. (Cornelius, 1978; North and

This is an abridged synthesis of two papers published by the author: "Undocumented Migration from Mexico: Some Geographical Questions," *Annals, Association of American Geographers* 72 (1982:77–87); and "Channelization of Undocumented Mexican Migrants to the U.S.," *Economic Geography*, vol. 58 (1982):156–76). The author would like to further thank the Association of American Geographers for a research grant that resulted in the author's obtaining the Mexican CENIET (ENEFNEU) data, by permission of the Executive Director (AAG) and Editor (Economic Geography).

Houstoun, 1976). He seldom makes a planned, discretionary move, but is driven by episodic economic necessity at the origin (Frisbee, 1975; Jenkins, 1977) and thus is most properly referred to as an "economic refugee" (Cornelius, 1976, 1978; Stoddard, 1977). He spends six months to a year in the U.S. before returning to Mexico, and makes four or five such trips in a lifetime (Cornelius, 1978; North and Houstoun, 1976; Reichert and Massey, 1979). Therefore, he is a temporary as opposed to a permanent migrant. Finally, while sending home one-third of his earnings on the average, he makes few claims on local social services and is quite pleased to work at wages below the legal minimum (Bustamante, 1977; Cornelius, 1978; North and Houstoun, 1976). Because of his limited participation in skilled occupations, his high productivity in unskilled work, his temporary status, his scant demand on social services, and his acceptance of low wages, the undocumented Mexican's impact on the host society may well be positive or at least neutral.

Unfortunately, previous research on this particular question has been piecemeal and sketchy from a geographer's point of view. Generalizations about the migration process have frequently been made from a case study of a single origin or destination. Spatial patterns, where they appear, are accorded little discussion (an exception is Dagodag, 1975), and changes in these patterns in recent years are ignored altogether (an exception is Bustamante, 1977). A more thorough treatment of spatial patterns would indicate, at least, that there is not one "wave" of migrants but a number of spatially channeled flows composed of migrants with different characteristics. Furthermore, the analysis of such flows would suggest important communication linkages and transportation routes which have come to shape the migration channels. Finally, the relative magnitudes of flow to different regions would provide a quantitative basis for gauging impacts on the labor force and on social service systems at different destinations.

In this study, three geographical questions are posed: (a) Where in the United States are undocumented migrants from Mexico concentrated, and how have these locations changed over time? (b) Does the density of recent arrivals (of undocumented migrants) show a regular decline away from the border, i.e., are patterns continuous (contagious), or are they discontinuous (hierarchical), and how have they changed? (c) To what degree are migration flows channelized between certain Mexican origins and certain U.S. destinations? Answers are sought to these questions, within the limits of available data.

Locational Concentration of Mexican
Undocumenteds in the U.S.

The first question involves the locations of Mexican undocumenteds in the United States, and how these locations have changed. The best and most recent data available on destinations of Mexican migrants to the U.S. come from the Mexican government's ENEFNEU project (Encuesta Nacional de Emigración a la Frontera Norte del País los Estados Unidos). The principal consultant on this project is Jorge Bustamante, an internationally known sociologist with the Colegio de Mexico in Mexico City. One research report from this project (Zazueta and Corona, 1979) focuses upon some 400,000 "absentee" workers whose families were interviewed in various Mexican localities in December 1978, and January 1979. Although the question of illegal status was not asked in the absentee questionnaires, other research has shown conclusively that labor migration from Mexico at this time was overwhelmingly illegal. More than half of the absentee workers were concentrated in California, approximately a quarter in Texas, and a tenth in Illinois, with no other state accounting for more than 2.2 percent (Table 3.1, column 1). California's dominance of the distribution is the most important piece of information from these data. There are other interesting findings, e.g., Illinois's third-place position, and the fact that 95.6 percent of the Mexican workers were in only eight states. The question of whether California leads simply because it has such a large population mass for attracting migrants can be answered in the negative. California's density of Mexican workers (measured per 1,000 of total state population) is greater than that for any other state, though the margin is less than for the percentage distribution (Table 3.1, column 2). It is unfortunate, given the known participation of such states as New York and Montana in undocumented migration, that more states are not included in the ENEFNEU absentee data report (Zazueta and Corona, 1979). Nevertheless, INS (Immigration and Naturalization Service) data on deportable aliens for 1978 (Statistical Division, INS, 1980) suggest that among the remaining states, only Montana may have a higher density ratio than those shown for Oregon and Florida in Table 3.1.

It is worth noting that the proportion of total undocumenteds in California, Texas, and Illinois (87 percent) is quite similar to the proportion of permanent resident aliens from Mexico living in these same three states in recent years (88 percent) (North and Houstoun, 1976:24). This suggests that undocumenteds tend to be located where the Mexican-origin population has already established itself, where they are able to use kinship chains and to blend in culturally. It is

Table 3.1 Distribution and Density of Mexican Workers in the US by Major
          States of Destination, 1978-79

US state of destination	Percentage distribution	Density, in workers, per 1,000 of state population
California	55.4	87.0
Texas	23.1	62.1
Illinois	8.6	26.8
New Mexico	2.2	63.5
Colorado	2.0	26.2
Arizona	1.8	26.8
Oregon	1.3	18.6
Florida	1.2	4.9
Other States	4.4	----

[a]Source: Zazueta and Corona (1979:137).

[b]Source: Percentage distribution from Zazueta and Corona (1979) applied to
estimate of 3.5 million workers from assumptions and data in Heer (1979);
Corwin (1978:128); and Fogel (1978:24-25). 1978 state population estimates
from Statistical Abstract of the United States.

significant that Portes (1977) found that more than 60 percent of a
sample of Mexicans legally residing in the United States had been
undocumented at some prior point in time; this proportion probably
understates the true case.

The pronounced "Californization" in the pattern of Mexican migrant
workers that we observe today has evolved over the past two centuries.
California had relatively few Mexican-origin persons 130 years ago.
At that time, New Mexico exhibited the greatest concentration of
Mexicans—some 75 percent of the country's Mexican-origin population
in 1850 (Corwin, 1978:31)—followed by Texas, which surpassed New
Mexico around 1900 (Corwin, 1978:113–19). These changes have
historical explanations. California had easy access to Far Eastern labor
for its farms and industries until the late 1800s and early 1900s, when
the Chinese Exclusion Act and the Gentlemen's Agreement with Japan
dried up these sources (Ehrlich, Bilderback, and Ehrlich, 1979:55–65).
In addition, California was not directly connected by rail to central

Mexico until the early 1920s (Corwin, 1978:49). On the other hand, in the late 1800s the Southwest Plains were in great need of a labor supply for erecting factories and building railroads. Furthermore, they had direct rail connections (via El Paso and Laredo) with central Mexico during this period (Corwin, 1978:45–50). Thus, until the 1920s, the Mexican-origin population increased much faster in New Mexico and Texas than in California. By then, California had met the prerequisites for the attraction of Mexican labor, and soon it had surpassed Texas as the chief state for Mexican-origin population. California's current predominance is chiefly a testimony to its superior wages, working conditions, and social milieu. For example, average Los Angeles wages for the occupational category of "laborer" are today around double those in San Antonio (Fogel, 1978:120). Additionally, there is evidence that illegal workers' rights are respected more by California employers than by those in Texas, New Mexico, and Arizona. The legal climate in California is also better, and the practice of discriminatory tactics by the Border Patrol is less severe (Ehrlich, Bilderback, and Ehrlich, 1979; Taylor, 1930). In addition, the power base of Chicano groups (who tend to support undocumenteds' rights) is stronger in California. More than Illinois, New York, or Texas, to the undocumented worker California is the "promised land." Several of these factors are discussed in detail in the last section of this paper.

Migrant Density Gradients in the U.S.

The second question is this: Do density patterns of recent undocumented arrivals show a regular decline away from the border, i.e., are such patterns continuous as opposed to discontinuous; and how are these patterns changing? To answer this, we need data on Mexican migration to a number of places within the United States over time. Fortunately, INS tabulations of deportable aliens by nationality and year for each of 35 districts and 21 border patrol stations were made available to the author (Statistical Division, INS, 1980). The district data are most appropriate for addressing the question, because they give a more representative spatial sample of undocumented aliens. The districts cover the whole country whereas the border patrol stations are in more narrow areas. These data suffer from the major problem that they are based upon INS apprehensions; the degree to which these represent the total population of such aliens is unknown. It is difficult to discern, for example, whether INS policy or migrant behavior is responsible for apprehension rates that are significantly higher in some districts than in others. Although for these reasons one must interpret the results from such data with considerable caution, this is the only detailed information available at present. It should be noted that INS apprehension data have been used in a number of studies (Cárdenas and Flores, 1978; Dagodag, 1975; Frisbee, 1975; Jenkins, 1977; Jones, 1981), with results that are consistent with those from studies of unapprehended undocumenteds (Baca and Bryan, 1980; North and Houstoun, 1976; Roberts, 1980; Zazueta and Corona, 1979).

Twenty-five INS districts are used in this test. The time period allowed by these data is 1973–78. As the cities for which these districts are named tend to be demographically central to their districts (the only significant exceptions are Miami and New Orleans), and as apprehensions tend to be greatest in the vicinity of such cities (which are INS district headquarters), it is plausible to construct isoline density maps using INS district city-nodes as points (Figures 3.1 and 3.2). The measure of density used is the number of Mexican aliens apprehended in a given year per one million (estimated) population in the district in that year. This is a surrogate for the flow of undocumenteds relative to the size of the population and labor force in the district.

From the figures it is evident that high flow density ratios are widespread, covering the entire U.S. Southwest and penetrating the Rockies and Intermontane Basin. The 1973 and 1978 patterns are basically similar. They show a distance-decay effect with certain interesting departures from perfect concentricity, viz., (a) a thrust of above-average densities into the intermontane West (especially Colorado and Wyoming), which is largely explained by the northward penetration of the Atchison, Topeka, and Santa Fe Railroad, built one hundred years ago, channeling migrants from central Mexico to the agricultural, manufacturing, and construction jobs of the region (Corwin, 1978: 48–49); and (b) a thrust toward Chicago, which, based upon newspaper accounts and research, has the high wages, availability of manufacturing jobs, and ethnic diversity (including Hispanics) to make it a magnet for undocumented migrants (Cornelius, 1978:21). In addition, one also notes (c) the locally higher densities around New York City, attractive for reasons analogous to those for Chicago; and (d) the enclave of locally lower densities around New Orleans, partly explained by fewer enticing job opportunities in the region and a less familiar culture. Note that the pattern of isodensity lines is much the same in 1978 as in 1973, despite increases in density figures for all but three districts over the period.

What is hidden in these maps is the fact that relative increases are considerably larger in the areas farther from the Southwest. An

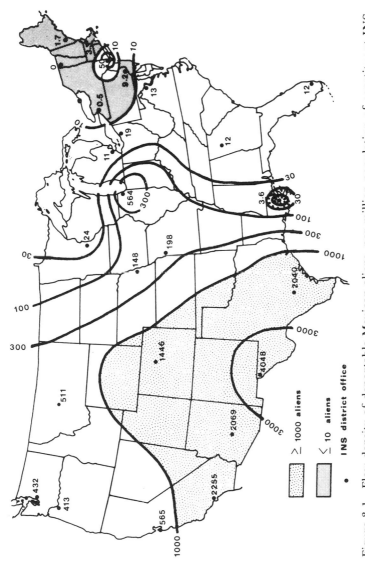

Figure 3.1 Flow density of deportable Mexican aliens, per million population of constituent INS districts, 1973

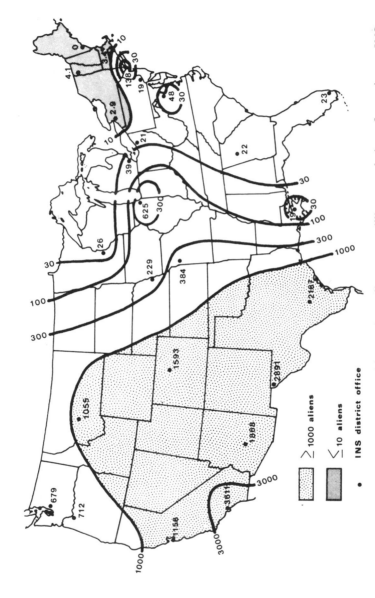

Figure 3.2 Flow density of deportable Mexican aliens, per million population of constituent INS districts, 1978

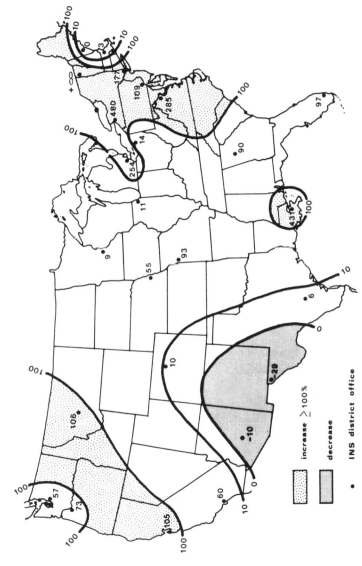

Figure 3.3 Percentage increase in flow density of deportable Mexican aliens, 1973–1978

increase ≥ 100%

decrease

• INS district office

additional isoline map (Figure 3.3), giving percentage increases in density between 1973 and 1978, shows this clearly. Flow densities in the Northwest, lower South, and Northeast more than doubled. If apprehensions accurately reflect the flows of undocumented migrants, and if this trend continues, we can expect that within each directional sector away from the Southwest, the center of gravity of the undocumented Mexican population will move outward.

Two other pieces of evidence tend to support the thesis of regular density decline away from the border. The first of these comes from a redefinition of our density measure. If we divide the number of Mexican apprehensions in a district by total apprehensions (all nationalities) for that district, we get an index that is less sensitive to the absolute numbers of immigrants. By thus placing all locales, whether in the Southwest or elsewhere, on a percentage scale, comparisons among them are facilitated. This index is also less sensitive to variations in INS enforcement among districts, because such variations would likely affect Mexicans and other migrants in similar ways. The resultant distributions (not shown) confirm the previous conclusions regarding the diffusion of migrants. In 1973, the 90 percent isoline encompassed the Southwest; by 1978 it blanketed nearly the whole western United States. Furthermore, the 10 percent isoline in 1973 separated the Middle Atlantic and New England regions from the rest of the country, whereas by 1978 it separated only New England. Otherwise, most of the familiar attenuations and enclaves of Figures 3.1 and 3.2 are present.

A second piece of supporting evidence involves patterns of Mexican workers in California in the mid-1970s. Cornelius (1976) was able to obtain (from the local priest) a detailed address list of 285 villagers from La Unión, Jalisco, working in the United States as of July 31, 1975. La Unión is representative of many emigrant villages in the Los Altos region (northeast of Guadalajara), one of the most important sending areas in all of Mexico (Winnie, Guzman-Flores, and Hernandez-Saldaña, 1979). The distribution of the 149 villagers living in major urban areas in California indicated the same sort of density-decay away from the border that we have noted in the apprehension data: Los Angeles had 7.64 and San Francisco had 5.43 sample migrants per one million resident population. These sketchy data do not, of themselves, prove a distance-decay relationship, but other data do corroborate such a relationship. Data in Taylor (1930:265) and Corwin (1978:118–26) suggest, for example, that the center of gravity of the Mexican-origin population in California has shifted northward considerably since 1926. It is interesting that both sets of data reveal a much clearer relationship for urban than for rural population clusters.

This fact suggests different migration processes. From close inspection, rural clusters of Mexican-origin population are present at spatially disjointed locales all over the country: the Imperial, San Joaquin, and Sacramento Valleys; southern Idaho; eastern Washington; southern Colorado; the High Plains of Texas; and several places in the Midwest. One explanation for this (and it is speculation at present) is that cultural and communications barriers as well as job competition are much greater for undocumented workers in urban than in rural areas. Thus they move more freely among agricultural areas, but their penetration of northern cities is slower, proceeding as kinship and cultural ties are built up. Cities such as Chicago and New York are exceptions for reasons indicated already; but the density gradient that we have observed would, by such an argument, be explicable in terms of kinship and cultural barriers in urban areas of the country.

Despite the evidence that undocumented migrants are dispersing throughout the country as well as moving up the urban hierarchy, the magnitude of this effect is still quite small. The densities of undocumented flows in the East in 1978 were a hundred times smaller than those in the Southwest; in the central Great Plains, they were around ten times smaller. Given their aversion to the hurried life-style and cultural isolation Mexicans face in the northern U.S., it is likely that for decades to come they will remain heavily concentrated in the Southwest.

Migrant Channelization and its Explanation

Channelized migration is a disproportionately large flow of migrants between a specific origin and a specific destination. It tends to connect a nonmetropolitan origin with a metropolitan destination, which distinguishes it from hierarchical migration. It is also generally long-distance, which distinguishes it from hinterland migration (Roseman, 1971). Channelized migration is presumed to be a function of spatial biases in communications links and information flow, particularly interpersonal communications. Quantitatively, channelization (C_{ij}) may be measured by:

$$C_{ij} = (M_{ij}/M_{.j}) / (M_{i.}/M_{..}) \qquad (1)$$

or

$$C_{ij} = (M_{ij}/M_{i.}) / (M_{.j}/M_{..}) \qquad (2)$$

In both formulas, M_{ij} represents the size of the flow from origin i to destination j. In the first formula, the flow in expressed as a proportion of total inflows to destination j ($M_{.j}$); this proportion is then divided by the total outflows from i ($M_{i.}$) as a proportion of all migration flows among the set of places being considered (M..). The result is an index of the degree to which a specific destination's proportion of migrants from origin i exceeds the aggregated destinations' proportion of migrants from origin i. As such, C_{ij} is akin to the location quotient. On a given data set, equation (2) gives exactly the same results as equation (1); the only difference is that M_{ij} is expressed as a proportion of total outflows from origin i.

As points of reference, other research has uncovered such channelization values as 3.2 for Scandinavian immigrants to the West-North-Central region of the United States as of 1910; 1.8 for the Irish in New England at the same time; and 2.0 for West Virginian migrants to northeastern Ohio between 1950 and 1960 (Ward, 1971:62–75). Perhaps even more valuable than individual channelization values is the value $\bar{C}_i$. (or $\bar{C}_{.j}$), which gives the weighted average of channelization out of (or into) a place, the weights being the sizes of the migration streams. As an example, $\bar{C}_i$. for Scandinavian migration to all U.S. regions in 1910 was 2.2; for analogous Irish migration it was 1.2.

The evidence (data) for channelization of Mexican undocumenteds to the United States is, unfortunately, much more piecemeal and unstandardized than that for European immigrants to the United States. Data come largely from interviews with aliens at specific sites in the U.S. The sampling frame is biased in that apprehended migrants form the bulk of the interviews and some self-serving statements, protective of kin and friends at home and in the U.S., may be expected from the informants. The CENIET study mentioned earlier deals with the experiences and characteristics of returnee and absentee migrants to the U.S. from Mexico (Zazueta and Corona, 1979). By its comprehensiveness and by the fact that it seeks information from unapprehended aliens in Mexico, it should help to correct this situation. Another study which yields useful data on settlement patterns over time is that of Baca and Bryan on unapprehended Mexicans in Los Angeles (Baca and Bryan, 1980).

The base of the channelization measure of formula (1) is the overall distribution of migrants by states of origin in Mexico. North and Houstoun (1976:31–43) interviewed some 493 undocumented Mexican workers who had been apprehended by the INS at some 19 sites in the United States in May and June of 1975. The Mexican origin states which stand out in these data separate themselves spatially into two groups: highland states along the western edge of the Mesa Central (Jalisco, Michoacán, Zacatecas, Guanajuato); and northern border states (Chihuahua and Coahuila) (Table 3.2, column 1; Figures 3.4 and 3.5). The states of southern and southeastern Mexico each have a notably small proportion of the totals.

Table 3.2 Percentage Distributions of Undocumented Mexicans, by Origins in Mexico, Mid-1970s

Mexican States and Regions of Origin[a]	Destinations US 1975[b]	South Texas 1975[c]	Southern California 1973[d]	Channelization values South Texas [Col.2÷1]	Southern California [Col.3÷1]
STATES					
Jalisco	12.2	1.8	26.2	.15	2.15
Chihuahua	11.8	4.0	1.0	.34	.08
Michoacán	10.7	1.7	21.2	.16	1.98
Zacatecas	9.9	4.5	7.4	.45	.75
Guanajuato	8.5	12.0	8.1	1.41	.95
Coahuila	6.7	24.5	(.3)	3.66	
San Luis Potosí	4.8	11.7	(.7)	2.44	
Durango	4.8	3.8	3.9	.79	.81
Baja California[f]	4.4	(0)	8.5		1.93
Nuevo León	3.9	13.1	(.2)	3.36	
Tamaulipas	3.0	12.6	(.3)	4.20	
Sonora	3.0	(0)	2.8		.93
Distrito Federal	2.6	3.5	2.6	1.35	1.00
Guerrero	2.2	1.4	2.4	.64	1.09
Sinaloa	2.2	(0)	4.7		2.14
Aguascalientes	2.0	1.0	(.8)	.50	
Nayarit	2.0	(.6)	3.3		1.65
Colima	1.3	(0)	1.8		1.38
Veracruz	.8	1.0	(.3)	1.25	
México	.6	(0)	(.4)		
Querétaro	.6	.4	(.8)		
Hidalgo	.6	(0)	(0)		
Other States	1.4	2.4	2.3		
Total	100.0	100.0	100.0		
Weighted channelization ($\bar{C}_{.j}$)				2.55	1.67
REGIONS[g]					
Central	39.2	20.4	61.9	.52	1.58
Northwest	38.1	12.9	31.6	.34	.83
Northeast	18.4	61.9	1.5	3.36	.08
South	2.9	2.4	2.7	.83	.93
States not included	1.4	2.4	2.3		
Total	100.0	100.0	100.0		
Weighted channelization ($\bar{C}_{.j}$)				2.36	1.30

Notes: [a]States with less than 0.5% in the first column are omitted from the table.
[b]North and Houstoun (1976:53), sample of 493 Mexican migrants to the US.
[c]San Antonio INS District, 707 I-213 forms; data in Cardenas (1976:61).
[d]Dagodag (1975), sample of 3,204 I-213 forms from Chula Vista Border Patrol Sector.
[e]Figures in parentheses are less than 1%. Not used in channelization calculations.
These calculations follow channelization equation (1).
[f]Baja California Norte and Sur are combined.
[g]See Figure 3.4 for regional definition.

Figure 3.4 Mexican states and territories. Ag = Aguascalientes; BCN = Baja California Sur; Cam = Campeche; Coa = Coahuila; Col = Colima; Chia = Chiapas; Chih = Chihuahua; DF = Distrito Federal; Dur = Durango; Gto = Guanajuato; Gro = Guerrero; Hid = Hidalgo; Jal = Jalisco; Mex = Mexico; Mic = Michoacan; Mor = Morelos; Nay = Nayarit; NL = Nuevo Leon; Oax = Oaxaca; Pue = Puebla; Que = Queretaro; QR = Quintana Roo; SLP = San Luis Potosí; Sin = Sinaloa; Son = Sonora; Tab = Tabasco; Tam = Tamaulipas; Tlx = Tlaxcala; VC = Vera Cruz; Yuc = Yucatan; Zac = Zacatecas.

Several conclusions may be drawn from these patterns. 1) The most prominent sending states, with greater than five percent of total emigrants each, run down the center of the country. These states encompass traditional mining and agricultural areas of the country, zones which have been in economic decline for decades. 2) Both relatively poor states (Michoacán, Zacatecas) and relatively well-off states (Coahuila, Chihuahua) are evident among the prominent sending areas. Several of the poorest, most indigenous, and most distant states (Oaxaca, Chiapas, Yucatán), however, send few migrants to the United States at all (Roberts, 1980:20–21). 3) There is a relatively continuous decline in the magnitude of emigrant percentages from the most to the least prominent origin states. This suggests that the emigration process is relatively widespread in Mexico. In fact, only ten states (31 percent) are in the lowest category in Figure 3.5.

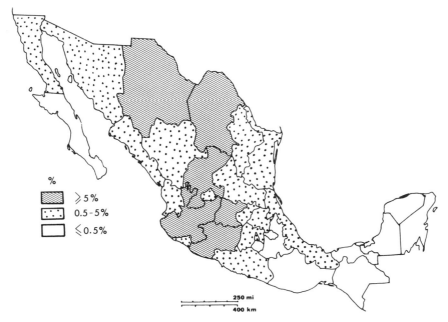

Figure 3.5   Percentages, by origin, of undocumented migrants to the United States, 1975

Data available from Cárdenas (1976:61) offer a sample of 707 I-213 forms from the 1975 records of the San Antonio INS District Office. This enables calculation of the migrant channelization index from the point of view of the South Texas destination region. The I-213 ("Record of Deportable Alien") forms are filled out by INS personnel who interview apprehended aliens at detention centers or at the site of apprehension. Some evasive answers are to be expected under such conditions. In actuality, however, several studies have found excellent cooperation from the aliens, who have a sort of "gentlemen's agreement" with the INS—cooperation in return for minimal harassment and rapid repatriation. This gives the migrant an early chance to attempt another crossing (Bustamante, 1977; Ehrlich, et al., 1979). The resultant distribution of migrant states of birth from the Cárdenas data (Table 3.2, column 2) indicates an emigrant hearth in northeastern Mexico, with Coahuila, Guanajuato, and San Luís Potosí together providing one-half. The data thus indicate that south Texas draws from both the northeastern Mesa Central and from the border states of the northeast. Chihuahua, Durango, and Zacatecas, toward the west, exhibit relatively low percentages because of the intervening opportunities represented by Juarez–El Paso and by California. Channelization values calculated from these data (Table 3.2) reveal that

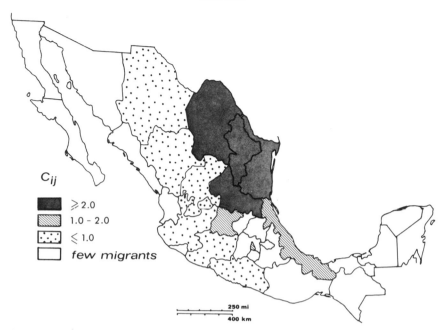

Figure 3.6   Channelization (C_{ij}), by origin, of undocumented migrants to the San Antonio INS District, 1975 ("Few migrants" indicates less than 1% of the total.)

Tamaulipas, Coahuila, Nuevo Leon, and San Luís Potosí are of much greater importance to San Antonio's undocumented migrant stream to the United States, and this is emphasized in Figure 3.6. The figure and table also show a tendency for states in the eastern part of Mexico to have higher channelization values than those to the west, with states in the northwest sending few migrants to South Texas at all. The overall pattern, then, is a highly channelized one. Notice the apparently close relationship of the channelization measure and distance from South Texas (actually, $r_p = -0.828$ between C_{ij} and distance from a state's population centroid and San Antonio).

Data made available to this writer by Tim Dagodag, from his 1975 study of a sample of Mexican illegals to the Chula Vista Border Patrol region of California (Dagodag, 1975) enables us to compare the South Texas undocumented migration field with that of southern California. Chula Vista is the major conduit for migrants to California, accounting for between fifteen and thirty percent of all Mexican undocumenteds apprehended in the United States in recent years (North and Houstoun, 1976:18–21; Samora, 1971:85). Dagodag used a sample of 3,204 I-213 forms, collected in 1973, in his study. The resultant distribution of migrant birthplaces (Table 3.2, column 3) shows a pronounced concentration in the western Mesa Central (Jalisco, Michoacán), with

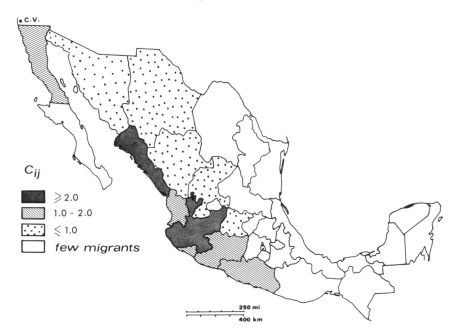

Figure 3.7   Channelization (C$_{ij}$), by origin, of undocumented migrants to the Chula Vista Border Patrol Sector, 1973

a secondary concentration in the state of Baja California Norte. The contrast between this distribution and that for the San Antonio district could hardly be more marked, with the important sending states in one distribution being of negligible importance in the other. Only in states which run down the country's central spine (Durango, Zacatecas, Aguascalientes, Guanajuato, the Distrito Federal) do the proportions for sending states approximate one another. These are states of "indifference" between the California and Texas in-migration fields, and they are also states for which the pull of El Paso and points north is strong. Channelization values for the Chula Vista stream (Table 3.2 and Figure 3.7) reveal a migrant hearth in the western Mesa Central (Jalisco, Michoacán) and Pacific Coastal (Sinaloa, Nayarit, Guerrero) regions. The map presents an inverse image of the previous map; it is as if the migrants were "poured" into southern California along the bottom of the Mexican horn. The California stream is a much less channelized stream than that for South Texas.

Factors Influencing Patterns of Migration
to the United States from Mexico

Any attempt to explain the aforementioned spatial patterns as they existed in the mid- and late-1970s must acknowledge both: 1) historical forces, particularly transport connections and employment attractions, operative over the past 50 to 100 years; and 2) current-day forces, particularly immigration policy and social/cultural attractions, operative over the last 10 to 20 years. Manuel Gamio has given us spatial data (based on postal money-order receipts) for the period of Mexican immigration in the 1920s, enabling us to compare origin-destination profiles then from that period with those of today (Gamio, 1930). Gamio's data, when compared to those of North and Houstoun for 1975 (1976), reveal a northward drift in the emigrant zones, in which traditional migration hearths in the western Mesa Central (Michoacán, Guanajuato, and Jalisco) have lost out to, or blended with, border sending zones (Chihuahua and Coahuila). It is not surprising that the Mexican origin pattern in 1975 is a less concentrated one than that for 1926. Gamio's data on United States destinations, compared to those of Zazueta and Corona for 1978/79 (1979), reveal a reverse phenomenon—a process of immigrant concentration in those states already dominant in 1926 (California and Texas) and a decline nearly everywhere else.

1. *Transportation linkages with Mexico.* The rail connections which were forged between central Mexico and Texas in the early 1880s had a compelling influence on both the origins and destinations of migrants. The connection of El Paso with Colorado, Kansas, and the Midwest was forged by the Atchison, Topeka, and Santa Fe Railroad in 1881; by 1884, the Mexican Central had completed its line all the way to El Paso from Mexico City (Corwin, 1978:48–9). At almost the same time, the Missouri Pacific connected Laredo and San Antonio to points north, while the Mexican National was completed from Laredo to Mexico City. In a few years, Mexican emigration became a phenomenon of the Mesa Central rather than the border states; and through El Paso and Laredo/San Antonio, came to be connected to all parts of the United States (California was not directly connected to central Mexico until completion of the Southern Pacific's Mexican line in 1923). It was during the ensuing 40-year period that El Paso became the major port of entry for Mexican migrants (Corwin, 1978:45), and Mexican migrant communities grew up in southern Colorado (e.g., the San Luis Valley), in Missouri (e.g., St. Louis), and elsewhere along the major trunk routes leading north and northeast from El Paso. It is interesting that the rail connections aided northern Mexico's economic development and slowed emigration from there, while accelerating emigration from central Mexico. After 1923, the year in which central Mexico was connected by rail with southern California, the rails were important in shifting the major streams to California. Because of its economic, climatic, and other attractions,

California now drew migrants heavily from the western Mesa Central, siphoning from the Texas and New Mexican streams. This process of concentration in California has lessened in recent years, as nonborder states have begun to receive undocumenteds (Jones, 1981). In addition, recent urban growth in northern Mexico, originally brought on in part by transport connections with central Mexico and the U.S., has been very rapid. The percentage of total population in cities with more than 15,000 people rose from 20 percent to 50 percent between 1940 and 1970 in the three north-central border states of Durango (Unikel, 1978:76), urban job and service creation have been unable to keep up. Thus, emigration to the U.S. is now proportionately much greater than it once was for states such as Chihuahua, Coahuila, and Zacatecas—all of which send their migrants primarily from urban instead of rural areas (Bustamante, 1977).

2. *Labor contracting patterns.* While railroads were the conduits for early migration streams, labor contractors for the railroads, farms, mines, and factories of the Southwest were the suction that kept the streams continuously flowing to the United States. The Santa Fe and Southern Pacific tracks were largely built and maintained by Mexican labor (Corwin, 1978:50). Furthermore, since this labor was often siphoned away by the new resource-based industries of the Southwest and Plains—meat packing, mining, metal refining, flour milling, warehousing, etc.—the labor contractors for the railroads were kept continuously at work. Later, farms and industries began to do their own recruiting directly (and illegally) in Mexico. The years prior to the 1920s were ones in which Texas garnered an increasing proportion of Mexican migrants, owing to pressing labor demands in the Rio Grande Valley coupled with a strongly pro-business political climate in Texas. Texas's position declined relative to California's in the late 1920s, only to resurge during the *bracero* period of 1942–1965. It was during the latter period that El Paso, located not too far from the major recruiting center for *braceros* in Mexico (Chihuahua City), regained its preeminence as a migration conduit. It is not surprising that the *bracero* epoch was one in which the Mexican states of Chihuahua, Coahuila, Zacatecas, and Durango greatly increased their shares of Mexican emigrants (Hancock, 1959:22). Today, in Baja California Norte and other Mexican states, networks of *coyotes, polleros,* and *enganchadores* (all terms for the middlemen who arrange for border crossing and transportation in the U.S.), etc. still strongly influence the channels of migrant entry. The predominance of California as a destination is partly attributable to the location of the numerous "middlemen" in Tijuana and Mexicali who, because of their experience and their "gentlemen's agreements" with the INS, can virtually assure

an aspirant with the necessary cash of a successful border crossing and safe arrival at his job (Ehrlich et al., 1979:296–310; Cornelius, 1978:23–24). Films such as *Alambrista* (Cinema 5, directed by Robert Young) and various new accounts of border crossings make it clear that *coyotes* play important roles in channeling migration through certain Mexican cities and into adjacent parts of the United States.

3. *Communication channels between destination and village.* At the macroscale (state, region) we have found substantial migrant channelization. Regarding the microscale, however, the process is not a simple one in which, through interpersonal communication, migrants from a particular village in Mexico settle in a particular town in the United States. Instead, the following conclusions are correct: (a) Within the major and comparatively dispersed emigrant zones in Mexico, a few subregions are responsible for much of the emigration. In support of this conclusion, see Johnson and Ogle (1978:85) and Hancock (1959) on the origins of migrants from Chihuahua; Cornelius (1976:53–57) on migrants from Jalisco; and Reichert and Massey (1979) on migrants from Michoacán. Within the villages of these subregions there is a high degree of shared knowledge concerning who has emigrated to the U.S., where they've gone, and their degree of success. (b) Focusing on the major and highly concentrated migrant destination zones in the U.S., we find considerable dispersion within the zones. The research on California, particularly, makes it clear that although migrants come from specific areas in Mexico, they quietly disperse toward locations where jobs are to be found (Villalpando, 1977). Thus, migrants may initially stay with relatives or village acquaintances (North and Houstoun, 1976:88–93) with whom they have maintained communications, but they then move on. In Cornelius's study of La Union, the sample of 285 emigrants were found to be living in no fewer than 110 different localities in the United States—57 of these in California alone (1976:16–19). In summary, the communications network informs and initially directs migrants to the destination regions which best fit their needs and means; but after that, migrants move rather freely in search of the best working conditions. They are not necessarily tied by kin or village associations to specific destinations. Thus, they may be unlike their Appalachian counterparts who moved to certain northern cities in the 1950s and 1960s, and either stayed there or dispersed slowly into urban hinterlands.

4. *Preference for an Hispanic social/cultural milieu.* Certainly an important factor in the concentrated pattern of undocumenteds in the United States is their sociocultural affinity for the Southwest, an affinity which they share with Mexican-Americans already living there. Price (1969) found that Mexican-Americans formerly residing in the lower

Rio Grande Valley in Texas, now living in Chicago, were much more likely to return home if the proper economic conditions prevailed, than were former residents now living in San Antonio. This greater affinity for San Antonio was reflected in significantly higher happiness levels and levels of participation in the urban locality—despite the better economic conditions of the Mexican-American respondents in Chicago. Affinity for the borderlands, within the generally-preferred southwestern region, has been found by Hansen (1971:165–77). Cornelius has given us a graphic description, from his interviews in Jalisco, of the aspects of U.S. life which are most disliked by Mexicans and thus which seem to discourage a permanent sojourn here: the fast pace of life; working constantly to survive; the dislike of U.S. climate; racial discrimination against Mexicans; the pervasiveness of vice; and the difficulty of attaining any social status in the U.S. (1978:26–27). These are negative views which seem to accelerate as one moves northward, and, of course, undocumenteds perceive the amenities of the Sunbelt vis-à-vis the Frostbelt, as does everyone else. In this regard, California possesses the Sunbelt climatic amenities and lacks the degree of racial discrimination one finds today in Texas. In addition, it possesses a large and powerful Chicano community to provide moral support and political representation. These advantages evidently more than offset the fast pace of life and high cost of living found in southern California cities.

5. *The U.S. legal climate.* Although scant data exist, there is considerable circumstantial evidence that California's legal climate is more favorable than that in other border states, particularly Texas. It also seems that this is perceived and acted upon by potential Mexican migrants. This legal climate has several dimensions: (a) stronger unions (particularly, in the farmworker, laborer, and service worker categories), which tend to increase wage levels and create a general respect for workers' rights (Corwin, 1978:266–69); (b) the lesser brutality and overt discrimination by Border Patrol personnel in California as compared to Texas (Ehrlich, 1979; Cárdenas and Flores, 1978; Texas Advisory Committee, 1980; (c) the generally stronger legal support for educating the children of undocumenteds in California versus Texas (as revealed in news accounts of recent court cases in Texas; and (d) fewer restrictions on the use of public services by aliens (recent studies in Los Angeles and San Diego have, in fact, found that aliens exact only marginal financial burdens on health, police, and welfare systems) (Villalpando, 1977).

6. *Job opportunities, wages, and working conditions.* A further rationale for California's dominance of recent undocumented patterns in the United States can be found in its superior economic environment, as

reflected in large numbers of available jobs, high wages, and relatively good treatment by employers. The existence of good working conditions in California has already been touched upon. Regarding job availability, the Border Industrialization Program, which employs tens of thousands of Mexican workers in Mexico and undetermined numbers in related industries in the United States, is especially evident along the California border. In the early 1970s, almost two-thirds of the 160 "twin plants" were in two California border areas: Tijuana/San Diego; and Mexicali/Calexico (Steiner, 1971). These plants were intended to keep would-be undocumenteds employed in Mexico; this has in general not occurred, because migration to the border from the interior has far outstripped available jobs; and U.S. jobs are still much higher-paying. In this regard, urban growth in northern Mexico has been phenomenal: Tijuana evidenced a 1500 percent increase in population between 1940 and 1970; and Mexicali, an 800 percent increase (Fogel, 1978:32). The Border Industrialization Program is now considered a prime cause of the recent surge in migrant crossings (Fogel, 1978:30–33). It is also notable that "borderland" wages in California are much superior to such wages in Texas, exceeding one dollar per day more (Steiner, 1971). Within the interiors of these states, California's wage superiority continues. For example, 1972 hourly wages in the category "laborer" were $4.88 in Los Angeles versus $2.80 in San Antonio, and $5.09 in San Francisco versus $3.14 in Dallas (Fogel, 1978:120). Similar differentials exist in many other employment categories. Thus, there is a relatively high-wage corridor along the West Coast, which attracts migrants from within Mexico both to northwestern border ciites and to California cities.

Conclusions and Discussion

The pattern of undocumented Mexicans in the United States at present apparently is a highly concentrated one, with more than 50 percent of the migrants in California. In contrast, the pattern of Mexican origins is a dispersed one. This implies that the attractive forces are spatially more specific, whereas the "push" factors are spatially more generalized and widespread. There are certain policy implications in these findings. California's heavy "burden" of undocumenteds (if they should prove to be a burden) may require federal subsidization in order to provide schooling, health care, etc., in the future, particularly as migrants become more assimilated. Analogously, U.S. aid to Mexico might be targeted to certain border states and to certain interior states where emigration is most pronounced. Proposals for a new guest-worker program and for tariff liberalization on products emanating from certain areas in Mexico have been made. These merit further consideration in regard to their impacts on specific parts of Mexico.

More importantly, the patterns of Mexican migrants within the United States have become more dispersed in recent years. During approximately 50 years prior to 1970, migrants were concentrating in California and the border Southwest. Since 1970, a gradual but unmistakable shift out of the Southwest has been taking place. This shift is occurring concomitantly with a large increase in the total number of undocumented migrants from Mexico who are apprehended by the INS, a surge of migrants comparable to those of the early 1940s and early 1950s (the *bracero* period). During these and earlier periods the patterns of destinations were more dispersed than they are today, with large flows moving into the central part of the U.S. Upon termination of the *bracero* program, there followed a more restrictive period. This in turn was superseded by a less-restrictive period beginning in 1976 with the Carter administration. There is some reason to believe that present-day dispersion is a compound influence of the increasing urban residential experiences and skill levels of Mexican migrants, a more lenient INS policy toward apprehensions in interior regions of the U.S., and the increasing awareness on the part of migrants of job opportunities and INS policies. It is interesting that the trend of larger increases outside the Southwest runs counter to the phenomenon of Sunbelt versus Frostbelt growth in the United States. Is it possible that undocumented labor may aid cities such as Chicago and New York in stemming the flight of certain labor-intensive industries to the Sunbelt and abroad? This is an intriguing question worth more study.

It is impossible to draw normative ("good or bad") conclusions from this process of migrant diffusion until more is known about the regional impacts of undocumented migrants on such economic phenomena as unemployment, wage rates, business profitability, and productivity. Not a single study in the literature has tested these relationships empirically, largely because unequivocal data on numbers of undocumenteds by regions are nonexistent. Yet such data are pivotal to the overall research on undocumented workers. Research underway by the author is uncovering weak, and in some cases insignificant relationships between changes in numbers of undocumented Mexicans apprehended, and changes in unemployment and wage rates over the same time period. This research has used complete years and INS districts as temporal and spatial units of analysis. It is possible that relationships by month and by individual states and cities will reveal closer relationships, but it is equally likely that the relationships will continue to be low. If so, we may have to revise the widely held assumption that labor-force impacts of undocumented workers are negative, or to acknowledge important intervening or exogenous forces in this relationship.

References

Baca, Reynaldo, and Dexter Bryan. 1980. *Citizenship Aspirations and Residency Rights Preferences*. Report for Sepa-Option, Los Angeles, California.

Bustamante, Jorge A. 1977. "Undocumented immigration from Mexico: Research report." *International Migration Review* 11:149–77.

Cárdenas, Gilberto. 1976. "Manpower Impact and Problems of Mexican Illegal Aliens in an Urban Labor Market." Ph.D. dissertation, University of Illinois.

Cárdenas, Gilberto, and Ray Flores. 1978. *A Study of the Demographic and Employment Characteristics of Undocumented Aliens in San Antonio, El Paso, and McAllen*. San Antonio: Avante, Inc., for the Texas Advisory Committee, U.S. Commission of Civil Rights.

Cornelius, Wayne A. 1976. *Mexican Migration to the United States: The View from Rural Sending Communities*. Cambridge, Mass.: Center for International Studies, Massachusetts Institute of Technology.

_____. 1978. *Mexican Migration to the United States: Causes, Consequences, and U.S. Responses*. Cambridge: Center for International Studies, Massachusetts Institute of Technology.

Corwin, Arthur F., ed. 1978. *Immigrants—and Immigrants: Perspectives on Mexican Labor Migration to the United States*. Westport, Conn.: Greenwood Press.

Dagodag, W. Tim. 1975. "Source regions and composition of illegal Mexican immigration to California." *International Migration Review* 9:499–511.

Ehrlich, Paul, Leslie Bilderback, and Anne Ehrlich. 1979. *The Golden Door*. New York: Ballantine Books.

Fogel, Walter A. 1978. *Mexican Illegal Alien Workers in the United States*. Los Angeles: Institute of Industrial Relations, University of California.

Frisbee, Parker. 1975. "Illegal migration from Mexico to the United States: A longitudinal analysis." *International Migration Review* 9:3–13.

Gamio, Manuel. 1930. *Mexican Immigration to the United States: A Study of Human Migration and Adjustment*. Chicago: The University of Chicago Press.

Hancock, Richard H. 1959. *The Role of the Bracero in the Economic and Cultural Dynamics of Mexico*. Stanford, California: Hispanic American Society, Stanford University.

Hansen, Niles. 1971. *Intermediate-size Cities as Growth Centers: Applications for Kentucky, the Piedmont Crescent, The Ozarks, and Texas*. New York: Praeger.

Heer, David M. 1979. "What is the annual net flow of undocumented Mexican Immigrants to the United States?" *Demography* 16:417–23.

Jenkins, J. Craig. 1977. "Push-pull in recent Mexican migration to the U.S." *International Migration Review* 11:178–89.

Johnson, Kenneth F., and Nina M. Ogle. 1978. *Illegal Mexican Aliens in the United States: A Teaching Manual on Impact Dimensions and Alternative Futures*. Washington, D.C.: University Press of America.

Jones, Richard C. 1981. "A geographical perspective on illegal migration from Mexico." Paper delivered at the annual meeting, Association of American Geographers, Los Angeles, April 21, 1981.

North, David S., and Marion F. Houstoun. 1976. *The Characteristics and Role of Illegal Aliens in the U.S. Labor Market: An Exploratory Study*. Washington, D.C.: Linton & Co., for the Employment and Training Administration, U.S. Department of Labor.

Portes, Alejandro. 1977. "Labor functions of illegal aliens." *Society* 14 (September/October):31–37.

Price, Daniel. 1969. *A Study of Economic Consequences of Rural-to-Urban Migration: Final Report*. Austin, Tex.: Tracor, for the U.S. Office of Economic Opportunity.

Reichert, Josh, and Douglas Massey. 1979. "Patterns of U.S. migration from a Mexican sending community: a comparison of legal and illegal migrants." *International Migration Review* 13:599–623.

Roberts, Kenneth D. 1980. *Agrarian Structure and Labor Migration in Rural Mexico: The Case of Circular Migration of Undocumented Workers to the U.S.* Austin: The Institute of Latin American Studies, University of Texas.

Roseman, Curtis C. 1971. "Channelization of migration flows from the rural South to the industrial Midwest." *Proceedings, Association of American Geographers.* 3:140–46.

Samora, Julian. 1971. *Los Mojados: The Wetback Story.* Notre Dame: University of Notre Dame Press.

Statistical Division, Immigration and Naturalization Service. 1980. "Deportable aliens located by nationality, 1974–78." Washington. (Grateful acknowledgment is made to Margaret Sullivan of the Division.)

Steiner, H. Malcolm. 1971. "The Mexican border industrialization program." *Texas Business Review* 65.

Stoddard, Ellwyn T. 1977. "Alternatives to immigration laws and policies." In Guy Poitras, ed., *Immigration and the Mexican National.* San Antonio: Border Research Institute, Trinity University, pp. 40–47.

Taylor, Paul S. 1930. *Mexican Labor in the U.S.*, Vol. 1. Berkeley: The University of California Press.

Texas Advisory Committee, U.S. Commission on Civil Rights. 1980. *Sin Papeles: The Undocumented in Texas.* San Antonio Press.

Unikel, Luís. 1978. *El Desarrollo Urbano de Mexico: Diagnóstico & Implicaciones Futuras.* Mexico, D.F.: El Colegio de Mexico.

Villalpando, Vic, *et al.* 1977. *Illegal Aliens: Impact of Illegal Aliens on the County of San Diego.* San Diego: Human Resources Agency, County of San Diego.

Ward, David. 1971. *Cities and Immigrants: A Geography of Change in Nineteenth Century America.* New York: Oxford University Press.

Winnie, William W., Jr., Elsa Guzman-Flores, and Victor Hernandez-Saldana. 1979. "Migration from West Mexico to the United States." In Barry Poulson & T. Noel Osborn, eds., *U.S.–Mexico Economic Relations*, pp. 193–200. Boulder, Colo.: Westview Press.

Zazueta, Carlos H., and Rudolfo Corona. 1979. *Los Trabajadores Mexicanos en los Estados Unidos: Primeros Resultados de la Encuesta Nacional de Emigración a la Frontera Norte del País y a los Estados Unidos (ENEFNEU).* Mexico, D.F.: Centro Nacional de Información y Estadísticas del Trabajo (CENIET).

PART TWO
Origins in Mexico

4

Illegal Mexican Immigration to California from Western Mexico

W. TIM DAGODAG

Although overlooked for decades, illegal immigration into the American Southwest from Mexico has not reached levels where considerable public interest has been evoked. Furthermore, the current scale and magnitude of illegal crossings induces a set of socioeconomic problems which beset the whole American Southwest. Concern for this topic can initiate public action involving domestic labor, which may result in the formulation of ameliorative policies dealing with labor force questions, migrant treatment, and citizenship status. This study reviews basic regional problems associated with illegal Mexican aliens. Through the use of a case study focusing on California, it generates a profile of illegal immigrants examined from several perspectives, both spatial and aspatial.

Regional Problems and Their Relationship to Illegal Immigration

While illegal immigration from Mexico has been recognized as a fact of life, deeper consideration of the process suggests several socioeconomic disequilibria endemic to the Southwest.

This is a revised version of "Source Regions and Composition of Illegal Mexican Immigration to California," *International Migration Review* 9 (1975):499–511. By permission of the publisher.

1. *Domestic Labor Patterns.* Domestic underemployment or unemployment in the region may be exacerbated by availability of a large illegal labor force which is regularly employed in agriculture, marginal industries, and services.
2. *Labor Law Violation.* Unskilled illegal aliens work for close to the legally prescribed federal, state, or local minimum wages. The willingness to work for lower wages has tended to depress compensation for domestic laborers in general and abet unemployment (Economic Development Administration, 1968:36).
3. *Loss of Revenues.* Some wages paid to illegal aliens are not subjected to federal or state taxation. In addition, because of cash exports to Mexico, a sizable portion of wages paid to aliens does not enter the regional economy.
4. *Health.* Tuberculosis, typhoid, hepatitis, and dysentery have been linked to illegal immigrants (*Los Angeles Times,* September 16 and November 12, 1973). A health hazard exists since aliens are frequently hired in food services or processing industries.
5. *Welfare.* Some illegal aliens are receiving public assistance (Swoop, 1973). This condition diverts resources from domestic recipients.
6. *Law Enforcement.* In addition to draining manpower resources of federal and local law enforcement authorities, illegal immigrants have been linked to the importation of drugs (INS, 1973).

Figure 4.1 indicates the number of aliens apprehended in the Chula Vista Border Patrol sector of Southern California. This number is symptomatic of impressive changes in illegal immigration experienced in the entire Southwest (609,673 apprehensions in 1973) (*Los Angeles Times,* January 17, 1974; November 9, 1972; and December 17, 1972). Two factors should be borne in mind when reviewing these data. Although the apprehensions represent an unknown number of repeat entries, those individuals attempting more than one illegal entry during a year are believed to be insignificant. This was primarily due to the former practice of transporting aliens back to interior states of Mexico. While this practice discouraged reentry by making it economically unfeasible, it was suspended in 1971. Subsequent to 1971, repeat entries may be surmised only from occasional notations in INS documents. Secondly, the number of aliens successfully eluding INS authorities cannot be documented.

Source Regions

In order to determine where immigrants to California originated, INS documents (I–213 forms) were analyzed. The sample consisted

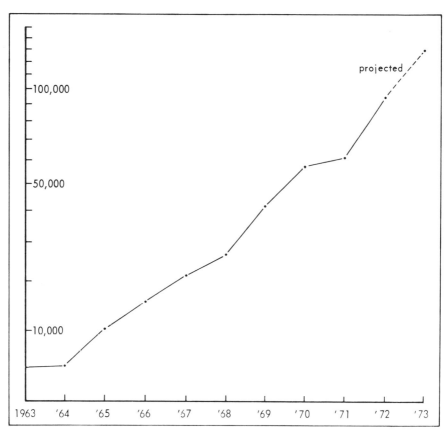

Figure 4.1   Number of illegal immigrants apprehended in the Chula Vista
Border Patrol sector, 1963–1973

of 3,204 selected documents—approximately five percent filed during
the period January 1 to August 31, 1973—for aliens seized in the
Chula Vista sector and its six outstations (Figure 4.2). Data retrieved
from these records were complete for questions regarding place of
birth, permanent residence in Mexico, sex, and age. Other questions
pertaining to marital status, occupation, length of stay in the United
States, place of apprehension, and amount of United States currency
held when arrested, were not uniformly answered because of an
inability to process fully each individual arrested.

In this study, place of birth was interpreted to be the source of
illegal immigration for two reasons. First, consideration of birthplace
reduces illegal immigration to its locational origins. Second, since the
question of state migration was anticipated, it was thought initially

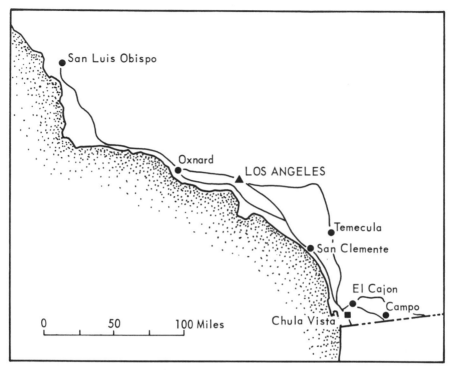

Figure 4.2   Location of U.S. Border Patrol outstations in the Chula Vista
sector

that a comparison of birthplaces and last place of residence would
allow identification of at least one internal movement within the
country. Later analysis revealed that last place of residence corre-
sponded closely (98 percent) with birthplace.

Figure 4.3 shows the location of source regions via a choropleth
mapping technique carried out at the level of Mexican states. Immediately, the western edge of the Mesa Central emerges as a hearth
of illegal immigration to California. To a lesser extent, adjacent states
and the northwest have participated. Above all, this cartographic
evidence indicates that contiguity alone is not sufficient to explain
levels of immigration. Instead, distances from the hearth to California
suggest that a set of well-defined and sophisticated motives must
underlie the decision to leave Mexico.

Despite the macroscale of Figure 4.3, several conclusions are possible.
First, this hearth is part of the most densely populated core of Mexico.
Second, it is well known that social, economic, and other maladjustments
beset this core area (Navarrete, 1967). Lastly, according to a division

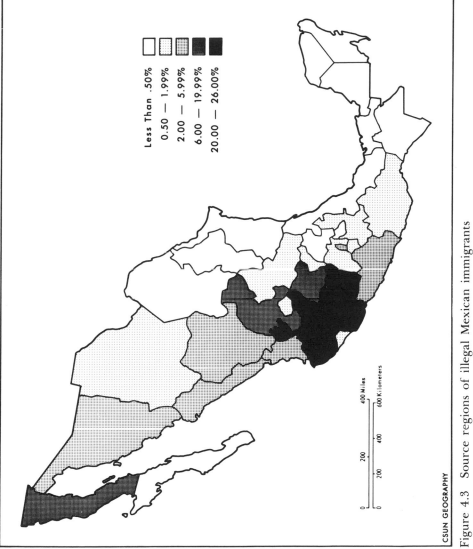

Less Than .50%
0.50 — 1.99%
2.00 — 5.99%
6.00 — 19.99%
20.00 — 26.00%

400 Miles
600 Kilometers
200
400
200
400
0
0

CSUN GEOGRAPHY

Figure 4.3   Source regions of illegal Mexican immigrants

of the country along cultural lines, most immigrants appear to originate in the mestizo areas of the western Mesa Central.

Within this national framework of illegal immigrant regions, two states, Jalisco and Michoacán, are conspicuous, and they account for over 48 percent of all immigrants seized (829 and 670, respectively). This observation is consistent with findings obtained previously by Gamio and others (Gamio, 1930; Carney, 1957; Grebler, 1966; Martinez, 1957; Redfield, 1929; Samora, 1971; Saunders and Leonard, 1951). Whetten noted that, except for the Distrito Federal, Michoacán led all other States in the number of migrant workers departing for the United States in the years 1942 through 1944 (Whetton, 1948). In a similar vein, most contract labor associated with an embryonic United States–Mexico Bracero Program was recruited from the Distrito Federal, Michoacán, and Guanajuato (Durán, 1955; Galarza, 1964). Although the origins of illegal immigration are outside the scope of the present study, one must acknowledge a relationship between these early labor contracting activities and later illegal migration of labor to California and elsewhere in the Southwest.

Because of apparent systematic immigration spanning at least four decades, Michoacán, the second largest contributor of immigrants to California, was chosen for detailed analysis. This intrastate examination eventually permits formulation of some basic conclusions regarding clandestine labor movement and regional problems already noted.

In the sample taken, 182 places in Michoacán were cited as points of origin. However, despite use of gazeteers and large scale maps, only 151 (83 percent) could be located. The distribution of those places (Figure 4.4) suggests both the rural-urban nature of origins, and the cultural subareas of these origins.

In the physically diverse landscape of Michoacán are nine urban places which yielded over 20 migrants each to California (Table 4.1 and Figures 4.4 and 4.5). Over 42 percent of the immigrants represented in the sample came from these towns. A more refined assessment, nevertheless, reveals a concentration of sources located in the highland complex of volcanic basins, plateaus, and lacustrine plains. Such discrimination also shows that six highland localities in the northern one-third of the state generated 32 percent of all immigrants, in addition to representing five of the largest cities.

Of the urban immigrants, most come from towns with a population of 10,000 or more. Still, the majority appear to be rural folk. This conclusion is warranted not only by the above findings but by recalling inherent shortcomings in the Mexican census wherein places with 2,500 or more inhabitants were classified as urban (Dirección General de Estadística, 1970). A generally more credible figure for defining

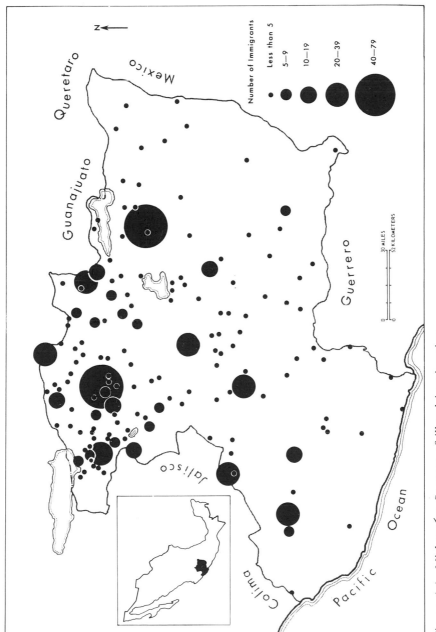

Figure 4.4 Michoacán: Sources of illegal immigration

Table 4.1   Michoacán, Mexico--Towns Yielding 20 or
            More Illegal Aliens[a]

Town	1970 population	Number
Apatzingan	44,849	29
Coalcoman	4,875	22
Tepecaltepec	9,002	21
Jiquilpan	15,960	23
La Piedad	34,963	23
Morelia	161,040	78
Puruandiro	9,956	24
Zamora	57,775	42
Uruapan	82,677	31

[a]Source: INS (1973)

urban functions in Mexico is at least 10,000. Therefore, most immigrants were rural dwellers at the time of departure.

Socio-economic Composition

In constructing a profile of the alien, several detailed characteristics
emerge. First, consider the ethnicity of the migrant sending areas
(Figures 4.4 and 4.5). Using the presence of 500 or more individuals
in each *municipio* who spoke only Indian (Tarascan, Mazahuan, Na-
huatl), or in each *municipio* who were bilingual, Indian culture areas
could be roughly delimited (Dirección General de Estadística, 1970).
If Uruapan and Morelia, sizable Hispanic-mestizo cities, are excluded
from the Indian culture area, only 32 individuals in the entire sample
of 670 came from predominantly Indian *municipios*. Thus, there is a
well-defined mestizo bias to the act of emigration, and Indians are
not significant participants in this international labor flow. This is a
logical finding. Indian communities have traditionally been conservative
and horizontally as well as vertically stable. They have strong norms
of social egalitarianism fostering coherence and stability of the society.
They have limited access to information. Mestizos, on the other hand,
are generally free from cultural and class constraints placed on

indigenous peoples; they are upwardly mobile, occupy enhanced positions of exposure to external sources of information, and, consequently, are more likely candidates for immigration.

Having established the basic mestizo character of illegal immigration, other aspects of age, sex, and economic composition complete the profile. For the following analysis, we focus on the total sample of 3,204 immigrants. Over 90 percent of all aliens were 40 years of age or younger, although the greatest frequency was registered for individuals between the ages of 18 and 27. Moreover, 92 percent of the aliens were males. Male preponderance here may be somewhat misleading since law enforcement techniques and perhaps a tendency to overlook females may distort the pattern of apprehensions. Nonetheless, these findings are not altogether surprising given the character of labor requirements in the United States.

The age distribution also suggests that young Mexican males are not participating in a process of domestic economic development. Exclusion from such participation, for whatever reasons, coupled with an evaluation of the penalties and rewards associated with illegal immigration, must constitute a primary motive to attempt unlawful entry. Furthermore, there appear to be few constraints on individuals deciding to leave their homeland (Table 4.2, for example, shows that marital responsibilities affect just over one-third of the sample).

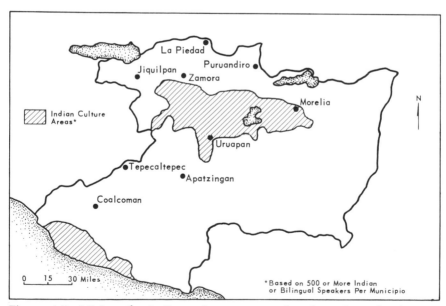

Figure 4.5   Michoacán: Indian culture areas and major urban places

Table 4.2 Selected Socioeconomic Characteristics of Illegal Immigrants Apprehended in California during 1973[d]

No. Responding in Sample of 3,204	Characteristic	No.	%
1,539	Marital Status		
	Single	959	62.3
	Married	579	37.6
	Divorced	1	.1
3,185	Length of stay in California		
	Apprehended at entry	1,405	44.1
	72 hours or less	1,056	33.1
	4 to 30 days	397	12.5
	1 to 6 months	261	8.2
	7 months to 1 year	41	1.3
	More than 1 year	25	.7
1,128	Occupation		
	Laborer	1,036	91.8
	Services	65	5.8
	Industry	20	1.8
	Student	7	.6
2,611	Activity when apprehended		
	Seeking employment	2,136	81.8
	In agriculture	384	14.7
	In industry	77	2.9
	In services	14	.5

[a]Source: INS (1973)

Other elements denoting economic composition and the nature of interaction in California are similarly confirmed in Table 4.2. Forty-four percent of the aliens were seized at one of the checkpoints upon entry into California and another 33 percent were arrested within 72 hours of initial crossing. This temporal pattern of apprehension is followed closely by a spatial pattern in which longer periods of illegal residency are related to increasing distance from the frontier. In fact, all those individuals who remained undetected for a period greater than one year were found in localities of Los Angeles.

Reference to Table 4.2 also shows that most aliens were low-skilled laborers searching for employment. There is, of course, a very high correlation between those individuals who were searching for jobs and the number arrested within 72 hours. Whether or not these individuals had specific employment destinations in mind can only be gauged from symptomatic evidence, such as recurrent employment of aliens by certain California industries, and the gravitation of townsmen or villagers to the same employer. Still, it is apparent that a considerable number of aliens cross the frontier without any definite job location in mind.

As for the economic success of the immigrants, an average of $30 was found among 512 aliens responding to INS interrogation. Using this seemingly small amount as a basic multiplier and recalling levels of migration, verifies the substantial nature of cash flow out of the United States. Of further importance to demographic theoreticians here is the potential contribution of illegal wage earners to other candidates, especially relatives, seeking to move directly from Mexico to the United States without engaging in any process of stage migration.

The absence of a stage migration process is definitely confirmed in cases involving aliens paying to be smuggled into California. These average payments (summarized in Table 4.3) indicate that young immigrants must be receiving monetary contributions which enable them to utilize organized smuggling services. Given the attributes of youth, average incomes in Mexico, and the length of time required to accumulate $200, some external funding of illegal immigration is certain. Evidence also points out that aliens may arrange to be transported across the frontier only to pay later upon procurement of steady employment (*Los Angeles Times*, February 2 and March 4, 1974).

Succinct as the above depiction is, enough characteristics emerge to note a general correspondence between the circumstances of illegal immigration and migratory labor in Latin America. In this regard, Bagu and Palermo (1966) have noted:

The most poor and ignorant remain [at home], involved in growing misery. Those who leave are those who have the physical energy and mental capacity to remake their destinies.

The decision to migrate, and the act itself, often entailing a journey of over 1200 miles, certainly bespeaks possession of some mental and physical advantages on the part of Mexican aliens. Moreover, the uncertainty and the real dangers associated with such immigration, lend additional support to this contention.

Table 4.3 Dollar Amounts Charged for Smuggling Services[a]

Amount (in U.S. Currency)	Number of Aliens	Percent
less than $50	5	3.6
$50 to $99	12	8.5
$100 to $199	78	55.7
$200 to $299	44	31.4
$300 or more	1	.8
Total	140	100.0

[a]Source: INS (1973)

Conclusions

The magnitude and acceleration of illegal migration from Mexico poses some very basic health, labor, and other related problems for U.S. destinations. An analysis of INS-apprehended aliens enables an examination of spatial distributions and personal characteristics of these migrants. This study, focusing on Mexico and California, has attempted to arrive at generalizations about the origins and composition of illegal immigration which may be applicable to the Southwest as a whole. These findings can be summarized as follows:

1. The major hearth of illegal immigration is centered in west-central Mexico in a region of existing socio-economic disequilibria.
2. Illegal immigration is related to historical patterns of legal labor recruitment, and most certainly to contemporary smuggling.
3. Illegal immigration is largely a rural phenomenon, although urban areas may become increasingly important points of origin.
4. Immigrants are preponderantly young, mestizo males.

5. Economic objectives of illegal immigrants appear to be tied to the acquisition of low-skill occupations in the secondary labor market.
6. Stage migration, as a form of interaction, is not applicable to illegal immigration since movement from the Mexican hearth to California is largely a single-stage, long-distance activity.

References

Bagu, Sergio, and Epifamio Palermo. 1966. "Condiciones de vida y salud de los trabajadores migrantes y sus familias en America Latina." *Cuadernos Americanos* XXV:15–24.

Carney, John Philip. 1957. "Postwar Mexican Migration: 1945–1955, with Particular Reference to the Policies and Practices of the United States Concerning Its Control." Ph.D. dissertation, University of Southern California.

Dirección General de Estadística, Mexico. *IX Censo General de Población.* Estado de Michoacán.

Duran Ochoa, Julio. 1955. *Población.* Mexico, D.F.: Fondo de Cultura Económica.

Economic Development Administration, U.S. Department of Commerce. 1968. *Industrial and Economic Potential of the United States–Mexico Border.*

Galarza, Ernesto. 1964. *Merchants of Labor: The Mexican Bracero Story.* Santa Barbara, California: McNally and Loftin.

Gamio, Manuel. 1930. *Mexican Immigration to the United States.* Chicago: University of Chicago Press.

Grebler, Leo. 1966. *Mexican Immigration to the United States: The Record and Its Implications.* Los Angeles: The University of California.

Immigration and Naturalization Service (INS), Interview with INS Commissioner, October, 1973.

Martínez, Ramón. 1957. *Mexican Emigration to the United States, 1910–1930.* Los Angeles.

Navarrete, Ifigenia M. 1967. "Income distribution in Mexico" in Enrique Perez Lopez, et al., *Mexico's Recent Economic Growth.* Austin: University of Texas Press, Latin American Monograph No. 10:146–51.

Redfield, Robert. 1929. "Antecedents of Mexican immigration to the United States." *American Journal of Sociology* 35 (November).

Samora, Julian. 1971. *Los Mojados: The Wetback Story.* Notre Dame: The University of Notre Dame Press.

Saunders, Lyle, and Olen E. Leonard. 1951. *The Wetback Worker in the Lower Rio Grande Valley of Texas.* Austin: Interamerican Education Program, University of Texas, Occasional Paper 7.

Swoop, David B., California State Welfare Director. Interview, November 11, 1973.

Whetton, Nathan L. 1948. *Rural Mexico.* Chicago: University of Chicago Press.

5

Agricultural Development and Labor Mobility: A Study of Four Mexican Subregions

KENNETH D. ROBERTS

This article examines the economic factors that affect labor allocation of rural landholding households in four areas of Mexico. The original research was considerably narrower, focusing on the "push factors" causing illegal migration to the United States. However, it soon became apparent that restricting the analysis to U.S. migration would make it impossible to distinguish between factors that cause members of households to work off-farm in general, and those that condition this wage labor to take various forms, such as local labor, circular or permanent migration within Mexico, or migration to the United States.

At its broadest level, this is a study of the relationship between rural development and labor mobility. There are a number of interesting theoretical issues involved, especially those raised by the emerging literature on circulation and on peasant household decision-making. This study, however, will keep the issue of undocumented migration

This is a revised version of "Agrarian Structure and Labor Mobility in Rural Mexico," *Population and Development Review* 8 (1982):299–322. It is based on a report prepared for the U.S. Department of State and the Employment and Training Administration, U.S. Department of Labor. The research was a collaborative effort of the Institute of Latin American Studies, The University of Texas at Austin, and the Centro de Investigaciones Agrarias, Mexico City, and benefited greatly from the assistance of Gustavo Treviño Elizondo and discussion with Ina Dinerman. By permission of the publisher.

as its central theme. Its conclusions challenge the assumption of an inverse relationship between rural economic development and undocumented migration. There are important implications for the effectiveness of development programs in slowing the long-term outflow of rural migrants. This study also sheds light on the suitability of a guest-worker program as an "interim" solution to the current insufficiency of job opportunities in Mexico and high levels of illegal migration to the United States.

Migration and Rural Development

Much of the literature on the relationship between economic development and migration in less-developed countries can trace its lineage to the dual-economy model of Lewis (1954). In his model, the economy is composed of two sectors: rural agricultural and urban industrial. There is surplus labor in the agricultural sector, and the urban wage is set at a fixed premium above the level of rural subsistence. Capital accumulation is the driving force of the model, providing increasing numbers of jobs that attract rural migrants. Rural-to-urban migration continues until there is no longer a labor surplus in the countryside, and rural and urban wages are equal.

These assumptions are echoed in numerous characterizations of the causes of Mexican migration to the United States. Thus, Reubens asserts that undocumented immigration is a result of "economic dualism, in which the expanding modern sectors exist side by side with lagging traditional sectors [and in which] surplus workers are accumulating in the hinterlands of agriculture, industry, and services" (1978:15). According to this widely held viewpoint, circular migration to the United States represents an interim strategy to cope with lagging job opportunities in rural and urban areas of Mexico. There is theoretical support for this role of circulation in the model of Zelinsky (1971), which posits a series of migration stages in which circulation is gradually replaced by permanent migration as urban opportunities expand.

Further development of the dual-economy model specified the rural conditions that define underdevelopment and cause migration: a lack of land and capital and the use of traditional techniques of production, resulting in low agricultural yields; rapid population growth resulting in a low marginal product of labor; resistance by economically insecure farmers to new agricultural technology and new crop varieties. An important implication of this theory is that if agriculture can be made more productive, the tide of migration to the cities will be slowed. Programs of rural agricultural development in the 1960s and 1970s, promoting the adoption of a mix of new grain varieties and the greater use of purchased inputs, often claimed the reduction of migration as one of the potential benefits. The dual-economy model also implies that the process of illegal migration from rural Mexico to the United States will not abate until Mexico develops its agricultural areas or provides an adequate number of jobs in the cities to compensate for the lack of rural development (Cornelius, 1977).

Several recent studies have challenged the empirical validity of this theory for many less-developed countries. The identification of the rural population with agricultural labor has been found to provide an incomplete description of rural economic activity. A study of off-farm employment in rural areas of 15 developing countries found that 20–30 percent of the labor force was engaged primarily in nonfarm employment (Anderson and Leiserson, 1980). On the basis of his research on peasants in Oaxaca, (a poor and predominantly rural state in Mexico), Beals concluded that "farming is neither their primary occupation nor is it their main source of income. The ways of making a living are numerous and varied" (1975:15).

Employment off one's own land (called "off-farm employment" throughout this study) may involve agricultural wage labor or other types of work in the local area, commuting to nearby towns, or circular migration between regions. While patterns may differ greatly between countries and between regions within the same country, many rural areas exhibit what White (1976) has termed "extreme occupational multiplicity." Goldstein has observed, "What evidently varies from country to country is not the variety of forms of movement relied upon, but rather the particular mix of alternatives and the exact conditions under which one or the other is relied upon more heavily" (1978:55).

Nor does agricultural "development" necessarily result in reduced migration or even reduced off-farm employment, as implied in the traditional theory. In many instances, new varieties of seeds and new techniques adopted in less-developed countries during the 1960s not only decreased labor requirements but also lowered incomes for certain strata of farmers and for landless laborers (Hewitt de Alcantara, 1976). The new technology requires a higher level of purchased inputs. It also gives the farmer less latitude with respect to the timing and amounts of labor and machinery inputs. A new cropping pattern or technology might have potential for increasing income and employment but, within a particular socioeconomic context, could cause greater concentration of land. This would be due to the inability of small farmers to afford the necessary level of purchased inputs and to assume higher levels of risk. Seasonal concentration of labor inputs for the new varieties might cause labor-supply bottlenecks and stimulate compensating changes in cropping patterns and increased mechanization.

These findings imply that circular migration does not necessarily represent a transitional phase between traditional agricultural employment and permanent migration from a region. In contrast to the portrayal of circular migration as corresponding to a period of declining agricultural production per worker, it would appear that agricultural development may stimulate circular migration. Circulation may provide a means to earn money to meet the higher level of cash requirements of agricultural production. This earning capacity might also offset the risks accompanying decreased production of the subsistence crop, and compensate for the decline in demand for local agricultural wage labor. Circular migration allows the peasant producer to maintain primary residence in the rural area and to obtain income from both farm and nonfarm sources. Circular migration may therefore provide higher income at less risk than either farm production or permanent migration (Fan and Stretton, 1980). This preliminary assessment of an expanded role for circular migration within less-developed countries is supported by recent research. Chapman and Prothero summarize this literature as follows: "Circulation, rather than being transitional or ephemeral, is a time-honored and enduring mode of behavior, deeply rooted in a great variety of cultures and found at all stages of socioeconomic change" (1977:5).

This article considers these challenges to the accepted theory of economic development and migration in greater detail, within the context of patterns of farm and off-farm employment and permanent and circular migration in four rural areas of Mexico. The following section sketches the nature of agricultural production in each of the four survey areas. Then we examine the allocation of household labor to off-farm activities, including circular and permanent migration, and the role played by regional agrarian structure. The last section derives some general conclusions concerning the relationships observed in the four zones.

Production and Employment in Agriculture

This study is based on farm survey data collected in the Mixteca Baja, Oaxaca State; Las Huastecas, San Luis Potosí; Valsequillo, Puebla; and the Bajío, Guanajuato (Figure 5.1). The four surveys were conducted in 1974, covering the year 1973. The first three were conducted by the Centro de Investigaciones Agrarias and the last by the author in collaboration with several Mexican agencies. The emphasis of each

Figure 5.1 Location of the four survey areas

survey was on farm structure as it affected farm and off-farm labor. The topic of migration was treated secondarily in the context of off-farm labor. The unit of analysis was the farm household. This included all members who live with the household head, work on the family farm, or contribute money to the farm household. The total sample consisted of 482 farm households.

The fieldwork in Oaxaca, San Luis Potosí, and Puebla was conducted in 1974 as part of a project examining the conditions of employment in rural Mexico. The results were published in three volumes (Barbosa Ramírez, 1976, 1977, 1979). They were conducted by the Centro de

Investigaciones Agrarias. The data are based on random samples, within farm size categories, of landholding households. Extensive data were collected on agricultural production and agricultural labor, distinguishing between household and hired labor and household off-farm employment. Migration emerges in this data at the location of off-farm employment during the year 1973, or through remittances sent by a household member from employment elsewhere, allowing circular migration to be explicitly examined. The fieldwork in the Bajío involved sampling 218 farms in the seven Bajío *municipios* (counties). The questionnaire included items on farm production, income, costs, labor, and household off-farm employment. The labor data were exhaustive, including the number of days worked by each household member, machinery and animals on the household plot, and off-farm labor for each household member by occupation. The definition of the household encompassed all persons living with the household head who contributed income from off-farm sources to the household or worked on their land. Thus migrants, circular or permanent, were captured if they either returned home and worked or sent remittances.

Table 5.1 summarizes the major agricultural characteristics of the four survey areas. These areas together span the major forms of agriculture found in Mexico (the major omission being any example of the highly mechanized agriculture of the irrigated areas of the Northwest). By almost any measure of development, the Mixteca Baja, located in the mountainous coastal region of the state of Oaxaca, occupies the lower end of the socioeconomic spectrum. The Bajío occupies the other end of the spectrum, having undergone significant agricultural modernization in the 1960s and rapid growth of the urban areas and infrastructure during the 1970s. A variety of commercial crops now dominate agriculture in this region.

Any notion of a linear progression from traditional to commercial agriculture that may be implied in the contrast between the Mixteca Baja and the Bajío breaks down when the characteristics of the other two regions are examined. Las Huastecas exhibits many aspects of traditional agriculture, with reliance on family labor and traditional inputs. Subsistence crops, though, are mixed with commercial crops, and farm incomes are relatively high. Valsequillo, by contrast, is closely linked with the commercial and semiurban economy of the Puebla area, and agriculture is partially mechanized. However, farm incomes are low for most households, and corn, the primary subsistence crop in Mexico, dominates the cropping pattern.

The *Mixteca Baja*, Oaxaca, conforms closely to the common perception of underdeveloped, traditional agriculture. Subsistence crops produced using traditional inputs and techniques are dominant; farm

Table 5.1 Major Agricultural Characteristics of the Four Survey Areas

Item	Mixteca Baja (67 house-holds)	Las Huastecas (98 house-holds)	Valsequillo (99 house-holds)	The Bajío (198 house-holds)[a]
Population[b]				
Density (persons per square kilometer)	26	39	560	100
Total	91,383	98,804	49,908	276,570
Labor force in agriculture (percent)	79	81	56	64
Population speaking Indian language (percent)	41	50	0	0
Dwellings with running water (percent)	10	25	52	n.a.
Agricultural production				
Average farm size (hectares)	2.8	7.1	6.1	10.4
Cultivated land in subsistence crops (percent)	76	66	87	46
Corn production sold (percent)	10	14	37	88
Value of agricultural capital per hectare (pesos)	$907	$285	$1,798	$4,070
Value of farm production per hectare (pesos)	$1,234	$3,273	$2,218	$4,250
Farm income (pesos)	$2,639	$16,816	$21,487	$22,306
Farms with income less than 5,000 pesos (percent)	79	20	64	23
Agricultural labor				
Household farm labor (person-days)	172	275	78	86
Hired farm labor (person-days)	68	52	87	85
Total farm labor (person-days)	240	327	165	171
Total farm labor per hectare cultivated (person-days)	118	75	37	22
Household farm labor in corn production (person-days)	127	105	58	30

Notes: [a] Excludes households possessing large irrigated farms.

[b] The population data are from the 1970 Censo de Población, Mexico, for the municipios of the survey area. All other data are from the household surveys.

n.a. indicates not available.

incomes are extremely low; and local employment opportunities are limited. The population of the region is impoverished; the 1970 census shows that most of the region's rural population live in one-room dwellings with dirt floors and (despite the presence of two towns of over 10,000 people) only 10 percent of the households have running water (Barbosa-Ramírez, 1976).

Las Huastecas, San Luis Potosí, is a more prosperous agricultural zone than the Mixteca Baja. This is true despite the fact that agriculture as practiced in both zones would be classified as traditional, employing few purchased inputs and devoting a relatively large percentage of cultivated land to production for home consumption. Households in Las Huastecas were able to increase farm income by devoting a large amount of household labor to high-value, labor-intensive crops—particularly sugarcane. Sugar provided a source of cash income without requiring much monetary outlay, while corn provided much of the subsistence consumption of the household. The fact that the value of agricultural output was relatively high without reliance on the market for hired labor, purchased inputs, or food explains the differences between off-farm household labor allocation in Las Huastecas and the other zones.

Agricultural technology in *Valsequillo*, Puebla, is more capital-intensive than in the first two zones. Tractors are commonly used in preparing the land for planting, with the smaller farms renting tractor services from the larger farms. If labor inputs are calculated per hectare, the differences between Valsequillo and the other survey areas are evident: total farm labor input per hectare in Valsequillo was less than half that in Las Huastecas and one-third that in the Mixteca Baja. Mechanization, primarily in land preparation, appears to have substituted for household labor, although substantial hired labor was used. The higher level of integration of Valsequillo into the market system, requiring heavier use of purchased inputs and hired labor, does not appear to have increased agricultural incomes for the majority of households. Most had farm incomes well below those in Las Huastecas. What agricultural modernization accomplished was a decrease in household farm labor inputs, thus freeing labor at the disposal of the household for alternative uses.

The *Bajío* of Guanajuato is by far the most urban and commercially developed zone of the four surveyed in this study. Most economic activity in the zone is in agriculture, but the area also contains strong industrial, commercial, and service sectors. Yet prosperity has not benefited the population equally. A high degree of rural stratification, manifested in wide disparities in farm size, capitalization, and farm income, makes averages over all farms meaningless.[1]

Incomes derived from large and medium-sized irrigated farms in
the Bajío were high, but even on the small irrigated farms they
exceeded those in the next most prosperous zone, Las Huastecas. All
but 23 percent of the farms in the Bajío produced incomes greater
than 5,000 pesos. However, the form that this income takes and the
methods used to produce it are far different from those in Las
Huastecas. Besides commercial crops, most corn produced in the Bajío
is sold, even by farms in the unirrigated and small irrigated categories.
Farms in Las Huastecas manage to generate relatively high levels of
income by growing high-value crops without spending much money
on labor and other purchased inputs. Farms in the Bajío employ a
capital-intensive technology and have to produce good crop yields just
to break even on cash expenses.

This brief survey of the agricultural situation of four areas in
Mexico emphasizes the importance of separating two potential effects
of agricultural modernization. With such modernization, agriculture
almost inevitably becomes more commercialized; hybrid seeds, fertilizer,
and machinery are substituted for more traditional inputs; and a
greater percentage of crop production is sold, linking the farm
household much more closely to the market economy. Farm incomes
may also rise, but only in regions where access to the improved inputs
and infrastructure such as irrigation is not restricted to the large
farms.

Off-Farm Employment and Migration

Table 5.2 compares farm and off-farm income and labor in the four
zones.

THE MIXTECA BAJA, OAXACA

Out of the 259 person-days worked by the average household in the
Mixteca Baja, 88 person-days, or 34 percent, were applied in off-farm
income-producing activities. This off-farm labor produced an income
of 2,329 pesos, bringing total household income to the (still very low)
figure of 4,968 pesos. Most households in the sample were poor and
earned close to the average level of household income for the zone.
Thus wage income formed a critical supplement to farm income for
most households; 69 percent of all households engaged some of the
labor at their disposal in a gainful activity other than farming their
own parcel of land. Most off-farm labor was local agricultural wage
labor, paying 15 to 20 pesos per day. Seventy-seven percent of the
off-farm labor days were employed within the same *municipio.* This is

Table 5.2 Off-farm Income and Labor in the Four Survey Areas

Item	Mixteca Baja (67 households)	Las Huastecas (98 households)	Valsequillo (99 households)	The Bajío (198 households) [a]
Income (pesos)				
Farm	2,639	16,816	21,487	22,306
Off-farm	2,329	4,211	12,293	12,257
Total	4,968	21,027	33,780	34,563
Labor (person-days)				
Farm	171	275	78	86
Off-farm	88	139	253	101
Total	259	414	313	187
Off-farm labor days as _jornalero_ (percent)	72	100	63	23
Average number of adults per household (over age 16)	3.1	3.3	3.7	5.4

Note: [a] Excludes 20 households possessing large irrigated farms.

a reflection of the difficulty of transportation in the region and the uniformity of wages throughout the zone.

As might be expected in a region with limited income-earning opportunities, permanent outmigration is a fairly regular feature: 43 of the 75 *municipios* in the larger Mixteca region lost population between 1960 and 1970 (Aguilar, 1974; Butterworth, 1975), largely due to the migration of young people to Acapulco or Mexico City. About one-fourth of the households in the sample had members working outside the zone at the time of the interview. Perhaps because of this, household size in the Mixteca Baja was the smallest of the four zones, averaging about 5.3 persons, with 3.1 of these over 16 years old. There was no circular migration to the United States, which is not surprising given the geographic and cultural distance separating the two societies and the lack of resources to finance the journey, the border crossing, and the necessary job search.[2]

LAS HUASTECAS, SAN LUIS POTOSÍ

Wage labor plays a less significant role in Las Huastecas than in the other three zones. This is not surprising, since household farm labor input and farm incomes are relatively high. During the study period, off-farm labor was 34 percent of total household labor. However, much of this labor was in unpaid community service still common in some indigenous regions of Mexico. Few households worked off-farm to earn money, and the income contributed by off-farm labor is only about 20 percent of total household income. The share of off-farm labor to total labor tends to be higher for households with greater numbers of adult workers and for households with lower farm incomes. The number of days worked in off-farm labor is distributed evenly over the year, with monthly variations in total household labor due almost entirely to variations in farm labor input.

Most off-farm labor is agricultural, and 63 percent of this occurs in the *municipio* in which the household resides. None of the households in the sample had members who had worked in the United States during the study year, despite the proximity of the zone to the border. Agricultural wages in the surrounding region, at 64 pesos per day, exceeded local agricultural wages of 31 pesos per day for work in the *municipio.* Households whose members engaged in work outside the *municipio* tended to invest more days in this activity than did households whose members worked locally. This difference probably reflects the less casual nature of regional *jornalero* (day-worker) labor; the higher costs of travel and job search are presumably overcome by higher wages and longer periods of labor. In addition to this salaried labor by persons living with the household head at the time of the interview, 18 households had members working in another area who had sent remittances during the year, averaging 2,135 pesos per migrant household.

The pattern of labor allocation that emerges in Las Huastecas is thus heavily weighted toward intensive use of on-farm labor. The pattern is of less permanent migration but more regional circular migration and commuting than in the Mixteca Baja. Earning off-farm income is less critical to most of the households in Las Huastecas, where farm incomes are relatively high and purchased inputs are kept to a minimum. Most households are able to earn sufficient cash to meet their minimal needs by growing surgarcane or coffee on a portion of their household land.

VALSEQUILLO, PUEBLA

Valsequillo is a more commercial agricultural zone than either Las Huastecas or the Mixteca Baja. But farm incomes are low for the majority of households, while levels of purchased inputs are higher than in either of the two indigenous zones. This creates the need for off-farm income, and much lower farm labor inputs and a higher proportion of hired labor allow households to devote the majority of their time to off-farm labor. Households in Valsequillo allocated 76 percent of their work time to wage labor during the survey period.

The large farms cause the averages to understate the importance of off-farm income to the majority of households in Valsequillo. For the 70 households with more than one-fourth of their total earned off-farm, farm income averaged only 4,180 pesos, and four out of five households received income from wage labor.

Off-farm labor for the average household was divided between agricultural wage labor and a wide variety of unskilled employment, including construction and domestic labor. Of the average household's total of 253 person-days of off-farm labor, 63 percent were employed in agriculture. Workers in nonagricultural occupations worked more days per year and earned a higher average income, 48 as opposed to 37 per day for agricultural laborers.

Only about 20 percent of off-farm labor occurred outside the *municipio*. Households whose members worked in other *municipios* did not tend to record more working days than those whose members worked entirely within the *municipio*, possibly reflecting the good transportation network, which makes local travel comparatively easy. In addition to earning wage income locally, ten households received remittances from temporary and permanent migrants, averaging 6,966 pesos per migrant. None of these migrants worked in the United States.

THE BAJÍO, GUANAJUATO

Wage income in the Bajío is a significant portion of total household income for all but the largest farm categories. Two-thirds of the households in the sample engaged in wage labor, and for these households wage income was between 26 and 44 percent of total income. Remittances were also important to the smaller categories of farm, with more than one-fourth of the households in these categories receiving remittances averaging 5,936 pesos.

Agricultural wage labor is a much less important component of off-farm labor in the Bajío than in the other zones because of the diversified economy. Households with large irrigated farms recorded high wage incomes because their members often held full-time positions as professionals or in commercial enterprises.

Perhaps the most striking characteristic of household labor in the Bajío is its low absolute amount: household labor for all categories in the Bajío averaged only 183 person-days per household, compared with 331 days in Valsequillo, 414 days in Las Huastecas, and 259 days in the Mixteca Baja (see Table 5.2). Households in the two indigenous zones worked more on-farm than in the Bajío, while those in Valsequillo worked more off-farm. Certainly the higher incomes from farm production in the Bajío were instrumental in reducing the need for wage income, but the fact that two-thirds of the households in this zone engaged in off-farm labor indicates its importance in supplementing farm income.

The seasonality of on-farm and off-farm labor reveals the role played by off-farm labor in total household labor allocation. If off-farm labor were to vary inversely with farm labor, this would indicate that the household subordinated its off-farm labor to farm labor demands. However, monthly off-farm labor did not vary much for the medium category of irrigated farms, which are the most representative of the average farm in the sample. Thus off-farm labor played an independent role in total household labor allocation; households worked a rather constant amount of time off-farm each month, and during months of high farm labor inputs they hired labor to enable them to continue working in these activities.

Circular migration in the Bajío was more common than in any of the other zones studied. Data on the location of household members indicate that about 40 percent of the 622 males of working age lived apart from the household head. Over half of these were in the same village, but a significant number were also found in the local cities of Celaya and Salamanca (7 percent), in Mexico City (3 percent), and in the United States (5 percent). These men could have been engaged in either circular or permanent migration, but the fact that they maintained a relationship with the household by either sending remittances or helping with farm work supports the thesis that they were probably absent only temporarily.

Survey respondents were asked to approximate the number of days worked by household members as agricultural laborers in different locations. The United States was the most frequent destination for *jornalero* labor outside of the *municipio* of residence.

Table 5.3 presents data on the differences between households that had members who had worked in the United States and those that did not, excluding the large irrigated farms, which sent no members to the United States. These two groups are not significantly different with respect to the major economic variables—farm size, farm income, purchased inputs per hectare, off-farm income, or off-farm labor. However, it is of great interest that households that sent migrants to the United States had an average labor force (males age 16 or more) that was 46 percent larger than those that did not, a difference that is statistically significant at the .001 level. The implication is that a larger household labor force permits a diversification of income sources that offsets the increased risk of migration to the United States.

This analysis indicates that circular migration to the United States would only be undertaken by households with multiple sources of income, which would not be too dependent on this risky income source alone. Moreover, households in the Bajío are larger than those in the other zones.

It may be postulated that households in the Bajío are larger *because* farm income is higher, permitting more members to share in the income from farm production.[3] The incorporation of adult members into the extended household, combined with low farm labor requirements, allows one or more household members to work almost entirely off-farm. Enjoying the security of the extended household and a share in farm production, household members can leave the community for long periods of time. Total household income is increased by their remittances, and the larger extended household permitted by higher farm income enables them to choose these relatively more risky off-farm alternatives. By contrast, in Valsequillo, farm incomes are lower and there are fewer adult members in each household, so that the failure to obtain a job in a more distant location could have serious consequences.

Table 5.3 Mean Values of Selected Variables for Households With and Without Members Working in the United States: the Bajío

	Households with U.S. labor (N = 30)[a]	Households with-out U.S. labor (N = 168)[a]	Level of signifi-cance of difference in mean values[b]
Farm Size (hectares)	8.4	10.7	.586
Farm income (pesos)	$21,131	$22,515	.936
Value of purchased inputs per hectare (pesos)	$1,409	$923	.590
Off-farm income (pesos)	$10,138	$9,708	.935
Remittances (pesos)	$4,173	$1,198	.001
Off-farm wage labor (person-days)	75	52	.245
Education (years)	9.1	8.7	.810
Male labor force (persons)	4.1	2.8	.001

Note: [a]Excludes the 20 large irrigated farms.

[b]T-test of pooled variance.

Discussion

The data presented in this study cast doubt on some of the distinctions often perceived between traditional and modern agriculture and on the common explanations for rural outmigration. Households in each of the four survey zones work a significant amount of time off-farm and use hired labor to permit them to continue to engage in off-farm economic activities even in months of heavy farm labor inputs. Thus off-farm labor is not a residual that absorbs part of the difference between household labor supply and farm labor demand. Rather, the household makes simultaneous decisions concerning the allocation of farm labor between household and hired labor, and the allocation of household labor between on-farm and off-farm labor.

This conclusion has important implications for the validity of simpler theories relating agricultural development and migration. If off-farm employment does not vary inversely with household farm employment and farm income, the assumption that a lack of agricultural development triggers increased circular migration, is called into question. That circular migration, in turn, leads to permanent migration as urban opportunities expand and rural opportunities decline relative to the size of the rapidly growing population is an assumption which must also be reexamined.

Two potential consequences of the concept of agricultural development, increased commercialization and higher farm incomes, have been shown to be important factors in the determination of household labor allocation. Agricultural commercialization, loosely defined as the substitution of purchased inputs, commercial crops, and marketed production for traditional farming, unequivocally has caused a decline in total farm labor inputs in the Bajío and Valsequillo and in the portion of these inputs contributed by the household. However, only where local agricultural conditions are favorable, as in the Bajío, can small farms raise farm incomes by participating in this improved technology. Agricultural development is not invariably associated with higher farm income. In Valsequillo, modern technology fails to produce adequate levels of income for most farms and serves only to reduce household labor inputs.

In contrast, farm incomes are relatively high in Las Huastecas because the soil and climate permit high-value crops to be grown with minimal levels of purchased inputs.

Agricultural development also has different effects on risks associated with total household income and therefore on the allocation of household labor to various off-farm activities. Higher levels of purchased inputs and the substitution of commercial for subsistence production link the household closely to the market economy. This increases the fixed monetary costs of production and the potential variability of farm income. Higher farm incomes, on the other hand, decrease the risk that the household will earn an income below subsistence level.

These concepts may be used to explain the patterns of household labor allocation observed in the four zones. In the Mixteca Baja, primitive techniques on poor soil yield insufficient farm incomes for the bare necessities of a small household. With few local opportunities for wage labor, young people often migrate permanently to cities in which networks of migrants from the local area live. Farm incomes are too low to finance the riskier alternative of circular migration to other areas, especially to the United States. In Las Huastecas, farm production yields a relatively high income with few purchased inputs. The necessity for wage labor is reduced by minimal household cash requirements resulting from the low commercialization of agriculture. Heavy inputs of household labor leave little opportunity for extended stays away from the farm. Clearly, farm income plays an important role in determining migratory patterns in these two zones of traditional agriculture. Were the analysis to stop here, it might be concluded that rising farm incomes would decrease circular migration.

The patterns of household labor allocation observed in Valsequillo and the Bajío provide little support for this conclusion. Both of these zones are much more commercially developed than the two indigenous zones, yet farm incomes are low in the former and high in the latter. The monetization of production in these zones has increased both the relative importance of off-farm labor and its diversification. However, circular migration is not an important component of the off-farm labor mix in Valsequillo. Circular migration in the Bajío though, especially to the United States, is quite common.

The function of farm income in reducing the risk of obtaining below-subsistence income is central to an explanation of the differences in patterns of labor allocation between these two zones. While households must work off-farm in Valsequillo to earn an adequate income, they cannot afford to support a circular migrant along with the accompanying risk that he will not quickly obtain a job and send remittances. Therefore, they work locally for long periods in a variety of occupations. Households in the Bajío use higher levels of farm income to support circular migrants, generating more off-farm income and partially offsetting the risk associated with their greater dependence on monetary sources of income. The total portfolio of income-producing activities is the important consideration. Higher farm incomes permit the relatively risky alternative of United States migration, while this activity produces high cash income and may reduce the variability of the total income portfolio.[4]

These conclusions are of course tentative. They are based on assumptions about the relative riskiness of farm income and particular types of off-farm employment in the four zones, and on incomplete data on labor migration. Yet the data on agrarian structure and patterns of off-farm labor allocation indicate clearly that the simple preconceptions that often guide policy do not apply. Circular migration has emerged in the Bajío as an integral part of a complex response to agricultural change, while other patterns of labor mobility in the other zones resulted from their particular circumstances. In order to understand this response, it was necessary to specify the impact of agricultural change upon purchased inputs, crop composition and seasonality, marketed production, hired labor, farm income, and household composition. While other explanations of the data may prove equally useful, it is clear that no general theory of a mobility transition can be applied to a region without an examination of its agrarian structure.

Notes

1. Barbosa-Ramírez (1973) characterized the Bajío as a polarized agricultural zone; Baring-Gould (1974) emphasized the growing gap between the *ejido* community and modern agriculture; and Díaz-Polanco and Montandon said it is a "zone where relatively modern agriculture and a dynamic modern commercial sector are combined with peasant communities at various levels of development" (1977:9)

2. Arizpe, in her study of migration from rural Mexico to the United States, wrote, "in Oaxaca, Young did find that the poorest migrated, first expelling children, then as whole households, but practically all went only so far as Mexico City or Oaxaca City" (1981:643).

3. Dinerman, in a study of U.S. migration from two villages in Michoacán, Mexico, noted that "migration tends to maintain, if not create, a preference for a particular form of household organization, the extended household" (1981:76).

4. A relatively risky asset may reduce the risk of a portfolio of assets by having its returns uncorrelated with the returns of the other assets (Markowitz, 1959). In this sense, U.S. migration might reduce the risk of the household income portfolio, although the returns from this activity alone might be expected to be quite variable.

References

Aguilar, M., J. Inigo. 1974. "Diferencia Étnica y migración en la Mixteca Baja." *Cuadernos de Trabajo*. Instituto Nacional de Antropología e Historia (September).

Anderson, Dennis, and Mark W. Leiserson. 1980. "Rural nonfarm employment in developing countries." *Economic Development and Cultural Change* 28:227–47.

Arizpe, Lourdes. 1981. "The rural exodus in Mexico and Mexican migration to the United States." *International Migration Review* 15:628–49. Reprinted in *The Border*

That Joins, eds. Peter G. Brown & Henry Shue. Totowa, New Jersey: Rowman and Littlefield, 1983.

Barbosa-Ramírez, A. René. 1973. *El Bajío.* Mexico City: Centro de Investigaciones Agrarias.

————. 1976. *Empleo, Desempleo y Subempleo en el Sector Agropecuario (Dos Estudios de Caso: Sub-Valle de Toluca y Mixteca Baja.)* Mexico City: Centro de Investigaciones Agrarias.

————. 1977. *Empleo, Desempleo y Subempleo en el Sector Agropecuario (Los Casos de los Distritos de Riego: Valsequillo y Costa de Hermosillo).* Mexico City: Centro de Investigaciones Agrarias.

————. 1979. *Empleo, Desempleo y Subempleo en el Sector Agropecuario (Los Casos de Las Tuxlas y Las Huastecas).* Mexico City: Centro de Investigaciones Agrarias.

Baring-Gould, Michael. 1974. *Agricultural and Community Development in Mexican Ejidos: Relatives in Conflict.* Ithaca: Latin American Studies Program, Dissertation Series, Cornell University.

Beals, Ralph L. 1975. *The Peasant Marketing System of Oaxaca, Mexico.* Berkeley: University of California Press.

Butterworth, Douglas S. 1975. *Tilantongo: Comunidad Mixteca en Transición.* Mexico City: Instituto Nacional Indigenista.

Chapman, Murray, and R. Mansell Prothero. 1977. "Circulation between home places and towns: A village approach to urbanization." Paper presented at a Working Session on Urbanization in the Pacific. Association for Social Anthropology in Oceania, Monterey, California (March).

Cornelius, Wayne A. 1977. "Illegal migration to the United States: Recent research findings, policy implications and research priorities." Cambridge: Center for International Studies, Massachusetts Institute of Technology (May).

Díaz-Polanco, Héctor, and L.G. Montandon. 1977. "La burguesía agraria de Mexico: Un estudio de caso en el Bajío." *Cuadernos de CES*, no. 22, El Colegio de Mexico.

Dinerman, Ina R. 1981. *Migrants and Stay-at-Homes: A Comparative Study of Migration from Two Communities in Michoacán, Mexico.* Monographs in U.S.–Mexican Studies no. 5. La Jolla: Center for U.S.-Mexican Studies, University of California, San Diego.

Fan, Yiu-Kwan, and Alan Stretton. 1980. "Circular migration in South East Asia: Some theoretical explanations." Research paper no. 8002, Department of Economics, University of Southern California.

Goldstein, Sidney. 1978. "Circulation in the context of total mobility in Southeast Asia." Honolulu, Hawaii: Papers of the East-West Population Institute, no. 53 (August).

Hewitt de Alcantara, Cynthia. 1976. *Modernizing Mexican Agriculture: Socioeconomic Implications of Technical Change 1940–1970.* Geneva: United Nations Research Institute for Social Development.

Lewis, W. Arthur. 1954. "Economic development with unlimited supplies of labour." *The Manchester School* (May):139–92.

Markowitz, Harry M. 1959. *Portfolio Selection: Efficient Diversification of Investments.* New York: John Wiley.

Reubens, Edwin P. 1978. "Illegal immigration and the Mexican economy." *Challenge* (November-December):13–19.

White, Benjamin. 1976. "Population, involution, and employment in rural Java." *Development and Change:*267–90.

Zelinsky, Wilbur. 1971. "The hypothesis of the mobility transition." *Geographical Review* 61:219–59.

6
Patterns of U.S. Migration from a Mexican Town

JOSHUA S. REICHERT
DOUGLAS S. MASSEY

Introduction

Guadalupe[1] is a small town located in the state of Michoacán at the western edge of Mexico's central plateau. This area has a long history of migration to the United States. Emigration from this region dates back to the turn of the century (Gamio, 1930). Among migrant-sending states, Michoacán has always been a leading contributor (Saunders and Leonard, 1951; Samora, 1971; Dagodag, 1975; North and Houstoun, 1976; Cornelius, 1978). Migrants from Guadalupe began going to the United States for seasonal work as early as 1911. For a variety of reasons, migration from Guadalupe grew over the years. Today, a majority of its people are committed to seasonal U.S. migration as a way of life. Indeed, migrant income is the primary source of support for nearly three-quarters of Guadalupe's families. This paper documents the extent and nature of this town's participation in the seasonal migrant flow. It also examines demographic and geographic aspects of migrants' movement in the United States.

The primary focus will be a comparison of legal and illegal[2] migrants. While in theory legal migrants from Guadalupe have the status of permanent resident aliens in the United States, in practice all maintain permanent residences in Mexico. Most do enter the United States for varying periods each year, but not to establish permanent homes.

This is a revised version of the authors' "Patterns of U.S. Migration from a Mexican Sending Community: A comparison of legal and illegal migrants," *International Migration Review* 13 (1979):599–623, by permission of the publisher.

Rather, their "green cards," or U.S. resident visas (INS form I–151), serve as work permits giving them unrestricted entry privileges. Few intend to abandon their homes in Mexico and settle permanently in the United States. These people exhibit very different patterns of migration than do illegal migrants.

The purpose of this paper is to explore how legal status affects the demographic profile of migrants from Guadalupe. How demographic characteristics interact with legal status to produce distinct patterns of movement within the United States will also be examined. We begin by describing the nature of the data and how they were gathered and use them to document Guadalupe's intense involvement in the U.S. labor market. We then compare legal and illegal migrants to demonstrate and explain basic demographic differences between the two groups—differences in the size of migrating units, their age-sex composition, and the amount of time spent away from home each year. Finally, we show how legal status affects patterns of migration, or patterns of spatial movement within the United States. The paper concludes by summarizing the findings and discussing their relevance to broader patterns within Mexico.

Data

Data were gathered over the course of a twelve-month investigation conducted in Guadalupe during 1977–78. This was part of a larger study examining the effects of U.S. migration on the social, economic, and political organization of the town (Reichert and Massey, 1979; 1980; Reichert, 1981; 1982). Guadalupe was selected as a research site because of the prevalence of seasonal U.S. migration among townspeople, and their dependence on migrant income. In addition, a preliminary survey conducted in northern Michoacán and parts of Guanajuato indicated that it was similar to other rural towns where a significant portion of the resident population migrated north on a regular basis.

Our analyses are based on two sources of information. First, a house-to-house census of the town's population was conducted to provide the name, age, sex, and kin relationship of each household member. This census was revised every two months over the course of the fieldwork to add data on migrant families who had returned. In the few cases where family members did not return during the study period, data were gathered from relatives and neighbors. This census provided the base population for all rates and comparisons included herein.

Since the census data were of a non-threatening nature, and because the project was endorsed by the president of Guadalupe who urged all townspeople to respond, little resistance was encountered from residents. In order to insure accuracy, however, information was checked with a variety of other records. These included an educational census conducted by local school teachers in 1976, and the files of two public works projects which listed all town households together with the age and sex of individual members.

While general demographic data could be compiled by direct census, it was not possible to use the same method to collect information on migration. Many residents work in the United States without legal documents. Naturally, these people worry about being discovered and reported to U.S. immigration authorities. They are unlikely to respond truthfully to direct questions asked by a reviewer. Therefore, information on migration was obtained from informants who trusted the investigator enough to provide information on other residents with whom they were familiar. A total of 26 people, representing a cross-section of the adult community, assisted in compiling the information. Reports were methodically cross-checked across a minimum of six informants, and usually more. When discrepancies were discovered, further inquiries were made until the investigator felt certain that accurate information had been obtained. When it was not possible to resolve conflicting reports, entries were classified as unknown. In this way, data were gathered on all persons who had ever been to the United States. Information collected included legal status, destination, work performed, movement patterns, number of trips made, and prior migrant experience. Repeated analyses and checks for internal consistency have established the reliability and accuracy of these data (Reichert and Massey, 1979; 1980).

Guadalupe as a Migrant Community

The town of Guadalupe consists of 2,621 people living in 379 households. Because joint-family households are quite common, the number of families (465), considerably exceeds that of households. As can be seen from Table 6.1, the community is very heavily involved in migration to the United States. Thirty-five percent of the town's entire population is actively engaged in U.S. migration. Among families and households, the dramatic commitment to migration as a way of life is even more evident. Roughly three-quarters currently send migrants to the United States.

Yet even these figures do not adequately express the overwhelming role that migration has played in the lives of Guadalupeños. This is

Table 6.1   Number and Immigration Status of Individuals Currently Migrating to
            the US and of Families and Households Currently Sending Migrants,
            Guadalupe, Michoacán, 1978

Immigration Status	Individuals	Families	Households
Currently Migrating	919 (35.1%)	342 (73.5%)	283 (74.7%)
Legal	723 (27.6%)	194 (41.7%)	154 (40.6%)
Illegal	196 (7.5%)	124 (26.7%)	101 (26.6%)
Mixed[a]	— —	24 (5.2%)	28 (7.4%)
Not Migrating	1697 (64.9%)	123 (26.5%)	96 (25.3%)
Total	2617[b] (100%)	465 (100%)	379 (100%)

Note: [a]Families and households sending both legal and illegal immigrants to
        the U.S.

        [b]Excludes four native-born U.S. citizens married to Guadalupe residents.

depicted in Table 6.2, which shows the number of people who have
ever migrated to the United States in addition to the number of
families and households containing such individuals. Forty-two percent
of townspeople have been to the United States at some point in their
lives, and 88 percent of all families and households contain at least
one individual who has been there.

These tables make two important points. First, they show the
extraordinary scale of Guadalupe's involvement in U.S. migration.
Nearly three-quarters of all families (containing nearly 80 percent of
the town's population) currently send migrants to the United States.
The great majority of these are supported exclusively by wages earned
in the United States. Among the remaining families, other sources
of income are typically dwarfed by migrant earnings (Reichert, 1982).
Second, they indicate the pervasiveness of return migration among
supposedly permanent U.S. residents. Of the town's 919 active migrants,
79 percent are green card holders. Furthermore, a majority (51 percent)
of Guadalupe's families contain at least one person legally entitled to

Table 6.2 Number and Immigration Status of Individuals Who Have Ever Migrated to the US and of Families and Households Ever Sending Migrants, Guadalupe, Michoacán, 1978

Immigration Status	Individuals	Families	Households
Ever Migrating	1095 (41.8%)	410 (88.2%)	335 (88.4%)
Legal[a]	827 (31.6%)	238 (51.2%)	199 (52.5%)
Illegal[a]	345 (13.2%)	272 (58.5%)	231 (60.9%)
Bracero[a]	130 (5.0%)	130 (28.0%)	128 (33.8%)
Never Migrating	1522 (58.2%)	55 (11.8%)	44 (11.6%)
Total	2617[b] (100%)	465 (100%)	379 (100%)

Note: [a]Frequencies for legal, illegal, and bracero categories will not sum to total ever migrating because they are not exclusive of one another.

[b]Excludes four native born U.S. citizens married to Guadalupe residents.

work in the United States. These people are not U.S. residents in the usual sense. The vast majority return to Mexico each year after a period of temporary employment in the United States (see Table 6.4). Since 1910, only 70 residents have left Guadalupe permanently to live in the United States (Reichert and Massey, 1980).

These figures suggest that a significant proportion of theoretically permanent U.S. immigrants are, in fact, de jure residents of Mexico who travel to the United States only for periods of temporary employment. Legal migrants may thus comprise a larger share of the seasonal Mexican migrant flow than has been generally recognized. For many Mexicans, the green card has become a de facto work permit enabling unrestricted access to the U.S. labor market rather than the permanent residence document it was intended to be (Reichert and Massey, 1982).

Legal migrants from Guadalupe are not the "green card commuters" described by North and Houstoun (1976) (i.e., Mexicans who live near the border and commute daily to work in the United States). Guadalupe

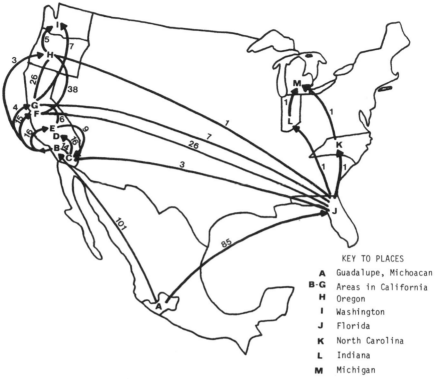

KEY TO PLACES

A	Guadalupe, Michoacan
B-G	Areas in California
H	Oregon
I	Washington
J	Florida
K	North Carolina
L	Indiana
M	Michigan

Figure 6.1   Migration routes for legally migrating family units from Guadalupe, Michoacán, to the United States (Specific place names have been deleted for reasons of confidentiality.)

is about 500 air miles from the closest U.S. border crossing at McAllen, Texas. However, migrants from Guadalupe do not work in Texas. They work primarily in California and Florida (see Figures 6.1 and 6.2). Effective commuter distance is 1200 miles or more.

Migration between Mexico and the United States is primarily a movement of laborers from areas of low to high wages (North and Houstoun, 1976; Mines, 1981; Conroy et al., 1980; Reichert and Massey, 1982). When one considers the incidence of migration among Guadalupeños of labor force age, as in Table 6.3, very high rates of migration are therefore found. Roughly 57 percent of all townspeople aged 15 to 64 are active U.S. migrants. There are, however, pronounced differences by sex. While 75 percent of males of labor force age are migrants, the figure was only 40 percent for females in the same age group. Moreover, females are particularly unlikely to migrate as illegals.

KEY TO PLACES

A   Guadalupe, Michoacan
B-E   Areas in California
F   Florida
G   North Carolina
H   Pennsylvania
I   Michigan

Figure 6.2   Migration routes for illegally migrating family units from Guadalupe, Michoacán, to the United States

These figures document the very high rate of participation by Guadalupe's male labor force in the migrant workforce. This finding has also been reported in other Mexican towns (Mines and Massey, 1982). Moreover, a clear, if quantitatively smaller, participation of women in the migrant force is revealed. Forty-four percent of currently migrating legals are women, as are 19 percent of active illegals. These figures have been increasing rapidly in recent years (Reichert and Massey, 1980). Combined with information coming from other studies (North and Houstoun, 1976; Keely et al., 1977; Avante Systems, 1978; Orange County Task Force, 1978; Van Arsdol et al., 1979; Maram, 1980; Poitras, 1980; Mines and Massey, 1982), they suggest the growing importance of women in the migrant workforce (Massey, 1982). Indeed, women from Guadalupe migrate not simply as marital companions, but to work. Of the 213 legally migrating women, 93 percent performed some type of wage labor during their last stay in the United States.

Table 6.3   Count of Individuals 15-64 Currently Migrating to the US
             by Present Immigration Status and Sex, Guadalupe, Michoacán,
             1978

	Males	Females	Total
Currently Migrating	415 (75.0%)	247 (40.2%)	662 (56.7%)
Legal	272 (49.2%)	213 (34.7%)	485 (41.5%)
Illegal	143 (25.9%)	34 (5.5%)	177 (15.2%)
Not Migrating	138 (25.0%)	367 (59.8%)	505 (43.3%)
Total	553 (100%)	614 (100%)	1167 (100%)

Sociodemographic Background

SIZE AND COMPOSITION OF MIGRATING UNITS

Migration from Guadalupe to the United States occurs primarily within the context of the family. U.S. earnings are important principally as a source of family support. If a migrant is accompanied by other people, they are usually members of his or her immediate family. Wages earned by various family members, such as wives and unmarried children, are generally turned over to the male family head. There is therefore a direct correlation between a family's income and the number of workers in the migrant party. For this reason, most migrants are eager to bring as many working family members with them as possible, in order to increase overall earnings.

There is a pronounced difference between legal and illegal migrants in size of the migrating party[3]—i.e., in the number of members of a given family currently working in the United States. On average, legal families send 3.5 migrants to the U.S., while illegal families send an average of only 1.3 migrants. Three-quarters of illegal families send only one person, while only 21 percent of legal families do so. Virtually no illegal families send more than two persons north. In contrast, 58 percent of legal families send three individuals or more.

Since illegal families tend to be larger than those containing legals, these differences cannot be attributed to variability of average family size. Rather the size differential between legal and illegal migrant parties relates to the fact that migrants from illegal families are unlikely to be accompanied by wives and children while working in the United States. Viz., only 17 percent of wives in illegal families went to the United States, compared to 74 percent in legal families. Similarly, only 26 percent of illegal families with unmarried children aged 15 or over included such children in the migrant party, as opposed to 84 percent for legal families.

There are also significant differences in the number of non-working dependents included within parties of legal and illegal migrants. Legal migrant parties carry an average of 1.00 non-working dependents to the United States, while among illegal parties the average is only 0.06—quite close to zero.

In spite of this contrast, among legal as well as illegal migrants, there is a strong disinclination to travel north with family members who cannot work. Sixty-two percent of legal parties contained no non-working dependents. The difference is that while illegals almost never carry dependents (only 3.2 percent of migrating families), among legals the practice is reasonably common (38 percent of migrating families). If a family member cannot work, the only incentive to migrate is to prevent the long-term separation of family members. In the case of illegals, this benefit is far outweighed by the perceived liabilities of increased vulnerability and greater risk of detection. There is also a strong desire on the part of illegal male migrants to avoid exposing their wives and children to the risk of arrest and deportation. Since these liabilities do not exist for legal migrants, there is a certain motivation to carry even those who cannot work in order to keep the family together.

TIME SPENT IN THE UNITED STATES

Migration from Guadalupe to the United States is highly seasonal. There is a strong tendency for migrants to return home each year for rest and relaxation, typically during periods when agricultural work in the United States is slack. However, as Table 6.4 demonstrates, this tendency is more pronounced for legal than for illegal migrants. Parties comprised of legal migrants returned to Guadalupe after an average of 9.4 months in the United States, compared to 12.4 months for parties of illegal migrants.[4] Ninety-four percent of illegal parties did so.

Illegal migrants tend to remain in the United States longer than legal migrants because of the high risk of detection they face when crossing the border. Studies have shown that once an illegal migrant

Table 6.4   Duration of Last Trip to the US of Migrant Parties from
            Guadalupe, Michoacán, 1978

| | Number of months spent in the US | | | | | |
	1-12 mo.	13-24 mo.	25-36 mo.	37+ mo.	Total	Average
Legal families[a]	183 (94.3%)	8 (4.1%)	1 (0.5%)	2 (1.0%)	194 (100%)	9.4 mo.
Illegal families[b]	96 (81.4%)	13 (11.0%)	7 (5.9%)	2 (1.7%)	118[d] (100%)	12.4 mo.
Mixed families[c]	20 (91.0%)	0 —	1 (4.5%)	1 (4.5%)	22[d] (100%)	12.6 mo.
Total migrating families	299 (89.5%)	21 (6.3%)	9 (2.7%)	5 (1.5%)	334[d] (100%)	10.7 mo.

Note: [a]Send only legal migrants to the US

        [b]Send only illegal migrants to the US

        [c]Send both legal and illegal migrants to the US

        [d]Duration of last trip could not be determined for 6 illegal and 2 mixed
           family migrant units.

has entered the country and secured employment, the chances of
apprehension diminish rapidly, since most apprehensions occur within
72 hours of entry (North and Houstoun, 1976; Cornelius, 1978). Once
across the border and working, illegal migrants therefore tend to
maximize earnings by staying longer, putting off the time when they
msut risk another border crossing. In contrast, legal migrants can
enter the United States at will and remain as long as they want. They
return home during the off-season, after only eight or nine months
of work, knowing that they can re-enter the U.S. whenever they
please. Thus, the net effect of illegal status is to induce migrants to
remain in the U.S. for longer periods than they would were they able
to migrate legally.

Migration Patterns

Information was collected on the number of moves made by migrant
parties during their most recent trip to the United States. Number

of moves was derived by defining 13 geographic zones based on Guadalupeños' reports of where they had worked during their latest trip. Six zones correspond to different areas within California. The rest represent particular areas within the states of Oregon, Washington, Florida, North Carolina, Indiana, Pennsylvania, and Michigan. A move was defined as movement between any two of these 13 zones. To see the location of these zones, refer to Figure 6.1.

Table 6.5 cross-classifies number of moves by migrant status to reveal yet another difference between legal and illegal migrants: the former are far more mobile within the United States than are the latter. Legal migration parties made an average of 1.2 moves in the United States, compared to only 0.4 for illegal parties. Seventy-one percent of illegal parties did not move at all once inside the United States, while for legal parties this figure was only 54 percent. Legal migrants are far more likely to make multiple moves than illegals.

However, Table 6.5 is not a fair comparison between the two groups. Illegal migrants rarely travel north with dependents. Legal migrants, however, are quite likely to be accompanied by spouses and, in many cases, children.

The presence of dependents obviously hinders mobility, and a more accurate comparison would contrast parties containing the same number of dependents. Table 6.6 therefore restricts consideration to migrants traveling alone. When size and dependency are controlled in this way, the mobility differential between legals and illegals is enlarged. The average number of moves for individual legal migrants is 1.8, six times the figure of 0.3 for illegal migrants.

The contrast between legal and illegal migrants is further heightened when distance of moves is taken into account. Figures 6.1 and 6.2 present maps of migration routes, or *corridas,* followed by legal and illegal migrant parties to their respective work places in the United States. These maps depict only those *corridas* originating in California and Florida, which together account for 94 percent of all routes followed by Guadalupeños. The few *corridas* originating at other points in the United States are not shown for the sake of simplicity.

These two figures clearly demonstrate the great spatial mobility of legal migrants, compared to a relative lack of mobility among illegals. Whereas 37 legal parties begin work in Florida and then make a transcontinental jump to west coast employment, none of the illegal parties does so. Moreover, with one exception, there is no movement among geographic zones of the west coast by illegal migrants. This is in contrast to the pervasiveness of such movement by legals. Rather, there is a marked tendency for illegal migrants to secure employment

Table 6.5　Families Currently Sending Migrants to the US by Immigration Status of those Migrating and Number of Moves Made in the US, Guadalupe, Michoacán, 1978

	0	1	2	3	4	5	Total	Average
Legal Families[a]	103 53.9	19 9.9	19 9.9	29 15.2	15 7.9	6 3.1	191[d] 100%	1.2
Illegal Families[b]	85 71.4	27 22.7	6 5.0	1 0.8	0 -	0 -	119[d] 100%	0.4
Mixed Families[c]	10 41.7	10 41.7	1 4.2	2 8.3	0 -	1 4.2	24 100%	1.0
Total Migrating Families[d]	198 59.3	56 16.8	26 7.8	32 9.6	15 4.5	7 2.1	334[d] 100%	0.9

Note:　[a]Number of moves could not be determined for three legal and five illegal families.

[b]Send only legal migrants to the U.S.

[c]Send only illegal migrants to the U.S.

[d]Send both legal and illegal migrants to the U.S.

Table 6.6 Individuals Currently Migrating to the US by Immigration Status and Number of Moves Made in the US, Guadalupe, Michoacán, 1978

	0	1	2	3	4	5	Total	Average
Legal Migrants Traveling Alone	17 42.5	1 2.5	6 15.0	8 20.0	6 15.0	2 5.0	40 100%	1.8
Illegal Migrants Traveling Alone	67 76.1	17 19.3	3 3.4	1 1.1	0 -	0 -	88 100%	0.3
Total Migrants Traveling Alone	84 65.6	18 14.1	9 7.0	9 7.0	6 4.7	2 1.6	128 100%	0.8

in southern California or Florida and to remain there, without moving, for the duration of their stay in the United States.

Conclusions

Data presented in this paper suggest several points regarding the phenomenon of Mexico–United States migration, as exemplified by the migrant population of Guadalupe. First, the commitment to U.S. migration as a way of life is widespread. Most of the town's families are supported almost exclusively by U.S. earnings. This participation in the U.S. labor market is possible because migration from Guadalupe is primarily seasonal. Over 90 percent of migrants return home each year for periods ranging from two to four months. This seasonality is facilitated by the fact that most migrants from Guadalupe are permanent resident aliens of the United States who use their green cards as work permits rather than residence documents. Among these legal migrants are many women, but there are also some women among illegal migrants. The number of women in both groups has been increasing in recent years. The pervasiveness and long history of U.S. migration have had dramatic impacts on patterns of socio-economic organization and development in Guadalupe (Reichert, 1981; 1982).

Legal and illegal segments of the migrant population differ in several important respects. Illegal migrants travel to the United States in smaller groups than do legal migrants. They are much less likely to be accompanied by wives, children, or non-working dependents. Illegal migrants also tend to spend more time in the United States per trip than do their legal counterparts; and they are much less mobile.

The relevance of these patterns to Mexican migration in general depends, of course, on the degree to which Guadalupe is representative of other towns and villages. It is clear that data from this town cannot be extrapolated to estimate the extent of outmigration from Mexico as a whole. Migration is generally much more common from rural areas than from urban centers. Moreover, Guadalupe is located in a region characterized by traditionally high rates of migration to the United States.

Even within this region, Guadalupe faces conditions that are unusually conducive to outmigration. In the years following the Mexican Revolution, Guadalupe lost most of its traditional land base. As a result, an unusually large share of its families were left landless. For many breadwinners, migration was the only rational thing to do. Were it not for the fact that a tradition of U.S. migration arose very early in Guadalupe (ca. 1911), many Guadalupeños would have long since joined the ranks of permanent outmigrants destined for Mexico's urban centers.

While push factors may have been exacerbated in Guadalupe, the town is not unrepresentative of conditions in rural Mexico. For a variety of reasons, Mexico is plagued by a critical shortage of cultivable land. The proportion of adult rural dwellers owning land fell from 42 percent in 1940 to 33 percent in 1970 (Cornelius, 1978). This occurred in spite of the transfer of land to some 3 million peasants since 1930. There are now an estimated 3.2 to 3.4 million landless peasants, more than existed in 1930 before the intensification of Mexico's agrarian reform (Hewitt de Alcantara, 1976). In many ways Guadalupe is merely a more extreme example of conditions already endemic to rural Mexico. Land shortages, poor agricultural conditions, low wages, a lack of jobs, and an expanding population have led many Mexicans to migrate in search of a better living.

Whether these data reflect wider patterns prevailing elsewhere in Mexico must await the results of studies now in progress. While results from Guadalupe may overstate the volume of U.S. migration compared to other rural communities, one can assume that findings on the relative importance of legal and illegal migration, as well as the differences between them, are representative of broader patterns within the rest of rural Mexico.

Notes

1. Guadalupe is a fictitious name chosen to ensure the anonymity of townspeople.

2. This uses the term "illegal migrants," or simply "illegals," to refer to migrants entering the United States without valid immigration papers. The term includes people who are simply undocumented because they do not hold any entry permit, plus those who have obtained fraudulent documents, as well as those who have been granted temporary entry permits, the terms of which have been violated by overstaying the designated time and working.

3. Throughout this paper, migrating groups or parties are defined within family contexts. This does not mean that the entire family necessarily migrates. It simply means that one or more members from the family leaves Guadalupe for a common destination in the United States.

4. Duration of last trip was measured as the length of time spent away from Guadalupe, not necessarily all of which was in the United States. A small portion of time is typically spent in transit between the two countries. Moreover, illegals are often apprehended and deported. In many cases, these individuals do not reutrn directly home after being ejected from the United States, but simply turn around and re-enter the country once again. In fact, one Guadalupeño was deported seven times during the course of a single trip, yet, in each instance, was back at work within a few days. If an illegal did not return home after deportation, but re-entered the United States to work again, he was not counted as having returned.

References

Avante Systems. 1978. *A Survey of the Undocumented Population in Two Texas Border Areas.* San Antonio, Texas: U.S. Commission on Civil Rights.

Conroy, Michael E., Mario C. Salas, and Filipe V. Gonzalez. 1980. "Socio-economic incentives for migration from Mexico to the United States: Cross-regional profiles, 1969–1978." Paper presented at the Annual Meeting of the Population Association of America, Denver, Colorado.

Cornelius, Wayne A., 1978. *Mexican Migration to the United States: Causes, Consequences, and U.S. Responses.* Migration and Development Monograph c/78-9. Cambridge: Center for International Studies, Massachusetts Institute of Technology.

Dagodag, W. Tim. 1976. "Source regions and composition of illegal Mexican immigration to California." *International Migration Review* 9:499–511.

Gamio, Manuel. 1930. *Mexican Immigration to the United States.* Chicago: University of Chicago Press.

Hewitt de Alcantara, Cynthia. 1976. *Modernizing Mexican Agriculture: Socio-economic Implications of Technical Change, 1940–1970.* Geneva: United Nations Research Institute for Social Development.

Keely, Charles B., Patricia J. Elwell, Austin T. Fragomen, and Sylvan M. Tomasi. 1977. "Profiles on undocumented aliens in New York City: Haitians and Dominicans." Staten Island, New York: Occasional Paper, Center for Migration Studies.

Maram, Sheldon L. 1980. *Hispanic Workers in the Garment and Restaurant Industries in Los Angeles County.* Working Papers in U.S.–Mexican Studies No. 12. La Jolla: Program in U.S.–Mexican Studies, University of California at San Diego.

Massey, Douglas S. 1982. *Patterns and Effects of Hispanic Immigration to the United States.* Washington, D.C.: Technical Report, National Commission for Employment Policy. Summer.

Mines, Richard. 1981. *Developing a Community Tradition of Migration: A Field Study of Rural Zacatecas, Mexico, and California Settlement Areas.* Monographs in U.S.–Mexican Studies No. 3. La Jolla: Program in U.S.–Mexican Studies, University of California at San Diego.

Mines, Richard, and Douglas S. Massey. 1982. "A comparison of patterns of U.S.–bound migration in two Mexican sending communities." Paper presented at the Annual Meeting of the Population Association of America, San Diego.

North, David S., and Marion F. Houstoun. 1976. *The Characteristics and Role of Illegal Aliens in the U.S. Labor Market: An Exploratory Study.* Washington, D.C.: Linton & Co.

Orange County Task Force. 1978. *The Economic Impact of Undocumented Immigrants on Medical Costs, Tax Contributions, and Health Needs of Undocumented Migrants.* Santa Ana, California: Report to the Orange County Board of Supervisors.

Poitras, Guy. 1980. *International Migration to the United States from Costa Rica and El Salvador.* San Antonio, Texas: Border Research Institute, Trinity University.

Reichert, Joshua S. 1981. "The migrant syndrome: Seasonal U.S. wage labor and rural development in Central Mexico." *Human Organization* 40:55–66.

——————. 1982. "Social stratification in a Mexican sending community: The effect of migration to the United States." *Social Problems* 29:411–23.

Reichert, Joshua S., and Douglas S. Massey. 1979. "Patterns of U.S. migration from a Mexican sending community: A comparison of legal and illegal migrants." *International Migration Review* 13:599–623.

——————. 1980. "History and trends in U.S.–bound migration from a Mexican town." *International Migration Review* 14:475–91.

——————. 1982. "Guestworker programs: Evidence from Europe and the United States and some implications for U.S. policy." *Population Research and Policy Review* 1:1–17.

Samora, Julian. 1971. *Los Mojados: The Wetback Story.* Notre Dame: University of Notre Dame Press.

Saunders, Lyle, and Olen E. Leonard. 1951. *The Wetback in the Lower Rio Grande Valley of Texas.* Austin: Interamerican Education Program, University of Texas, Occasional Paper 7.

Van Arsdol, Maurice, Joan W. Moore, David M. Heer and Susan Haynie. 1979. *Non-apprehended and Apprehended Undocumented Residents in the Los Angeles Labor Market: An Exploratory Study.* Washington, D.C.: U.S. Department of Labor, Manpower Administration.

7

External Dependency and the Perpetuation of Temporary Migration to the United States

RAYMOND E. WIEST

Migration of Mexicans to the United States is increasing and is not likely to decline, despite official actions in both countries to discourage or control it. The current financial crisis stemming from Mexico's vast foreign debt, and the accompanying devaluation of its currency, is beginning to stimulate an unprecedented amount of illegal entry to the United States. In the U.S., the demand for labor from Mexico or elsewhere is not likely to diminish. The underlying causes of such extensive human spatial mobility, here and elsewhere, are being penetrated in recent analyses, as a result of the development and refinement of critical theory. The works of Amin (1976), Frank (1969, 1979), Petras (1978), Portes (1978, 1981), and Wallerstein (1979), among others, have demonstrated the importance of viewing migration as part of a world economic system, and of understanding the process historically.

This essay is an elaboration of data and arguments presented in an earlier article (Wiest, 1979a). The research was begun in 1966–67. Additional research in the same community was conducted in 1968, 1971, 1972, 1974–75, and 1983. In all, 32 months were spent in the field. I am grateful for support from the following sources in the order indicated: NDEA-Related Fulbright-Hays Fellowship; NIMH Predoctoral Fellowship, No. 6-FI-MH-24,159-01A3; The Canada Council; University of Manitoba Research Board; International Development Research Centre (Ottawa); and the Social Sciences and Humanities Research Council of Canada.

My objective in this essay is to analyze migration from a single rural community in northern Michoacán in terms of recent theoretical developments that for general purposes may be referred to as dependency theory. The essay first treats the explanation of migration and its effects. It deals briefly with the essential elements of the "dependency" approach, and argues for attention to long-term structural features of social systems based in the production process which involves all humans. The specific context of migration dealt with in this essay is then treated. This provides some sense of the history of the process as well as the peculiarities of the case discussed. The main part of the essay details several specific impacts of migration that perpetuate and increase external dependency. Various elements of this increased dependency are discussed.

Explanation of Migration and Its Effects

One of the processes unleashed by the development of capitalism has been widespread rural exodus (Stavenhagen, 1975). This migration has become a focal issue of virtually every social science discipline. Migration studies formerly emphasized acculturation, assimilation, and individual adjustment at the destination. Recently, however, attention has shifted to the impact of migration on the countries, regions, and communities from which large numbers of people migrate (see Downing, 1979).

Migration has come to be viewed in extremes, partially because of strong theoretical differences among authors. Some see migration as a real hope for the underdeveloped areas, while others feel it is yet another mechanism of their exploitation. Certain theorists have seen migration as a potential equalizer—realigning population and resources, both by removing excess population from the rural sector and by stimulating transformation of rural areas through new experiences of migrants (e.g., Brandes, 1975; Griffin, 1976; Shadow, 1979). Some see advantage to the underdeveloped rural sectors and the less developed countries in the form of a "safety-valve" for political unrest (e.g., Hancock, 1959; Lewis, 1960), or in a more favorable balance of payments (e.g., Frank, 1969:306; Randall, 1962). Other researchers have argued to the contrary that widespread migration is detrimental to rural regions of origin (e.g., Brettell, 1979; Piore, 1979; Rhoades, 1978; Swanson, 1979; Wiest, 1979a). They believe that the lowered cost of labor provided by migrants is an essential part of the process of capitalist expansion (e.g., Alba, 1978; Amin, 1974; Jenkins, 1978; Portes, 1978). While migrant remittances are probably increasingly important to Mexico's balance of payments, the suggestion that they facilitate economic development has not been substantiated by research conducted with an adequate time frame or using adequately critical theoretical tools. Recent analyses in Mexico by such writers as Bustamante and Martinez (1979), Cross and Sandos (1981), Dinerman (1978), Reichert (1981, 1982), and Wiest (1973, 1979a, 1980), and in other parts of the world, e.g., Lipton (1980), Piore (1979), and Rhoades (1972), are providing new insights on the long-range impacts of migration to the United States upon local economies in Mexico.

These contrasting views of migration may be summarized as (a) those utilizing an equilibrium model and accompanying orthodox "development" theory; and (b) those focusing on the historically-generated structural conditions which, interacting with the dominant capitalist mode of production, impinge upon development in peripheral regions—i.e., "dependency" theory and the "historical-structural" approach. Drawing upon the latter of these contrasting views, the case analyzed here focuses on international and national political economy, to illustrate several features of dependency.

THE DEPENDENCY APPROACH

The works of Amin (1976), Frank (1969, 1979), Stavenhagen (1975), Emmanuel (1972), Downing (1982), and numerous others articulate the dependency argument. This approach postulates that under the capitalist mode of production, underdevelopment is a product of capitalist development, the expression of class interests, and structured social inequality. Satellite (peripheral) economies are designed primarily for exports (including labor). Their economic surplus is basically international, with historical roots in colonialism and imperialism. It is replicated at the national level as internal colonialism.

A serious problem of the dependency approach is its focus on external, at the expense of internal, relationships. The tendency to reify the poles (center and periphery) in ways that obscure the dynamic interrelationships (see Petras, 1978:33–39) is a result of this focus. The poles of the model are not the active units, nor are geographic regions for that matter. Rather, social classes give the system its dynamics. Class analysis, combined with a historical perspective and a careful analysis of the production process, is necessary to more fully understand the migration process.

THE HISTORICAL-STRUCTURAL APPROACH

This paper deals with several underlying forces influencing migrational impacts at the origin. The nature of expenditures and investment, the land tenure system, the distribution of wealth and access to resources, and the social structure to which migrants relate are all forces affecting these impacts. As such, it provides quite a different perspective from research focusing on the more superficial, *surface* effects such as income levels and material acquisitions. As an integral part of this "historical-structural" approach, class analysis focuses upon the control of productive means and thus on the social relations of production and distribution. Utilizing a class conflict model, class analysis penetrates the myths that are part of the ideology of capitalism and central to orthodox social science—e.g., that of social mobility.

Human beings are active parts of a dialectical process producing change. Thus, an analysis of their ideology and ideological changes contributes to the historical-structural approach. The development of class consciousness and the politicization of the peasantry and proletariat are basic elements of change often ignored by orthodox social science (see Bach and Schraml, 1982).

Surface effects of migration to the United States are most visible from the perspective of individual decision-making and household economics, although there are also immediate and conspicuous effects on the distribution of cash in the community. The surface effects of migration are generally considered beneficial. Although deceptive, these surface effects are the ones noted by most analysts and cited as evidence of development. The most significant underlying effects elude many analysts. They are inconspicuous not only because their consequences are delayed, but also because they are obscured by traditional orthodox economic models. These effects may contradict more superficial indices of change; I shall argue that they are detrimental to the community and the households. These "underlying" effects are often the "structures" exposed and examined through the historical-structural approach (see Bach and Schraml, 1982; Wiest, 1979b; and Wood, 1981, 1982).

Thus, the historical-structural approach focuses on class relations and the production process, while the dependency approach provides a framework for understanding spatial and historical dimensions of migration. These approaches are synthesized in the case study which follows.

The Context of Migrant Origins

The small rural *mestizo* municipality of Acuitzio in the state of Michocán shares with much of the region a relatively high rate of underemployment and unemployment. This is manifested in the form of tremendous wealth differences, extensive petty commerce, and a high rate of outmigration, both to urban centers and to the United States.

Acuitzio lies some 35 kilometers south of Morelia, capital of the state. Its 1970 population was 7,500 (a net loss of 4,500 since 1950). The *cabecera* (head town) population is approximately 3,600 (a net increase of 600 since 1950, but still below the 4,000 of pre-1930). The remainder of the population dwells in small hamlets.

Like most other communities of this region, Acuitzio has long been a source of labor for extra-community and extra-regional industry. As early as the 16th century, large-scale industries of Michoacán required a steady source of labor to supply produce. This produce found an especially ready market in the mining areas to the north. In addition, workers were needed in the mines. New settlements had to be built in the rapidly expanding northern frontier. Finally, men were needed to serve as native allies of mercenaries to the Spanish armies (Staley, 1974, pp. 82–83; West, 1948, p. 50). Acuitzio became an independent community with its own specializations. The production and repair of cart wheels and the production of leather goods, principally *huaraches* (sandals) and shoes, were an integral part of the development of mining and *hacienda* agriculture.

Located on the route for transport of goods between the lowlands (to the south) and the markets and mines (to the north), Acuitzio gradually became a center of commerce and services. It retained this reputation until the 1930s. With the construction of roads into Tacámbaro through Pátzcuaro and into Huetamo in the late 1930s, the heavy traffic of goods through Acuitziuo was diverted. The village that once relied on income from services, provision of night lodging, small businesses, and crafts, suddenly had too many retail outlets and services. The change had a marked effect on the entire municipality. It stimulated the beginning of a rural exodus which produced a general demographic shift in the municipality. The population shifted from the rural hamlets and isolated housesites into the *cabecera* (county seat), and of *cabecera* residents to the large cities, principally Mexico City. Migration to the United States for labor began about the same time, and has continued to the present.

In 1975, the *cabecera* population began to grow slightly in response to a new road and anticipated employment. A sawmill began to operate in a neighboring village, and a factory was being built in Acuitzio to manufacture furniture and other wood products. Most households currently depend on a combination of several income sources. A mix of subsistence and small-scale market-oriented agriculture still forms the principal economic base in Acuitzio (37 percent of the households). A sizeable number of households, however, depend primarily on retailing (16 percent), handicrafts or trades (17 percent), and wage labor, much involving migration (24 percent). Even prior to completion of the factory, wage labor had become important as a primary or secondary source for more than half of the households in the *cabecera*. Nearly 50 percent of the *cabecera* households are landless, although about 10 percent of the landless households work land as sharecroppers.

Dependence on migration for sole or supplementary household support is widespread in Acuitzio. In any single year more than 50 percent of the households rely to some extent on remittances from migrants who have gone to the United States, to Mexico City, or to some other city or region of Mexico.

Far more males than females have left Acuitzio for seasonal or temporary work elsewhere. Females (usually dependent daughters) do, however, go to Mexican urban centers to work as domestics. Through 1975, women who left Acuitzio were still most likely to go to Mexico City for work. Men were still inclined to go to the United States. Based on my 1967 in-depth sample survey and my 1971 census, about 17 percent of the 654 males between ages 15 and 60 migrate to the U.S. each year. Local informal records and community hearsay indicate that the percentage of the migrating labor force was closer to 30 percent. However, these accounts often include individuals who are "permanently removed" but who may remit small sums of money to relatives (see Reichert, 1981, for a discussion of methodological problems associated with determining who migrates).

According to the 1971 census, nearly 90 percent of the migrants are adult men between the ages of 15 and 60. Fifty percent of working-age migrants go to the United States, and the other 50 percent to locations within Mexico. Among migrating *husband-fathers*, 80 percent migrate to the U.S., and only 20 percent within Mexico.

Most migrants to the United States from Acuitzio possessed immigrant visas through 1975, but some regularly go to the U.S. illegally. More than half of these migrants to the U.S. remain there from 7 to 12 months. About 25 percent stay for more than a year at a time. The remaining 25 percent go for shorter periods (3 to 6 months). Those migrating to other areas of Mexico for work generally stay for more than a year, although they may return for periodic brief visits. Illegal immigrants to the U.S. tend to remain for longer periods of time to minimize the risks of detection and to increase their chances of earning money (see Reichert and Massey, 1979). Women are rarely involved in illegal immigration. As legal immigrants, those women going to the U.S. accompany their husbands or fathers. The number of such cases has been limited in Acuitzio, but research in 1975 suggests a likely increase due to a recent trend among men to accept the wife in a wage-earning role. Not only has the incidence of female migration increased, but all indications from correspondence with informants is that illegal migration has increased substantially as well since 1975.

In 1967, an informal village list of 160 Acuitzio migrants to the United States indicated that about 70 percent of the migrants went to California for work in agricultural jobs (in 1975, several of these migrants preferred to go to Oregon and Washington to avoid labor union activity). Nearly 20 percent worked in factory or service jobs in the Los Angeles area. Fewer than 5 percent held similar jobs in Chicago. Another 4 percent worked in Alaska, and a very small number in Texas and other southwestern states. These data support the findings of Jones (1982), whose research shows a strong concentration of temporary Mexican workers in California.

Perpetuation of Migration

In this section I will address the growing external dependency of the Acuitzio migrants and of the village from which they migrate. What form the increasing dependency takes, how it is directly linked to migration, and why migration is thus perpetuated will be examined. Several specific elements of this increased dependency are as follows: (a) individuals who considered their migration temporary are finding themselves committed to regular recurrent migration for household maintenance; (b) the conspicuous consumption of return migrants and their families stimulates migration of others to the United States; (c) income derived from U.S. earnings flows disproportionately from the village to regional, national, and international centers; (d) investment of U.S. earnings in village land has inflated land values and perpetuated an exploitative sharecrop system; and (e) continued recurrent migration to the U.S. stimulates both rural-to-town and town-to-city movement in Mexico. I will elaborate on each of these elements.

SUSTAINING A NEW STANDARD OF LIVING

One of the most immediately obvious effects of migration is the substantial rise in the annual income of many households with members working in the United States. This increased income is displayed in the form of conspicuous house renovation, new and fashionable clothing, new appliances and furniture, and in some instances the purchase of motor vehicles (Table 7.1). It is also obvious from the fact that many migrants spend several months in the village each year essentially on vacation. A few make their relatively high earnings obvious by

Table 7.1   Percentage Distribution of Domestic Facilities and Selected
Consumer Goods Among Seventy Sample Households, Acuitzio, 1967

| | Migration Households | | | |
Facilities	Non-migration households	Member in Mexico	Member in the US	Totals
Number of Rooms (including kitchen)				
1 to 3	60%	72%	44%	61%
4 to 8	40%	28%	56%	39%
Floor Material				
Dirt	40%	28%	0%	31%
Some dirt, some brick	16%	33%	11%	20%
Brick or cement	33%	33%	56%	36%
Some tile	12%	6%	33%	13%
Sleeping Facilities				
Petates (reed mats)	35%	61%	11%	39%
Petates and mattresses	16%	6%	11%	13%
Mattresses	49%	33%	78%	49%
Toilet Facilities				
None	14%	33%	0%	10%
Privy	60%	56%	22%	54%
Drain	12%	27%	33%	19%
Flush	14%	11%	44%	17%
Cook Stove				
Hearth	58%	72%	22%	57%
Oil	21%	17%	0%	17%
Gas	21%	11%	78%	26%
Television				
No	88%	94%	44%	84%
Yes	12%	6%	56%	16%
Total Households	43	18	9	70

generously providing drinks for friends and/or publicly committing themselves to expensive *cargos* (religious obligations to the saints).

The families of U.S. migrants eat better than most non-migrant families. At the same time they spend a smaller percentage of household cash income for food (28 percent for U.S. migrant households, 65 percent for other households). They enjoy more frequent, thorough, and costly medical care. They are also more readily able to purchase prescribed medicines.

U.S. migrant households experience income increases of approximately 300 percent over the pre-migration incomes. Although dated by inflation and recurrent devaluations, my in-depth 1967 data are still instructive. At that time annual household income of those migrating to the U.S. ranged from over 12,000 to 70,000 pesos, compared to an overall range of 300 to well over 100,000 pesos. With a mean household income of over 35,000 pesos, all U.S. migrant households were well above the median annual household income of 7,000 pesos. Nearly all these households derive the income from the earnings of one household member, usually the husband-father. The sharp rise in income and the fact that migrant husband-fathers usually remain the sole supporters of the household, are striking when contrasted with households whose members migrate within Mexico. Among the latter, incomes are generally below the overall median and the income derives from several contributors. In families in which the husband-father migrates to Mexico City alone, for example, we find the wife-mother also working away from Acuitzio. This is due to the husband's low wages coupled with the poorly-developed local labor market (see Arizpe, 1981).

The households from which husband-fathers regularly migrate to the United States have thus come to depend on this source of income for their everyday welfare as well as for any attempts to raise their standard of living. This wage labor occupies migrants nearly full-time, although none of the migrants are fully proletarianized. Most of them supplement their wage incomes through some agriculture, commerce, or animal husbandry. These migrant families accumulate more consumer goods, more household conveniences and comforts, household labor-saving appliances. They also often have remodelled houses that are easier to care for. Some of these consumer goods reduce household drudgery and women's labor time while enhancing women's social status in a system increasingly based on invidious comparison.

Under these conditions, migrating men are able to maintain the dominant breadwinner role in the domestic group. The wives of these men remain heavily dependent (in many cases totally dependent) upon their husbands for economic support. This arrangement is consistent with the traditional agrarian division of labor characteristic of most domestic groups in Acuitzio. Migrating men consciously try to keep their wives dependent, and the threat of physical abuse is always present, though seldom carried out. The ideology surrounding male dominance remains strong. It is one of the reasons that few migrants have set up small familial commercial concerns such as housefront stores. These give their wives too much public exposure and too much independent power.

Recurrent migration of married men does not threaten conjugal relations when the men earn enough to retain their breadwinner role. Despite recurrent male absence, the women remain dependent on their husband's earnings. This serves to perpetuate the myth of male dominance. But this picture is incomplete without reference to the attitudes of migrants and their families concerning migratory wage labor and recurrent absence. The views are varied. Most women and men consider the arrangement to be a necessary evil, dictated by the economic circumstances. Nearly all view the period of migration as temporary, and are increasingly alarmed by the need to return year after year long beyond their original intentions. In balance, my research suggests that the economic consideration strongly overshadows other aspects deemed negative by the families of migrants. Two of the most obvious negative effects are the lack of companionship and the father's reduced contact with his children. It should be remembered, though, that most families have thought of a temporary involvement in migration. Conditions have led unexpectedly to a continued and increased dependence in nearly all cases.

All the migrants I interviewed expressed the desire or intention to earn enough to establish themselves in agriculture or a business in Acuitzio or nearby Morelia. Yet they return year after year for the relatively high wage of a U.S. job. In this way they are able to afford the increasing costs of a higher standard of living (see Amin, 1974: 282–83), and to enjoy the leisure and prestige of an annual vacation in the home village. The ideology of successful "establishment," together with the raised standard of living and the luxury of leisure time, are avenues to social mobility. Social mobility does occur. In fact, poor peasants are transformed into a temporarily comfortable proletariat. A few even challenge the established bourgeoisie with their new wealth. This status change and its maintenance is linked directly to labor migration and dependent on continued cyclical migration (see Bustamante and Martínez, 1979:268–76).

This view of social structure and class is severely limited and misleading. From a class analysis perspective, we must note that the availability of a large supply of foreign workers has allowed U.S. agribusiness and manufacturing industry to expand. It continues to profit at their expense and the expense of less-developed regions (cf., Bustamante and Martinez, 1979). Competition for available jobs has kept wages low, despite the organization of labor and its increasing demands. New reserve pools of labor are found in less developed areas. For example, the establishment of duty-free manufacturing zones, within Mexico's most heavily populated areas of high unemployment and low wages, is designed to reduce pressures in those areas. It is, however, acknowledged to be a direct aid to U.S. industry for whom border zone wage increases have made business unprofitable there (*Business Week*, 1976:42). This response of U.S. business vividly demonstrates the tenuousness of wage jobs, especially those tied to industries dependent upon cheap labor.

The history of Mexican migration to the United States has been one of abuses both by the U.S. government and employers and by the bureaucratic bourgeoisie of Mexico through *soborno* (graft). Yet the recent migrants from Acuitzio would for the most part deny this, arguing that treatment has been better, wages higher, and individual freedom greater than in Mexico. Bustamante and Martínez (1979: 275–76) point out that:

> [the migrant] has learned over the generations that his chances of getting work are better in the occupations that do not tend towards upward social mobility. . . . He has also learned that his earnings in the United States will buy him goods and services which in the community he comes from may signify upward social mobility among his peers.

The migrants view the surface effects, however, and are unconscious of their position in a class system. A guise for economic development, their good fortunes and social mobility obscure the material relations of production of which they are a part.

Most migrants from Acuitzio form a mobile rural proletariat whose job futures have little security. The location, duration, and nature of their annual treks is increasingly dependent on forces beyond their control. At the same time, migratory wage labor to the United States provides a substituted income rather than a supplementary one. Dependence on it is virtually complete. Despite intentions of establishing themselves in Acuitzio by eventually acquiring enough property or a business to maintain their standard of living, these migrants find it necessary to return to the U.S. each year as funds run low, and as their hopes for building a firm economic base in the town or elsewhere in Mexico diminish. They must contend both with strikes (not in their interest as they perceive it) and the threat of open hostility. Forced to continue as migrants, they seek employment in areas not controlled by unionized labor. However obscured their position, these migrants are part of a larger proletariat. This serves to build and maintain agribusiness and the lower paying city industries of both the U.S. and Mexico.

CONSPICUOUS CONSUMPTION AND INVIDIOUS COMPARISON

The increased earnings of recurrent migrants to the United States have been associated with consumption that is conspicuous in the village. This is not because return migrants uniformly flaunt their new wealth, but because their acquisitions are relatively rapid and difficult to hide. Villagers have thereby come to expect conspicuous consumption as a result of migration.

Among international migrants in Acuitzio, the highest priority is improvement of the domicile—adding new rooms or a second story, covering dirt floors with brick or tile, and installing indoor plumbing. The fact that existing houses are remodelled rather than new ones built, as in the village studied by Reichert (1981), reflects the existence of numerous vacant houses in Acuitzio—a legacy of an earlier boom period based on commerce and services. The acquisition of consumer durables has second highest priority. Mattresses and bed frames head the list. Gas stoves with ovens, furniture, television sets, and stereo consoles follow. Cars and pickups are purchased by a few. Clothing is an important consumption item—a readily-identifiable symbol of success. Table 7.1 compares migration households and non-migration households on a variety of household facilities and consumer goods possessed in 1967. It is obvious that U.S. migrant households are well above the majority of households on all of the indices.

This consumption is responsible for the widely-held belief in the village that migration provides the only way to improve one's standard of living. People expressed it to me in a variety of ways, but most agreed that migration to Mexico City was out of necessity whereas migration to the United States was an opportunity above necessity (Arizpe, 1981). Most people wanted to migrate legally, with "papers," but they saw little chance to acquire the necessary papers. Reichert (1982) draws attention to the intense pressure for migration through conspicuous consumption, and the changing attitude towards illegal migration that lays blame on those who did not take the chance (1982:40). In 1975, I encountered in Acuitzio a growing resistance to migration as the only solution to poverty and a locally depressed economy. Truck bumpers proclaimed "Y No Fuí Al Norte" ("And I Didn't Go North"); gunfights broke out between nonmigrants and return migrants to challenge the conspicuous display of return migrants. Most likely the more recent trend noted by Reichert is true of other villages as well. Correspondence with informants since 1975 indicates that there was subsequently a sharp increase in illegal migration to the U.S. from Acuitzio. Reichert's (1982) findings regarding the social consequences of increased consumption and invidious comparison confirm nearly all of my own. Social and economic differences have increased, resulting in rising social tensions. However, the belief that individual initiative rather than fate determines one's future is becoming more prevalent. This attitude encourages migrants to seek their fortunes through migration (Reichert, 1982).

Consumer goods are markers of the good life generally desired by villagers. However, the fact that they set off migrants from less fortunate nonmigrants in terms of standard of living is not the most significant point. Rather, as I argued in another part (Wiest, 1979a:92–94), some migrants from Acuitzio become rural bourgeoisie—small landlords, moneylenders, or commercial entrepreneurs whose interests are opposed to those of the landed peasantry, the sharecroppers, the landless, and the underemployed. They, in fact, perpetuate the structures that have precipitated migration in the first place.

Reichert (1982:416) suggests that the migrants, "by virtue of their high annual incomes, formed an elite segment of the town population." He recognizes the power advantage gained by migrants through acquisition of land and the use of motor vehicles for transport of commodities in the village. Yet he does not come to grips with the class relations involved and their implications for the organization of production in the village (Reichert, 1982:413–16).

DISPROPORTIONATE FLOW OF INCOME FROM THE VILLAGE

Capitalism is based on the appropriation of surplus value. While this is a class-relations phenomenon, it has its spatial dimension in regional and national inequalities that are a product of internal modes of production and external exchange relations (Frank, 1979:xiii; Amin, 1974; Emmanuel, 1972). Local bourgeois interests are allied with national and/or international metropolises in the process of surplus value appropriation. Thus, the predominant part of local commerce and wage labor in peasant villages exists to generate as much working capital as possible through super-exploitation (Frank, 1979). One of the offshoots of this process in the case of Mexican capitalism is that labor is a leading primary product export—an important source of foreign exchange for Mexico.

Measures of surplus value appropriation would provide a better understanding of the disproportionate flow of income from the village. It would also improve our knowledge of class relationships and relations between center and periphery (see Downing, 1982, for a discussion of measures of surplus value appropriation). In the absence of such measures, I will discuss the distribution of earnings conceptually. Figure 7.1 approximates the direct and indirect distribution of migrant earnings in a model that illustrates the role of village commerce and class interests in the metropolis-satellite structure.

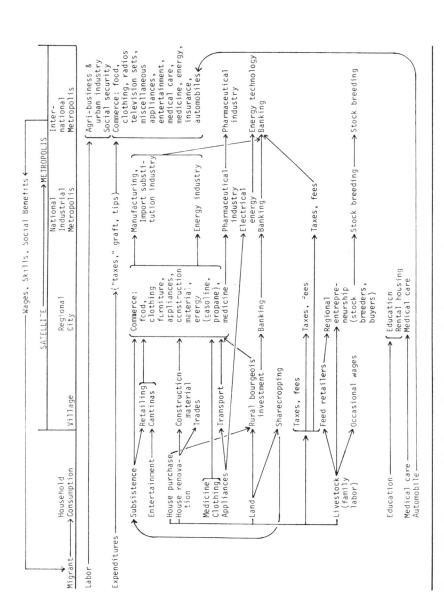

Figure 7.1 Direct and indirect distribution of migrant earnings

The disproportionate flow of earnings from the village to regional, national, and international centers is a function of the structure of expanding capitalism. The issue takes on an added significance in the light of relatively large infusions of cash earnings that theoretically could be applied for local benefit. Of particular interest here is how migrant earnings impact on the rest of the community. Are local jobs created? Is local commerce stimulated? Is there a multiplier effect?

Most striking has been the limited scope of perceptible spread of migrant earnings within the community. I found, instead, a conspicuous individualization of benefits centered on conjugal families (Wiest, 1973). Migrant labor, while occasionally involving cooperation between a more extended group of kinsmen, more often has resulted in growing assertions of independence. This response is consistent with reliance on wage labor and a consequence of loss of corporate kin group control over resources.

Moreover, only small percentages of the cash earnings of migrants are spent in Acuitzio. Aside from maize, purchased largely in the form of local machine-made tortillas, fresh meat, and breads, even foodstuffs are purchased outside of Acuitzio. The majority of Acuitzenses prefer a weekly trip to the Morelia or Pátzcuaro markets to buy fresh fruit and vegetables and convenient canned goods. Canned goods were increasingly popular with families of migrants, who were shopping more and more in urban markets. Retail outlets for fresh fruit and vegetables do exist in Acuitzio, and the supply of dry goods and canned goods is rapidly expanding there. But no Acuitzio retailer has yet been able to afford the quantity, variety, and quality of produce at a price to compete with urban center outlets.

Given such a high incidence of urban center buying, the established merchants in Acuitzio cater more to people from the rural hinterland. These people come to the *cabecera* on foot or by bus on weekends and festive occasions. The poorly-developed village commercial infrastructure is underscored by the large festive occasions. In another Michoacán village (Reichert, 1981), the dearth of retail outlets and the reluctance of migrants to invest in them is attributed to the high percentage of villagers absent each year. Acuitzio's outmigration, in comparison, was not nearly so high through 1975, and therefore did not have the same direct impact on local commerce. Rather, its proximity to larger centers, the difference in quantity, quality, and variety of goods and services, along with the prestige attached to more sophisticated urban tastes, account for its low level commercial development.

These individual preferences and strategies are accompanied by structural mechanisms which have exacerbated Acuitzense dependency.

Table 7.2 Number of People Entering and Leaving Acuitzio During a Week in June, 1972

	Mon.	Tues.	Wed.	Thurs.	Fri.	Sat.	Sun.	Totals
Entering	527	585	434	513	524	597	835	4015
Leaving	609	584	453	531	526	578	757	4038
Net Change	-82	+1	-19	-18	-2	+19	+78	-23

First, consider the movement of people in and out of the village. In 1972, a research assistant kept one week's records of the movement of people in and out of the town on the road to Morelia. The observations summarized in Table 7.2 are consistent with aforementioned interview and survey data. Many Acuitzenses live, work, visit, buy, and sell elsewhere. They then return to their home village on occasional weekends. Considering that hardly anyone commutes daily to Morelia or other nearby locations for work, this volume of traffic into and out of Acuitzio appears unusually high. Acuitzio is the terminus and origin of most of the traffic. Only one additional small village is accessible on this road. This mobility was apparent in Acuitzio even before the road was paved, when the 35 kilometer trip to Morelia took up to three hours. Now a new road has made the trip more comfortable and convenient, reducing the time to 30 or 40 minutes.

Return migrants rely heavily on urban centers for foodstuffs, dry goods, consumer durables such as furniture and appliances, medicine, health care, and education. They also spend a fairly high percentage of their income abroad for consumer durables which they bring to Mexico. The primary reason is that many of these items are less costly in the United States. They also consider the quality superior and the choice of marketed items much greater. The principal items purchased in the U.S. are clothing, radios, tape recorders, portable television sets, cameras, watches, small household appliances, cars, and pickups. Many of these are used items designed for resale in Mexico. The regular importation of such items has led to a fairly reliable source of income for police and government bureaucrats who collect "taxes," graft money, and tips on the movement of these goods. Return migrants often told me that they were obvious targets for *mordidas* (bribes), and that they had to plan on this expense in returning to Mexico with durable goods.

Contraband entry in the case of motor vehicles is difficult and not very widespread, but it does occur. Nearly all motor vehicles are purchased in the U.S. and entered into Mexico legally with 180-day permits—the same as applies to foreign toursits. The arrangement requires the regular return of migrants to the U.S.

Thus far I have argued that commercial activity in the village changes minimally in response to migrant remittances. One obvious exception is the sale of alcoholic beverages, both legal and contraband, which increases substantially while migrant men are home "on vacation." The annual return of migrants coincides with the increase in frequency of festivities from mid-September through December. This provides numerous occasions for conspicuous display of cash earned. These cash expenditures do not remain in the village, however. They are put into wider circulation through investments by the cantina-owning rural bourgeoisie. Thus the multiplier effects are insignificant for the local community. The expenditures are drawn to the center as a function of the alliance of local bourgeois interests with national metropolises in a dependency structure characteristic of dependent capitalism in the periphery.

House remodeling circulates some · migrant earnings within the community. House renovation and public works projects involve more use of brick, and because of this, the brick factories are expanding production and employing more laborers. At the same time, however, the production of adobe is declining. There is more work for local craftsmen, although much of the labor in renovating houses is done by the migrants upon their return from the United States. Employment that is generated by migrant earnings, as well as the demand for locally produced building materials like brick and roof tiles, is temporary, sporadic, and totally dependent upon continuation of migratory labor.

Public works projects in Acuitzio have been the subject of much discussion but little action. In 1975, a new municipal administration took office. It was headed by a young ex-migrant laborer on whom a younger group of PRI (Partido Revoluccionario Institucional, the dominant party in Mexico) political supporters were pinning their hopes for local change. Local initiative was instrumental in the construction of a secondary school; minimal state support was extended. But families of migrants had little involvement (see Reichert, 1981, for evidence of high migrant involvement in public works projects). It is my impression that many of them were more intent on sending their children to urban secondary schools.

In summary, a good portion of migrant earnigns never circulates within the village of origin, but is spent for consumer durables in the

United States or urban centers in Mexico. Those earnings that are returned to the village leave it and the region quickly and with little in the way of multiplier effects at the local or even regional level. The lack of a local commercial infrastructure and labor market encourages this flight of cash, as do the tastes and preferences of a rural proletariat attempting to mimic the rural bourgeoisie. Migrant earnings are increasingly important to the national economy for its balance of payments, however. Consistent with its peripheral position to dominant capital, the Mexican national level must extract as much surplus value from its own periphery as possible.

INFLATED LAND VALUES AND AN ARCHAIC TENURE SYSTEM

Ownership of land in a municipality that is still basically agricultural is considered one of the most desirable forms of long range security. For many years the majority of migrants were directly involved in agriculture, many as sharecroppers or owners of very small holdings. Thus, migration represented for many an opportunity to purchase their own land or to expand their holdings. In the early 1960s, at the end of the *bracero* program, the number of "green carders" (legal migrants) expanded rapidly. The majority of these new migrants were from outlying hamlets of the municipality, and from neighboring municipalities. Several of them managed to buy land at very reasonable prices.

As in the region in general, agricultural land is in short supply, especially fertile land and/or irrigable land. With demand high and supply severely limited, the cost of most parcels rose rapidly after 1965. Land "bargains" were still available, however, depending on the vendor's need to sell and the social relations between buyer and seller. There was an indication that some migrants were lending to small-holders who were subsequently forced to "sell" to the lender. By-and-large, land acquisitions appear to have been costly for the return migrants. The majority have been unable to purchase agricultural land. Instead, many have settled for village-edge garden-size housesites, often moving their families from rural areas. Non-migrants and migrants share the perception that local land prices have escalated. Word has spread that return migrants have money and are eager to acquire land at virtually any cost.

Table 7.3 compares migrant with non-migrant land holdings. Fifty-seven percent of the sample households have access to land. They either own, rent, or possess rights to *ejido* (communal) land. Among those migrating to the United States, about 78 percent own land or have rights to *ejido* land. The fact that more migrants hold land than

Table 7.3   Distribution of Seventy Sample Households by Land Tenure and
            Migration, Acuitzio, 1976[a]

Land tenure	Percent non-US migrant households	Percent US migrant households	Totals
Landless	46%	22%	42.9%
Land owners			
Large holdings (latifundia)	1%	0%	1.4%
Family farms	7%	11%	7.1%
Sub-family plots (minifundia)	26%	56%	30.0%
Ejidatarios (3 hectares)	15%	11%	14.3%
Sharecroppers (medieros)*	5%	0%	4.3%
Total landholdings	100%	100%	100%
Total households	61	9	70

Note: [a]The number of medieros in the sample is very small simply because
        the sample covered in the cabecera exclusively, and virtually all
        of the medieros live in ranchos, rancherías, or isolated house-
        sites.

non-migrants cannot be attributed to migration, however. The history
of its acquisition must be taken into consideration. Nearly half of the
migrants with land in my sample already possessed it before migrating.
It was acquired through inheritance or purchase prior to migration.
The others have purchased plots of land with migrant earnings, but
all of these purchases have been on a small scale. Most migrants
possess subfamily holdings that are inadequate to maintain the household. These holdings are certainly inadequate to sustain a lifestyle
which would no longer require wage-labor migration to the U.S. At
best, land acquisitions serve to supplement their U.S. wage incomes.
The same is true of investment in livestock—it does not provide an
income even closely approximating that from wage jobs in the U.S.
A wage income does facilitate income diversification and supplementation—e.g., more U.S. migrants enter hog-raising on a commercial
basis (56 percent) than do nonmigrants (19 percent)—but through
the use of unpaid household labor. Animals are usually tended by

wives when their husbands are absent, as an extension of women's domestic labor. Expanded use of unpaid household labor is evidently a widespread response of peasants-cum-rural proletariat (see Downing, 1982:274, for parallel evidence). In fact, the continuity of a peasant mode of production can have the effect of keeping the cost of commodities low through the utilization of household labor among noncapitalist peasant producers, thus permitting lower labor costs and higher profits in the capitalist mode of production (e.g., Bartra, 1975).

Seasonal workers continue to rely on income supplementation and continue to be guided by an ideology of establishing themselves on their own land. Thus, they are never completely proletarianized. A peasant mode of production is consequently maintained with the effect of providing a partially self-sufficient labor force that bears a good part of its reproduction cost. Thus, the cost of labor to capitalist enterprises is lowered.

The archaic, exploitative, tenure arrangement of leasing to share-croppers is well suited to the needs of migrants. Leasing to share-croppers allows the landowner to be seasonally absent. His ownership of land is protected, and a small but continued agricultural income in kind or cash is guaranteed. The effect is to encourage recurrent migration of the landowner, and to perpetuate an exploitative sharecrop system. It also provides the migrant laborer with a supplemental income requiring minimal investment of labor and capital. Share-cropping evens the risk between the landowner and the tenant, but it increases surplus value appropriation since "social labor" is drawn into appropriation, through the involvement of the tenant's domestic group. This sharecrop system also served to keep women in their traditional dependent position. Wives of migrants are kept from direct management of the agricultural operation. Some sharecroppers are able to consolidate several small but contiguous plots belonging to different owners, but such arrangements are usually short-lived. The tenuousness of these arrangements, compounded by the common belief that migration offers the only hope for improvement, has encouraged sharecroppers also to migrate (see Reichert, 1981:62).

In summary, migrant land purchases have not put more land into production nor provided additional jobs. Rather, land simply changes hands, and migrants become, in effect, absentee landlords. Their competition for land has inflated land values. This has placed the majority of landless persons at an even greater disadvantage, by removing them even further from their means of production. Those who sell land, usually at a premium, generally move to a city and enter commerce.

LABOR MARKET DECLINE AND INTERNATIONAL MIGRATION

Migration to the United States is necessitated partly by the poorly-developed labor market at the local and regional levels. With the development of the shoe industry of Guadalajara and Leon, local employment opportunities have become relatively less attractive. With the advent of new farm equipment (replacing ox-drawn carts), the number of local cartwheel manufacturers and repairers has dropped from seven to one in the last ten years, even though Acuitzio is still known throughout Michoacán for its quality of material and workmanship. Finally, farm mechanization among several *latifuindistas* (large landholders) has reduced agricultural labor jobs.

Despite the high incidence of households headed by women in the village, jobs available to women remain low-status and few in number. Most employed women work in service jobs as domestics; a few work as day laborers tending and feeding animals. Mechanization has substantially reduced tortilla making as a source of income for local women. A growing number of women are turning to petty commerce to supplement the meager income received from a variety of sources, including small contributions from daughters and sons in Mexico City (Wiest, 1973).

Most of the local wage labor is connected with agriculture and is seasonal. With the annual departure of one-fifth of the male labor force from Acuitzio a shortage of laborers would seem likely. In fact, there are agricultural entrepreneurs who claim that their productive potential is limited because they cannot get adequate help. Potential laborers are present, but they prefer not to work in the fields for the wages offered (12 pesos/day from 1966 to 1972; 20 to 25 pesos/day in 1974; this compares to U.S. wages of $15 to $20 per day in 1966–67). The shortage of hands willing to work for local wages is alleviated in large part by labor migration into the *cabecera* from outlying hamlets. Hamlet residents are in search of income supplementation as well as the amenities offered in the *cabecera*—particularly for their children. The *cabecera*-hamlet relationship is a first-level exploitative one in the metropolis-satellite structure. This is because it draws on a reserve labor force that is poor, undereducated, unpoliticized, and hence less costly to the local entrepreneurs.

Regional labor opportunities are also severely limited. There is intense competition for jobs in Michoacán and the surrounding states. The level of industrial development is low, with projects emerging only recently designed to alleviate the problem. A new paper mill in Morelia is in the early stages of operation. The steel mills on the coast at Lazáro Cárdenas are still under construction. In both cases, however, the demand for labor is already well outstripping job op-portunities. Construction projects such as the paving of the road through Acuitzio in 1972 provided temporary employment for a handful of Acuitzio laborers, but most jobs went to urban residents. A few Acuitzio women find employment as domestics in such places as Pátzcuaro, Uruapan, or Morelia, but this is the general limit of labor possibilities in the region. The regional centers extract less labor than surplus capital from the municipality; commercial financing, processing, packaging, and distribution are all located in the regional capital of Morelia.

The principal internal destination for Acuitzenses seeking to increase their chances of employment or economic betterment is Mexico City. The greatest number of rural-urban migrants are single sons and daughters who find work in construction, demolition, and services (domestics, gate keepers, waiters, cooks). Increasingly, they are turning to petty commerce because they cannot get wage jobs. Petty commerce is more consistent with the need to move back and forth between the rural town and the city (Wiest, 1973; Arizpe, 1981).

There are essentially two different classes of the Acuitzio population that migrate to Mexico City: (a) the upwardly mobile bourgeoisic and petty bourgeoisie who move to the city in order to improve their life style and their income; and (b) the landless underemployed poor who are destitute and have no options in Acuitzio. The former usually move as entire families, and tend to remain there. The latter usually involves individual migrants, often dependent sons or daughters, who work for several months in the city before returning to the rural village. For the upwardly mobile class, urban jobs and business op-portunities are generally available. For the landless class, rural-urban migration is a desperate search for a supplemental income source, and their life chances do not improve appreciably.

Furthermore, village outmigration removes local capital-generating potential in the case of the migrating bourgeoisie. At the same time, it supplies cheap labor for low-paying urban industry in the case of the landless unemployed. Among the latter, labor exportation tends to remove the most productive age group. Migration to Mexico City involves the relatively younger men, women, and families, leaving behind the elderly, infirm and very young. Consequently, international and rural-urban migration has lowered rather than raised overall productivity of the sending community. The most productive and best educated age group is drawn off, and abandonment of rural hamlets is encouraged. The previously cultivated land is thereby left idle or worked less intensively. Finally, the dramatic shift of population to

Mexico City has exacerbated an already enormous problem (Muñoz, Oliveira, and Stern, 1977).

While we see extensive shifts in the demography of the municipality, it is significant that labor exportation reinforces the existing social structure. This social structure has been an essential part of the conditions that lead to labor exportation in the first place. International migration sets into motion a hamlet to *cabecera* shift by freeing limited jobs in the *cabecera* and fueling the myth of social mobility.

Conclusion

The evidence is strong that migration perpetuates itself—a process that Reichert (1981) refers to as the "migrant syndrome." In this essay I have addressed a number of elements of this perpetuation, and I have explained it in terms of structures that generate external dependency. The evidence is that migrants to the United States (a) earn considerably more than they could earn in Mexico, (b) must continue to migrate to sustain a higher standard of living, and (c) have patterns of consumption which induce still others to migrate. Their earnings flow disproportionately from the village to virtually eliminate potential multiplier effects, and migrant land acquisitions at premium rates remove others still further from the means of production. A sharecropping arrangement allows them to continue to migrate while benefiting from land ownership. Finally, U.S. migration stimulates internal migration by creating a paradoxical labor shortage, through knowledge of preferable wage rates in the U.S., in a village with high unemployment.

Fundamental to this migrant syndrome are the underlying structural features characteristic of capitalism. In this system, labor is a primary product export from Mexico. Migration is but one manifestation of the appropriation of surplus value. To understand the origin of the labor migration process as well as the profound spatial mobility of labor today, attention must range from the class interests that have set the conditions for migration from the periphery, to the fluctuation of international exchange rates.

This long-term study of migration from one community in Mexico contributes to our understanding of the peasant village–world capitalist system interface. The analysis puts migration into a broader world system framework through the application of dependency theory and historical-structuralism. The dependency approach offers a dynamic spatial and structural interpretation of the division of labor and the class relations of the rural origin. The social structure—the relations of production—of which migrants are a part, becomes focal through attention to the production process.

Bustamante and Martínez (1979:273–74) make clear why it is essential to break through the ideological constraints of capitalism and determine the underlying structures. As they point out, Mexicans may cross a national border but they remain within a single system that is international in scope. A demand exists in the United States for Mexican labor, while institutions and practices exist to mark this required labor (as "illegals," "undocumenteds," or, I might add, "guest workers") and guarantee its temporality through deportation to assure that the greater portion of the social costs of labor are not borne in the U.S. As I have argued in this essay, the migrants are by-and-large unaware of their relationship to the productive process of international capitalism. The argument made by Bustamante and Martínez (1979) suggests that capital has a vested interest in obscuring that relationship. The next step in the analysis of migration and the international division of labor should be to address the political and economic implications of peasant and proletariat politicization and class consciousness potential. It is my hope that this essay contributes to such research.

References

Alba, Francisco. 1978. "Mexico's international migration as a manifestation of its development pattern." *International Migration Review* 12:502–13.

Amin, Samir. 1974. *Accumulation of a World Scale: a Critique on the Theory of Underdevelopment.* New York: Monthly Review Press.

———. 1976. *Unequal Development: An Essay on the Social Formations of Peripheral Capitalism.* New York: Monthly Review Press.

Arizpe, Lourdes. 1981. "The rural exodus in Mexico and Mexican migration to the United States." *International Migration Review* 15:626–49. Reprinted in *The Border That Joins*, eds. Peter G. Brown and Henry Shue. Totowa, New Jersey: Rowman and Littlefield, 1983.

Bach, Robert L., and Lisa A. Schraml. 1982. "Migration, crisis, and theoretical conflict." *International Migration Review* 16:320–41.

Barta, Rodger. 1975. "Sobre la articulación de modos de producción en América Latina: algunos problemas teóricos." *Historia y Sociedad* 5:5–19.

Brandes, Stanley. 1975. *Migration, Kinship, and Community: Tradition and Transition in a Spanish Village.* New York: Academic Press.

Brettell, Caroline. 1979. "Emigrar para voltar: a Portuguese ideology of return migration." *Papers in Anthropology* 20:1–20.

Business Week. 1976. "Mexico: New duty-free zones that aid U.S. industry." February 23, p. 42.

Bustamante, Jorge, and Gerónimo G. Martínez. 1979. "Undocumented immigration from Mexico: Beyond borders but within systems." *Journal of International Affairs* 33:265–84.

Cross, Harry E., and James A. Sandos. 1981. *Across the Border: Rural Development in Mexico and Recent Migration to the United States.* Berkeley: Institute of Governmental Studies, University of California.

Dinerman, Ina R. 1978. "Patterns of adaptation among households of U.S.–bound migrants from Michoacán, Mexico." *International Migration Review* 12:485–501.

Downing, Theodore E. 1979. "Explaining migration in Mexico and elsewhere." In F. Camara and R.V. Kemper, eds., *Migration Across Frontiers: Mexico and the United States.* Albany: Institute for Mesoamerican Studies, SUNY, pp. 159–67.

————. "The internationalization of capital in agriculture." *Human Organization* 41:269–77.

Emmanuel, Arghiri. 1972. *Unequal Exchange: A Study of the Imperialism of Trade.* New York: Monthly Review Press.

Frank, André Gunder. 1969. *Latin America: Underdevelopment or Revolution.* New York: Monthly Review Press.

————. 1979. *Dependent Accumulation and Underdevelopment.* New York: Monthly Review Press.

Griffin, Keith. 1976. "On the emigration of the peasantry." *World Development* 4:353–61.

Hancock, Richard H. 1959. *The Role of the Bracero in the Economic and Cultural Dynamics of Mexico: A Case Study of Chihuahua.* Stanford: Hispanic American Society.

Jenkins, J. Craig. 1978. "The demand for immigrant workers: Labor scarcity or social control?" *International Migration Review* 12:514–35.

Jones, Richard C. "Undocumented migration from Mexico: Some geographical questions." *Annals, Association of American Geographers* 22:77–87.

Lewis, Oscar. 1960. "Mexico since Cardenas." Pages 285–345 in R.N. Adams et al., eds., *Social Change in Latin America Today.* New York: Vintage Books.

Lipton, Michael. 1980. "Migration from rural areas of poor countries: The impact on rural productivity and income distribution." *World Development* 8:1–24.

Muñoz, Humberto, Orlandina de Oliveira, and Claudio Stern. 1977. Migración y desigualdad social en la ciudad de México. México, D.F.: Instituto de Investigaciones Sociales, Universidad Nacional Autónoma de México.

Petras, James. 1978. *Critical Perspectives on Imperialism and Social Class in the Third World.* New York: Monthly Review Press.

Piore, Michael J. 1979. *Birds of Passage: Migrant Labor and Industrial Societies.* Cambridge: Cambridge University Press.

Portes, Alejandro. 1978. "Migration and underdevelopment." *Politics and Society* 8:1–48.

————. "International labor migration and national development." Paper prepared for the Immigration and Refugee Workshop, Wingspread, Wisconsin, August 17–20.

Randall, Laura. 1962. "Labor migration and Mexican economic development." *Social and Economic Studies* 11:73–81.

Reichert, Joshua S. 1981. "The migrant syndrome: Seasonal U.S. wage labor and rural development in central Mexico." *Human Organization* 40:55–66.

————. 1982. "A town divided: Economic stratification and social relations in a Mexican migrant community." *Social Problems* 29:411–23.

Reichert, Joshua, and Douglas S. Massey. 1979. "Patterns of U.S. migration from a Mexican sending community: A comparison of legal and illegal migrants." *International Migration Review* 13:599–623.

Rhoades, Robert E. 1978. "Foreign labor and German industrial capitalism, 1871–1978: The evolution of a migratory system." *American Ethnologist* 5:553–73.

Shadow, Robert D. 1979. "Differential out-migration: A comparison of internal and international migration from Villa Guerrero, Jalisco (Mexico)." Pp. 67–84 in F. Camara and R.V. Kemper, eds., *Migration Across Frontiers: Mexico and the United States.* Albany: Institute for Mesoamerican Studies, SUNY.

Smith, Carol A. 1981. "Regional analysis in world-system perspective: A critique of three structural theories of uneven development." Paper prepared for the Society for Economic Anthropology Conference, Bloomington, Indiana, April 24–29. (Revised September 1981.)

Staley, Robert A., 1974. "An Ecological Approach to the Development of a Stratified Polity in Michoacan." MA thesis, University of Manitoba, Winnipeg.

Stavenhagen, Rodolfo. 1970. "Social aspects of agrarian structure in Mexico." Pp. 225–70 in R. Stavenhagen, ed., *Agrarian Problems and Peasant Movements in Latin America.* Garden City: Anchor Books.

———. 1975. *Social Class in Agrarian Societies.* Garden City: Anchor Books.

Swanson, Jon. 1979. "The consequences of emigration for economic development: A review of the literature." *Papers in Anthropology* 20:39–56.

Wallerstein, Immanuel. 1979. *The Capitalist World-Economy.* Cambridge: Cambridge University Press.

West, Robert C. 1948. *Cultural Geography of the Modern Tarascan Area.* Publication no. 7. Washington, D.C.: Smithsonian Institution, Institute of Social Anthropology.

Wiest, Raymond E. 1973. "Wage-labor migration and the household in a Mexican town." *Journal of Anthropological Research* 29:180–209.

———. 1979a. "Implications of international labor migration for Mexican rural development." Pp. 85–97 in F. Camara and R.V. Kemper, eds., *Migration Across Frontiers: Mexico and the United States.* Albany: Institute for Mesoamerican Studies, SUNY.

———. 1979b. "Anthropological perspectives on return migration: A critical commentary." *Papers in Anthropology* 20:167–87.

———. 1980. "The interrelationship of rural, urban, and international labor markets: Consequences for a rural Michoacán community." *Papers in Anthropology* 21:29–46.

Wood, Charles H. 1981. "Structural changes and household strategies: A conceptual framework for the study of rural migration." *Human Organization* 40:338–44.

———. 1982. "Equilibrium and historical-structural perspectives on migration." *International Migration Review* 16:298–319.

8

Network Migration and Mexican Rural Development: A Case Study

RICHARD MINES

The Mexican economy has grown rapidly since World War II. Import-substituting industrialization and agricultural development, spurred by technological change, irrigation, and a growing export market, have produced a 2–3 percent average annual growth rate despite rapid population increase (Felix, 1972). The income generated has been so unevenly distributed among regions, sectors of economic activity, and social groups, however, that the Mexican experience has been described as creating jointly "wealth and misery" (Aguilar and Carmona, 1967).

The biggest drawback to the so-called "Mexican miracle" is its inability to create adequate employment. With the decline of death rates in the postwar period, Mexico's population growth exceeded three percent per year for many years. Several large cities are growing at annual rates of 6–7 percent, while employment is growing at only 3 percent (Reynolds, in press). In fact, rapid employment creation associated with the early stages of import-substituting industrialization is now over. Employment growth generated by the oil boom has also leveled off.

In areas touched by the new agricultural technology and the expansion of farm exports, a large number of permanent jobs have

This is a revised version of "Migration to the United States and Mexican Rural Development: A Case Study," *American Journal of Agricultural Economics* 64 (1982:444–54). Special acknowledgement is made to Alain de Janvry, Carole Nuckton, and B. Delworth Gardner, all of whom assisted in the preparation of this essay, by permission of the editor.

not been created. Mechanization, which accompanied farm modernization, either displaced many workers or shortened their work season. More important, the vast majority of Mexican peasants are bypassed entirely by the new technology. Traditional rain-fed farming practices still predominate in the central highlands where most peasants live. Furthermore, an agricultural policy seeking cheap food for the urban industrial sector through price ceilings and grain imports has discouraged many peasants from planting corn (Gomez-Oliver, 1978). Much rain-fed land previously opened to cultivation is currently left idle or used for extensive cattle grazing (Barkin, 1980).

While development has brought some advantages to the poor rural dwellers, such as grammar schools, better roads, and—for Indians— greater fluency in the Spanish language, it has not led to improvements in their economic productivity. Rural inhabitants' aspirations and physical mobility have been enhanced, but not their buying power. At the same time, population growth rates have remained high in rural areas. Most peasants now generate more income by selling their labor than from the production of their farms (Centro de Investigaciones Agrarias, 1974). Not surprisingly, many villagers and peasants now depend on migration to the United States to supplement local earnings.

On the other side of the border, United States society has also undergone structural shifts which complement Mexican developments. They have been particularly noticeable in the last decade. The service sector of the economy has expanded, while the industrial core has remained stable (AFL-CIO, 1979). Most jobs created in recent decades have been without full-time hours, fringe benefits, or a chance for advancement (Ginzberg, 1977). In the 1950s, 1960s, and 1970s, women, blacks and the abundant young adults, products of the baby boom, filled these lower-level jobs. Now, rising aspirations and educational levels among women and blacks along with a declining population of young adults have left a potential shortfall of unskilled workers (Wool, 1976). Mexican workers with established pathways, job contacts, and settlement areas are the logical people to fill this gap.

United States migration policies and enforcement practices have adapted to the changing labor supply-demand situation. In the 20 years after World War II, Mexican immigrants were desired principally as field laborers in agriculture. The contract labor system of 1942–64, the *"Bracero"* program, and the deportation drive of 1954 (Operation Wetback) made it difficult for nonimmigrant Mexicans to find nonagricultural work. Operation Wetback cleared the undocumented migrants from the cities, forcing those interested in U.S. work to come as contract laborers in agriculture. By the late 1960s, however, as the demand for Mexican workers spread from agriculture to urban employment, immigration law enforcement could not keep up with events. Social security cards were easily obtained by undocumented workers until recently. Now the ebb and flow of hundreds of thousands of Mexicans across the border occurs largely outside the purview of U.S. immigration law.

The Evolution of a Migratory Community

In order to observe the microeconomic impacts of this migratory process on the emitting Mexican rural communities, one community— Las Animas, in the state of Zacatecas—was chosen for closer scrutiny.

Contemporary studies and work done in the 1920s identified six western and central northern Mexican states as the core source region for cross-border migration (Gamio, 1930; Dagodag, 1975). This area encompasses the western side of the central plateau. Within the core region there are areas which have widespread commercial agriculture and areas where the traditional rain-fed practices persist. Some areas have mostly small landholders, others have mostly *ejidal* land (land legally owned by the community but with total occupant usufruct rights). Among those areas with heavy migration rates, some sending areas specialize in cross-border migration and others in internal migration.

Las Animas, which is in the northwestern section of the core region, is typical of a migratory community where small land ownership, traditional rain-fed agricultural practices, and international migratory patterns predominate. The village has 1,333 people and is located three hours north of Guadalajara. Its economy is rooted in rain-fed corn and beans production supplemented by low-productivity cattle raising. A random sample of 67 village families in 1978 indicated that 11.8 percent of the land in the village is devoted to rain-fed corn/ beans production, 0.5 percent is irrigated and planted in chile peppers, and the remainder is used for extensive cattle grazing. Sixty percent of the agricultural production in the community is carried out by sharecroppers. The remaining 40 percent is done by small owner-producers. The home village is highly dependent on cash remittances from the United States. Today, over 50 percent of the village income is remitted from the United States. The reader should keep in mind that the generalizations derived below by analysis of Animeño migration are most useful when applied to areas with socioeconomic character-istics similar to Las Animas.

Las Animas was chosen because of its deeply rooted tradition of cross-border migration and its linkage to mature settlement colonies in the United States. By recording detailed job histories and village production data for a sample of villagers and migrants, it was possible to analyze the evolution of this village community as it became increasingly committed to international migration. The study of one community allows us to uncover certain tendencies inherent in the development of such villages. The maturing process that Las Animas has undergone in recent decades sheds light on the way many other migratory communities in central Mexico have developed or will develop as they insert themselves into the U.S. job market. Below, we describe the particular historical evolution of Las Animas and extract generalizations about migratory patterns, social differentiation, and the economic impacts on sending areas.

The first migration wave to the United States occurred in the 1920s. During this decade, Animeños worked in mines, agriculture, and one urban area—South San Francisco. With the depression of the 1920s, almost all Animeños returned home and resumed traditional farming activities. Starting in 1942, Animeño men again began coming north, this time as contract laborers. Soon they learned to desert their *bracero* contracts or cross the border illegally on foot. As undocumented workers they earned higher wages and stayed for longer periods than as contract laborers. By the 1950s, most men were working illegally in the United States. A small beachhead community of Animeños was forming in South San Francisco. In 1954, the first postwar wave of migration from Las Animas to the United States ended when Operation Wetback forced almost all migrants out of rural and urban areas. Between 1954 and 1956, the percentage of Animeño men spending part of the year in the United States dropped from 40 percent to 18 percent.

The next wave north began with the severe drought of 1957. Many Animeño men came across the border as *braceros* or undocumented workers, but by the early 1960s they again began locating urban jobs. Between 1960 and 1964, legal residents founded permanent settlement cores in South San Francisco and East Los Angeles. These pioneers began to house and job-place other villagers. Once the settler cores were established, a mass migration occurred including Animeños of both sexes and all ages.

By the late 1970s most villagers could rely on mature migratory networks to guide them in the United States. The mature status of the binational village community is illustrated by the stabilization of several migratory patterns. The average age of male Animeños in the United States stabilized at 36 years, as old returnees just balanced young arrivals. The proportion of legal immigrants among all male Animeños in the United States leveled off at about one-half, and the

proportion of U.S. Animeños living in urban areas stabilized at over
70 percent of the total male migrant population. Meanwhile, the village
population also has remained relatively stable over the last five years.
Las Animas appears to have achieved a migratory equilibrium at a
very high rate of outmigration and return migration.

Methodology and Conceptual Framework

Social scientists concerned with migration have concentrated on two
levels of analysis: the macrostructural or society-wide level and the
individual decision-making level. There is, however, an intermediate
level, consisting of migratory networks which have their own definite
structures. The network receives its signals from the larger society
and in turn creates options for its members. The networks are based
on the reciprocal exchange of favors among friends and relatives.
This exchange is traditional among poor rural people who have few
material assets and who must rely on social contacts (Lomnitz, 1975).
As the villagers turn to cross-border migration as a survival strategy,
the reciprocity networks become international.

The intermediate level analysis sheds light on theoretical formu-
lations carried out either at the macrostructural or individual decision-
making levels. The most common formulation at the individual decision-
making level is the push/pull hypothesis. Migrants under this theory
decide to migrate as a result of negative push factors in the receiving
area, and friction from obstacles in between (Cardona, 1976). Proponents of the push/pull approach have pointed to economic factors
as the primary cause of migration. Particular stress has been given
to wage differentials between rural Mexico and the U.S. Southwest
(Jenkins, 1977). The network model also supports the preeminence
of economic motivations. However, the superiority of the destination
area is dependent on a network of job and social contacts. This enables
the newcomer not only to find work and improve his material standard
of living but also to adjust emotionally to his new surroundings. Part
of the pull is inside the migratory network itself.

The network model is also applicable to macrostructural theories
of migration. The discussion at this level is part of a larger debate
between two theories of social change—modernization and dependency
(Portes and Browning, 1977). The two theories are similar in form
though different in substance; they both explain the spread of western
civilization to rural Mexico. The modernization school asserts that as
western culture spreads, rural Mexico becomes more secularized,
complex, educated, and democratic. Dependency theorists argue that
as the capitalist market spreads wealth, skills and capital are drained

from outlying areas. The study of network migration enriches this debate by demonstrating how integration into the international labor market can both increase the consumption level of almost all people in the migratory community and at the same time drain the sending area of much of its active labor force and promoters of change.

It is hypothesized in this study that well-established networks reduce the monetary and emotional costs to the migrating individual and increase his chances of success. This network hypothesis helps explain how patterns of migration develop. It sheds light on why migration tends to become concentrated geographically and by occupation in both sending and receiving areas (Swanson, 1979). It demonstrates why individuals in well-developed networks benefit from migration while others without strong network ties do not. This in turn helps explain the changes in social structure and the rural development process in the village.

In order to collect information about these networks, the migrants were categorized according to their relationships to the U.S. job market.

First, we distinguished between (a) U.S.-oriented migrants who have chosen the United States as their lifelong place of work, and (b) temporary migrants for whom the village economy remains an important source of subsistence. Among temporary migrants, two subgroups were distinguished: (i) the "two times or less" group composed of older migrants who never became seriously involved in the U.S. job market and younger migrants at the beginning of their migratory life cycle, and (ii) undocumented shuttles who are mainly men with a medium-term commitment to the United States and who normally return to the village in middle age. U.S.-oriented migrants were separated into three categories: (i) legal shuttles who have their families in the village but work in the United States; (ii) long-term permanents who "have their lives in the North" and visit the village only for vacations; and (iii) the beginner permanents, a new group in the Animeño population, made up predominantly of undocumented young men and their wives. Members of this last group intend to stay and become long-term permanents; they also visit the village only for vacations (see Table 8.1).

A random sample of 67 villagers was selected in 1979 in Las Animas. This group was complemented by ten representative Tijuana-based individuals from the village and 45 Animeño individuals working in the United States. Complete life histories were obtained for all 123 of these respondents. Data were also gathered on the kin networks of the interviewee: his parents, wife, children, siblings and his wife's siblings and parents. Information was thereby obtained on 1,454

Table 8.1 Definition of Kinds of US Migrancy

Kinds of migrants	US or village-based	Intend to work in US throughout working years	Shuttle or long-stay	Wife-child in village	Usual type of US work	Total years in US	Legal or undocumented
Temporary:							
Two times or less	Village	Undecided or no	Shuttle	Yes	Unskilled	2 or less	Undocumented
Undocumented shuttle	Village	No	Shuttle	Yes	Unskilled	3 or more	Undocumented
US-oriented:							
Beginner permanent	US	Yes	Long stay	No	Semi-skilled	3 to 6	Undocumented
Long-term permanent	US	Yes	Long stay	No	Semi-skilled	7 or more	Legal
Legal shuttles	Village	Yes	Shuttle	Yes	Semi-skilled	Any	Legal

Table 8.2 Most Frequent Type of U.S. Occupation by
Age Group, 1979 (in percentage)

| | Age Group | | |
Occupation	16 to 39 (N = 259)	40 to 54 (N = 120)	55 or more (N = 91)
Agricultural	21.2	43.3	67.0
Low-wage urban	38.6	21.7	23.1
Semiskilled urban[a]	40.2	35.0	9.9

Source: Sample of 1,454 observations

Note: [a]Defined as earning $4.50/hour or more (1978 dollars)

persons about their access to land, their work in the village, their migrancy, and their work experience in the United States. Each piece of data about noninterviewees was cross-checked by conversations with other community members. A final check was conducted by a paid informant at the conclusion of the data-gathering period.

The data provide a historical perspective on migration patterns, and the impact of migration on a village economy. Furthermore, the data reveal how these processes changed over time as the community became increasingly conditioned by migration. This maturation process can be characterized as a set of tendencies.

Migration Patterns

TENDENCY 1

At the beginning of migratory experience, a village network obtains access in California to agricultural, rural, unskilled, and temporary work. As the network matures, jobs become increasingly nonagricultural, urban, semiskilled and legal.

Tendency 1 can be observed by looking at the most frequent occupation of Animeño men of different generations (Table 8.2). While older men are still in principally agricultural jobs, most younger migrants have semiskilled urban jobs. The share of agriculture in total work performed by migrants while in the United States declined from 100 percent in 1944 to 70 percent in 1958, to 48 percent in 1966, and to 20 percent in 1978. In contrast, time spent in U.S. cities as a percentage of time spent in all places increased from zero in 1944

Origins in Mexico

Table 8.3 Type of Migrancy in the United States by Age Group, 1979 (in percentage)

Kind of migrancy[a]	Age Group		
	16 to 39 (N = 265)	40 to 54 (N = 121)	55 or more (N = 91)
Temporary:			
Two times or less	21.1	20.7	19.8
Undocumented shuttle	24.5	36.4	50.5
US-Oriented:			
Beginner permanent	16.2	2.5	1.1
Long-term permanent	32.8	38.8	22.0
Legal shuttle	5.3	1.7	6.6
Total:	99.9	100.1	100.0

Source: Sample of 1,454 observations.

Note: [a]See Table 8.1 for definitions of the types of migrancies.

to 35 percent in 1978. The share of legal migrants in the total number of U.S. migrants increased from 5 percent in 1951 to 50 percent in 1978.

The shift to urban employment reflects not only the maturing of the Animeño network but the growth in demand for Mexicans in the service, manufacturing, and construction industries in recent decades. However, it is not atypical today for less mature networks to have virtually all of their members working in agriculture (Reichert and Massey, 1979).

TENDENCY 2

As the village migrant community matures, the road to committed status is altered. Instead of passing through an undocumented shuttle stage, migrants tend increasingly to pass through a beginner permanent stage.

This tendency is best illustrated by age-cohort analysis (Table 8.3). In the two older age groups, almost all serious migration began as (and remains) undocumented shuttling. The traditional pattern involved seasonal migration to agricultural jobs. Eventually, some of these older men were able to regularize their status, find urban jobs, and stay for long periods in the United States. However, in the youngest age group, a new migrant category has established itself—the beginner permanent. Until the permanent settler cores were founded in the early 1960s, this path was not an option for Animeño migrants. The beginner permanent, instead of serving an apprenticeship as an undocumented shuttle, now comes directly to the urban colonies. If he is able to find a steady job and go undetected by the U.S. Immigration and Naturalization Service, he may eventually achieve long-term status.

TENDENCY 3

Although network migration is a male-led phenomenon, over time a greater percentage of total migrants are women and a higher percentage of women migrate without documents.

Accounts by older Animeño migrants indicate that in the 1920s virtually no village women went to the United States. In the oldest age-cohort group in the sample (55 years or more), only 11.5 percent of those who crossed the border were women. In the younger age cohorts, however, women are a growing percentage of all U.S. migrants, representing 23 percent of migrants in the age group 40 to 54 and 29 percent in the age group 16 to 39.

Although Animeño migration continues to be a male-led phenomenon, women whose husbands or close relatives have achieved U.S.-oriented status are now more likely than before to join them. If the ratio of U.S.-oriented females to the U.S.-oriented migrants is compared among the three generations, it appears that, over time, increasing percentages of U.S.-oriented males are bringing their women to the United States. In the younger cohorts, females represent 36 percent of the total U.S.-oriented migrants, but only 28 percent of the oldest group. Further, the percentage in the youngest cohort is biased downward since many of the single males in this group may still marry village women and bring them to the United States.

Although the proportion of legal migrants among all migrants has risen, there are two counter-tendencies to be explained. First, there is a tendency for a high percentage in the youngest male age group to be undocumented; this percentage is even higher than in the middle-aged groups (Table 8.4). However, undocumented status among many of the young is of short duration. The youngest group is at the beginning of its migratory cycle, and many will attain legal status in the future. The undocumenteds in the middle-income group, on the other hand, generally have given up on attaining legal status; many have returned permanently to the village. Second, there is a clear counter-tendency toward increased unauthorized migration among Animeña women (Table 8.4). This reverse tendency is directly related to beginner permanency observed among men. More men are settling in the urban colonies before they obtain legal papers; they find it

Table 8.4 Undocumented Migrants among US Migrants, 1979

Age	Number of all migrant men	Undocumented migrants[a]	Number of all migrant women	Undocumented migrants[a]
		(%)		(%)
16 to 39	265	61.9	110	47.3
40 to 54	121	59.5	35	27.8
55 or more	91	71.4	11	8.3

Source: Sample of 1,454 observations.

Note: [a]The number of total undocumented migrants equals the sum of one or two timers, beginner permanents, and undocumented shuttles.
The percentage of undocumented is calculated by dividing this sum by the total number of US migrants in each category.

convenient to bring their wives to the United States, also without papers. Animeña women are migrating earlier in their husbands' life cycles. They are coming before, instead of after, their husbands obtain legal status.

Social Differentiation

TENDENCY 1

In village migratory networks, a division into two groups occurs in the young adult period of the male migrant's life cycle. One group of young men unable to gain a firm foothold in the U.S. job market becomes permanently relegated to temporary cross-border migration. The other group attains regularized status and begins a career in the United States that lasts through the working years. This is the U.S.-oriented group.

Because of the long tradition of U.S. migration, young Animeños know that regularized status and a steady job in the United States are the paths to success in their binational community. Both U.S.-oriented and temporary migrants have similar objectives at the start of their migratory cycle. All begin with low-wage, low-prestige urban or rural work. Some are able to move out of this low-status work; others are not. The lives of the two groups continue along similar lines even after this differentiation by type of job. Both groups frequently visit the village, looking for marriage partners and houses. Both groups keep track of land sales in the village in the hope of

Table 8.5   Average Hourly Wages in Constant
            1967 US Dollars

| | Village-based | | U.S.-based | |
Year	Number of migrants	Average wage[a]	Number of migrants	Average wage[a]
1970	12	2.89	26	3.16
1971	15	2.59	28	3.28
1972	18	2.33	32	3.39
1973	21	2.26	34	3.45
1974	19	2.07	36	3.10
1975	15	1.79	37	3.06
1976	17	1.74	35	3.00
1977	23	2.01	35	2.99
1978	33	1.84	41	2.81

Source: Sample of 143 interviewees.

Note: [a]Each migrant was asked for his average hourly
          wage in a given year. The average wage for each
          group is an average of all those in the group
          who reported an average hourly wage for that
          year.

someday making purchases. In time, however, the differences in their
U.S. jobs lead to concrete distinctions in lifestyle.

Most men in the U.S.-oriented group bring their families to California. A small proportion, about 10 percent (the legal shuttles), leave
their families in Las Animas and commute for six months or more
each year for work. Their sons, however, are not left to make a living
in Las Animas, but usually obtain legal U.S. status as they reach
working age.

The temporary migrants leave their nuclear families in the village.
In middle age, members of this group return to the village to teach
their sons to plant. Without guaranteed access to the U.S. job market,
knowledge of local agriculture is necessary for the son's survival.

The better jobs held by the U.S.-oriented group give them numerous
advantages over the temporary group. The crucial difference is the
higher pay obtained by the U.S.-oriented group. The average yearly
U.S. earnings in 1978 were about $9,600 for U.S.-based men but only

$4,800 for village-based men. In the 1970s, the wages of the U.S.-
based group almost kept up with inflation, while the village-based
migrants suffered a severe decline in real wages (Table 8.5).

The U.S. wage differential gives the U.S.-oriented migrants another
advantage—greater access to village land. Despite long absences from
the village, a higher percentage of U.S.-based individuals has been
able to buy land (and at a younger age) than the village-based group.
Thus, 35 percent of the U.S.-based households are landowners, while
only 25 percent of village-based households own land.

By the time Animeño village migrants are middle-aged, they become
resigned to one of two destinies: (a) unskilled work in the United
States and sharecropping in the village, or (b) semiskilled work in the
United States and recreation in the village. The coexistence of these
two destinies has created two clear-cut social groups in the binational
Animeño community.

TENDENCY 2

Social mobility in village migratory networks depends principally on
kinship ties and not on education.

The indicators of success for Animeño village migrants are U.S.-
oriented status, work in the United States, and property in the village.
The young individual's chance of eventually achieving these success
goals is a function of how successful the older members of his kin
network have been in achieving these goals. Education is not a
differentiating factor because it is the same for all groups. It is very
rare for anyone in the village to have gone beyond primary school.

Tendency 2 is demonstrated by comparing network connections of
the U.S.-based with the border-based and the village-based networks.
These are three somewhat overlapping groups: the village networks
are composed of 67 village-based respondents and 911 close relatives;
the U.S. networks are made up of 45 U.S.-based respondents and 636
close relatives. If we eliminated the common relatives among the three
groups, the differentials discussed below would be even greater.

When U.S.-based networks are compared with either village or
border-based ones, it is apparent that kin ties to a U.S.-based migrant
increase a villager's chances for success. There are more than twice
as many people in the U.S.-based networks in U.S. cities at a given
moment than there are in the other two networks (Table 8.6). The
U.S.-based networks also include twice as many members with U.S.-
committed status than the other groups. Far fewer in the group related
to U.S.-based interviewees do agricultural work in the United States.
Despite the fact that members of U.S.-based networks spend less time

Table 8.6 Comparison of US-, Village-, Border-Based Networks

	(1) In US cities		(2) With US committed status		(3) US migrants whose usual work is agriculture		(4) Adults who own land	Small plots %	Large plots % [a]
Network	No.	%	No.	%	No.	%	No.		
1) US-based	526	44.7	520	46.3	284	22.5	365	11.5	10.1
2) Village-based	775	24.5	774	25.8	377	37.7	556	11.9	6.7
3) Border-based	125	19.2	124	24.2	57	47.4	89	10.7	6.0

Source: Sample A-1454

Note: [a] Large plots are greater than 12 hectares.

in the village, more of them own large plots than in the village or border-based networks.

Remittances from the United States have created and reinforced the class differentiation in the village.

There are two kinds of remitters sending checks back to Las Animas—young men (and women) sending money to their parents, and husbands sending money to their wives and children. These remittances can be used either for sustenance of the recipients or for asset purchases, usually land or houses. The undocumented shuttle migrants, because they hold seasonal, unskilled U.S. jobs, generally can only make sustenance remittances to their families. The legal shuttles and long-term migrants, particularly after they have worked several years in the United States, begin to make asset remittances. This differing remittance pattern between migrant types bestows on some village families the assets of land, houses, stores, and machinery while the families who receive no asset remittances must work and sharecrop for their better-endowed neighbors.

Impact on the Village Economy

TENDENCY 1

U.S.-oriented migration leads to more neglect of the village economy than does temporary migration.

Compared with shuttle migrants, both legal and undocumented, permanents are much less interested in working in the village. While 81 percent of the "two times or less" migrants worked at least two months a year in Las Animas (at least four out of the last five years), only 5 percent of the permanent migrants did the same. Even if comparisons are limited to landholders, who would be more likely to take time off to work their land, very few U.S.-based migrant landowners take an interest in working in the village. Yet most temporary migrant landowners do work their own land. In this case, 68 percent of the temporary migrants had worked at least two months a year in Las Animas for the last five years. Only 17 percent of the U.S.-oriented migrants had done so.

The influence of holding a good U.S. job on the amount of time worked in the village can be seen most clearly by comparing the legal with the undocumented shuttles. Despite the fact that three times as many legal shuttles hold land and twice as many own businesses in the village, they work significantly less in the village than the un- documented shuttles. Over the last five years, 33 percent of the legal shuttles worked at least two months in the village every year, while 53 percent of the undocumented shuttles had done so.

The temporary and shuttle migrants work more in the village because they earn less in the United States. The low remuneration gained, even from working one's own land, relative to U.S. standards, discourages most men from working in the village. Only those unable to earn enough in the United States are compelled to work in their native village.

TENDENCY 2

Migration leads to the improvement of the consumptive level of the sending area but diminishes its productive capacity.

The extreme U.S.-orientation of Las Animas has caused a severe labor shortage. The absence of most prime-age males from the village for most of the year is only part of the problem. Even men who are in the village when demand for their labor occurs, shun the traditional tasks, despite the protests of local employers, because they view the village as a place to rest, not work. Though wages in Las Animas are inflated by local standards, they cannot attract workers used to U.S. earning levels.

One might expect that a labor scarcity coupled with relative wealth among the U.S. employed land-owning class would lead to labor-saving and productivity-enhancing investments. Unfortunately, this has not occurred in Las Animas. The old productivity system is in place— men, using animals, do all the planting, weeding, and harvesting.

Despite the large volume of dollars entering the village, surprisingly few investments are made to improve productivity. On an individual level, remittances not used for sustenance are used to buy consumer durables such as stereo equipment or blenders. On a community-wide level, fund-raising drives among the U.S. settlement communities have resulted in village electricity, street lights, and church improvements. The two areas the local people agree need investment—rural industry and irrigation—have received little attention, however. In fact, the absentee landlord has invested more money in land and vacation houses in recent years than the whole community has in productive investments!

TENDENCY 3

As a village-migrant network becomes more deeply involved in the U.S. job market, the land becomes increasingly concentrated in the hands of successful U.S. migrants indifferent to village development.

When migrants are young, they hold little land. Later, as money is saved, land purchases occur. Not surprisingly, in the older age cohort, most of the U.S.-oriented migrants have bought land while less than one-third of the temporary migrants have sufficient resources to acquire land in this age group. Competition for land by Animeños with good U.S. jobs has bid up the price of land in the village and virtually eliminated all but those with a good U.S. job from access to land. As a result, paradoxically, those with plans to purchase and improve the land, the temporary migrants, are excluded by the price from carrying out their plans.

In the future, it is unclear if the tendency for land to be transferred only to successful U.S. migrants will persist. Access to the U.S. job market has inflated land prices. Furthermore, in the youngest cohort of migrants, there is a growing tendency to lose identification with the village entirely. Many young Animeño migrants have become acculturated to the Hispanic urban culture of California cities and lost the ambition to rise socially in their native village community.

TENDENCY 4

In a mature migratory network, long-term permanent migrants buy village land not for profit but for prestige, security, and to raise food for their parents.

U.S. migrants who own land in the village rarely transfer earnings from Mexico to the United States. Only one out of 19 landowners in the U.S. sample did this. In 15 out of the 19 cases, the migrant's village relatives retained the income from the land. U.S. resident migrants look at asset investments primarily as a substitute for cash remittances to their parents. Managing the land provides their parents with a steady supply of food and forage. In this way a single asset remittance absolves the migrant son of having to remit cash regularly. Also, land owned in the village means security in case of unemployment in the United States or repatriation.

Recently, land investments in Las Animas are clearly not for profit. Earnings from the corn/bean harvest for a small landowner yielded a four percent return on land bought in 1978; leased land, a rare practice in Las Animas, returned about five percent. At the time,

Mexican banks were paying 16 percent interest on long-term deposits. The possibility that the absentee landlords are speculating on the appreciation of the property can be ruled out because few lots are resold once acquired by U.S.-oriented migrants.

It is not surprising that despite a large flow of U.S. remittances there are few productive investments in Las Animas. Landowners comprise a nonprofit-seeking, absentee landlord class whose elderly fathers or less successful relatives manage the land with neither the money nor the motivation to make long-term capital improvements.

Conclusions

Network analysis of one community allows several generalizations to be made about the impacts of Mexican migration to the United States.

The history of Las Animas demonstrates that a deep commitment to migration does not lead inevitably to rural development. It was observed that the binational community tends to bifurcate into a successful U.S.-oriented group and a less successful temporary migrant group. The first group tends to buy up village land and businesses when they become available. They have little incentive to invest time or money in improving their investments since a semi-skilled job in the United States provides much more income than does improved land in the village. Instead, the migrants' fathers or less successful relatives manage their properties.

The second group, the temporary migrants, achieve few long-term benefits from migration, yet continue hoping to win the "prize" of permanent status. They generally sharecrop when in the village, but would find it attractive to farm improved land there. Although some have land, however, they lack the resources to make investments. As a result, both groups find it more in their interest to opt for an employment strategy based on the U.S. job market rather than the local economy. They correctly perceive that their best chances for social mobility do not lie in their native village but in the United States.

This U.S.-orientation has not led to the depopulation of Las Animas. On the contrary, the village still serves a definite purpose for the migratory community. It is a recreation area for visiting migrants, a retirement center for returnees, and a reproduction center for future migrants. Although there are a few productive investments made in the village, both the community and individual families use migrant remittances to make village life more comfortable.

Although the orientation toward work in the United States has shifted local production from stable crops to low-productivity cattle raising, Las Animas still does not import corn. Traditional corn production is maintained by the temporary migrant group who, due to inadequate earnings in the United States, must still plant in the village. Since their sons have no job guarantees north of the border, the temporary migrants feel obliged to teach their sons to make a living with a plow. Thus, the traditional economy of the village is maintained.

The tendency for wage migrants from developing countries to use their earnings for consumption rather than productive investments has been corroborated by other studies (Swanson, 1979; Piore, 1979; and Reichert, 1981). Examples where migrant earnings are invested profitably in rural industry are rare (Cornelius, 1976:37). The migratory network, since it spreads by word-of-mouth and kin contact, tends to become concentrated in one village or region. As a consequence, the few nonagricultural investment opportunities available in rural areas (bars, grocery stores, taxi and truck firms, etc.) tend to become quickly saturated by numerous returning and visiting migrants (Reviere d'Arc, 1975).

In the 1940s Las Animas sent out pioneers to the United States who established settlement communities and eventually placed most Animeños in jobs in California. Some obtained steady well-paying jobs; others had to settle for temporary seasonal work. Still, network migration from the Las Animas community has meant that most people in the village lead a more comfortable life. A large proportion, though a minority, also achieve security by obtaining a long-term job in California. Under the present political and economic organization of Mexico and the United States, however, these advances in comfort and security inevitably lead to a "freezing" of economic development and a reduction of production in the village. Until investment opportunities and secure income in rural areas are assured, network migrants will continue to view Mexico as the place to rest and raise their children and the United States as the place to make a living.

References

AFL-CIO. 1979. "The national economy, 1979." *Report of the Executive Council of the AFL-CIO, Thirteenth Convention, 1979.* Washington, D.C.

Aguilar, Alonso, and Fernando Carmona. 1967. *Mexico: Riqueza y Misería.* Mexico: Editorial Nuestro Tiempo.

Barkin, David. 1980. *Mexican Agriculture and the Internationalization of Capital.* Soc. Sci. Res. Rep. no. 68, School of Social Science. Irvine: University of California. May.

Cardona, Ramiro. 1976. "Toward a model of migration in Latin America." *Migration and Urbanization,* ed. Brian DuToit and Helen Safa. The Hague, Netherlands: Mouton Publishers.

Centro de Investigaciones Agrarias. 1974. *Estructura Agraria y Desarrollo Agrícola en Mexico.* Mexico: Fondo de Cultura Económica.

Cornelius, Wayne. 1976. *Mexican Migration to the U.S.: The View From the Rural Sending Communities.* Cambridge: Migration and Development Study Group, Massachusetts Institute of Technology.

Dagodag, W. Tim. 1975. "Source regions and composition of illegal Mexican immigration to California." *International Migration Review* 9:499–511.

Felix, David. 1977. "Income inequality in Mexico." *Current History* 72 (3):14.

Gamio, Manuel, 1930. *Mexican Migration to the United States.* New York: Arno Press.

Ginzberg, Eli. 1977. "The job problem." *Scientific American* 237:43–51.

Gomez Oliver, Luís. 1978. "Crisis agrícola, crisis de los campensinos." *Comercio Exterior* 28:714–27.

Jenkins, J. Craig. 1977. "Push/pull in illegal Mexican migration to the U.S." *International Migration Review* 11:178–89.

Lomnitz, Larissa. 1975. *Como Sobreviven Los Marginados.* Mexico: Editorial Siglo Veinte y Uno.

Piore, Michael. 1979. *Birds of Passage.* New York: Cambridge University Press.

Portes, Alejandro, and Harley Browning, eds. 1977. *Current Perspectives on Latin American Urbanization,* pp. 6–7. Institute of Latin American Studies. University of Texas.

Reichert, Joshua. 1981. "The migrant syndrome: Seasonal U.S. wage labor and rural development in central Mexico." *Human Organization* 40 (1981):56–66.

Reichert, Joshua A., and Douglas S. Massey. 1979. "Patterns of U.S. migration from a Mexican sending community: A comparison of legal and illegal migrants." *International Migration Review* 13:599–623.

Reviere d'Arc, Helene. 1975. "Tepatitlán: Terre d'emigration." *Cahiers des Ameriques Latines,* May.

Reynolds, Clark. "Labor market projections for the United States and Mexico and their relevance to current migration controversies." Food Res. Inst. Stud. (in press).

Swanson, Jon. 1979. "The consequences of emigration for economic development: A review of the literature." *Papers in Anthropology.* University of Oklahoma, Spring.

Wool, Harold. 1976. *The Labor Supply for Low Level Occupations.* Washington, D.C.: U.S. Department of Labor, Employment and Development Administration.

PART THREE
Destinations in the United States

9

Occupational and Spatial Mobility of Undocumented Migrants from Dolores Hidalgo, Guanajuato

RICHARD C. JONES
RICHARD J. HARRIS
AVELARDO VALDEZ

An unresolved question in research on Mexican undocumenteds is whether they improve their job status in the United States, or whether they remain in menial jobs in the "secondary labor market." Recent research has indicated that an increasing percentage of undocumenteds are finding urban-sector jobs (North and Houstoun, 1976; Cornelius, 1978), but this research does not answer several important questions. First, do individual migrants improve their job status, or is the observed trend simply the result of newer migrants beginning in higher status jobs? Second, assuming that individual migrants do improve their job status, is this chiefly a function of changing to a nonagricultural job, or does occupational status continue to improve after the migrant reaches the urban sector? Third, how contingent is job-status improvement on an individual's movement in geographic space?

The field research for this study was made possible by a grant from the Trull Foundation, Palacios, Texas. The authors were ably assisted by a Mexican Lecturer in Sociology at the Autonomous University of Nuevo Leon, Lic. Javier Burnes, and by four student interviewers: Patricio Morelos, Leticia Salazar, and Lisbeth Barron (from the UANL), and Abel Camarillo (from the Autonomous University of San Luís Potosí). Without their help, the field research for this essay would not have been possible.

Recent research on spatial mobility of undocumenteds to and within the United States (Jones, 1982a, 1982b) has shown that over time, undocumented patterns have dispersed northward. This research has not revealed much at all about successive moves of individual migrants. The most popular conception is of undocumented migrants rooted to particular geographic localities year after year, by reason of kinship ties, fear of apprehension, lack of awareness of new opportunities, poverty, and the problems associated with adapting to new surroundings. This chapter shows that this impression is erroneous. Not only do migrants exhibit substantial geographic mobility, but it is of a highly organized nature. Furthermore, there is significant upward occupational mobility as well. Subsequent mobility levels off, however, once the migrant reaches the urban sector, despite the fact that undocumenteds continue to travel long distances to undertake new jobs.

The basic purpose of this chapter, then, is to investigate the degree of occupational mobility among a sample of Mexican undocumenteds who have recently migrated to the United States, and to examine how spatial mobility as well as other factors are involved in this phenomenon. As such, it fits into the larger theme of economic impacts on U.S. receiving areas.

Previous Research and an Organizational Schema

Regarding the question of occupational mobility, many writers (North and Houstoun, 1976; Cornelius, 1978; Cross and Sandos, 1981:49–56; Mines, 1981; Zarrugh, 1974) have noted that since the *Bracero* program terminated in 1964, there has been a dramatic increase in the proportion of undocumenteds in nonagricultural jobs. This trend parallels one evident among Chicanos and blacks in the Southwest, both of whom are abandoning agriculture for urban jobs in large numbers (see Wood, 1974). Available research does not tell us, unfortunately, whether individual migrants are advancing occupationally. It is possible that first-time migrants are moving into urban jobs, while repeat migrants remain in agricultural jobs. Assuming that both types of migrants are moving into urban jobs, however, an important question remains—is their rate of advance steady and constant within the urban sector, or do migrants encounter a job-status ceiling marked by a leveling-off or decline in status over time? This question has become increasingly important as research reveals a larger and larger number of urban "settler" populations of undocumenteds in the United States (Cornelius, 1981; Baca and Bryan, 1980; Cardenas, 1976; Jones, 1982b). These urban settler populations hold jobs of markedly higher status than the urban "sojourners" whose characteristics have been revealed either in INS records, or in surveys of Mexican migrants in their villages of origin. If our analyses show a steady progression from low to high status jobs, this will provide circumstantial evidence that sojourner populations become settler populations over time. If not, we would have to conclude that settler populations have different origins and are characterized differently from sojourner populations; or, more likely, that a relatively small subgroup of sojourners with exceptional characteristics progress steadily toward settler status while most do not.

The question of job mobility after reaching the urban sector has been addressed (obliquely) by several researchers. One group argues that rural-urban moves are consistent with low occupational mobility after reaching the urban sector; i.e.,

> The shift among Mexican illegals from agriculture to nonagricultural employment in the U.S. does not necessarily mean that the Mexicans are competing more successfully than before with American workers for desirable jobs in other sectors of the economy. It mainly reflects the fact that there are proportionately more unskilled or low-skilled jobs available today in commerce, industry, construction, and services, than in agriculture (Cornelius, 1978:55).

This argument implies that undocumenteds do not progress beyond low-skilled jobs in urban areas (see also Stoddard, 1976). They become, to themselves and to the public at large, "commodity migrants"— human raw material for U.S. industry, business, and households which enable these sectors to cut costs and compete in today's economy (Bustamante, 1978). This argument is consistent with a sort of "ceiling" on job advancement once migrants reach the urban sector. A small minority of migrants do become "settlers," holding relatively higher-status jobs in manufacturing and services (Cornelius, 1981:27–34). But most migrants are stuck in blue-collar jobs in construction, warehousing, and the lowest-status jobs in manufacturing.

A second group argues that the shift to nonagricultural jobs has been accompanied by substantial occupational mobility:

> The conclusion is justified that many illegals are employed in jobs which are more than marginally attractive to domestic workers. All the jobs filled by the illegals are not of the farm, food-handling, household service type. Some are *better-paid positions* in manufacturing plants and the construction industry. . . . The illegal Mexican worker is gaining acceptance for some jobs which provide much better than minimum wages and working conditions . . . (Fogel, 1978:91).

This argument is also supported by other research. Briggs (1975:29) noted that undocumenteds are increasingly found in craftsman positions, while Portes's (1979) study of legal Mexican immigrants with residential experience in the United States prior to legalization, found a marked increase in the proportions employed in semiskilled and skilled urban jobs, and a decline in both agricultural, minor urban service and unskilled urban worker categories over time.

On the question of spatial mobility, conclusions differ as well. On the one hand, it would appear that some undocumenteds move directly to their destinations within the United States, and once there, do not tend to move about. This has been illustrated for migrants from a Michoacán village to California (Reichert and Massey, 1979), in which it was found that 71.4 percent of illegal migrant parties did not move at all once in the U.S. Other studies have found that migrants from Chihuahua to the San Luis Valley of Colorado (an agricultural and food processing area) returned each year to the same jobs (Guttierrez, 1981:40–67; Kelly, 1978). On the other hand, other evidence seems to suggest substantial relocation after arrival in the U.S.—for example, the aforementioned study of migrants from Las Animas, Zacatecas, to California (Mines, 1981:91–92), and another study of migrants from northeastern Mexico to South Texas (Jones, 1982b). Macro-studies of migration flows in the U.S. (e.g., Jones, 1982a) imply spatial mobility, but data are most often cross-sectional rather than longitudinal, and therefore definitive conclusions cannot be drawn.

Overall, much less attention has been paid to spatial mobility than to occupational mobility in the literature. Although occupational mobility may be more important from a policy standpoint, spatial mobility is an essential consideration in understanding the mechanism through which occupational mobility takes place.

A simple schematic model illustrates this mechanism, while at the same time summarizing several of the arguments presented (Figure 9.1). This model is similar to the life-path migration models formulated by Wendel (1953) and Conway (1980), except that it focuses on only the most theoretically relevant of outcomes, not on a large number of possible outcomes.

In each sub-figure there appear the migration paths of two hypothetical, representative migrants to the United States from Mexico; these paths direct migrants to one of three occupational status levels (low, medium, high), to one of two sizes of urban place (small, large), and to one of two possible regions of the U.S. (border, nonborder). Each path may have either one or two steps. There are nearly 370,000 possible permutations here, but we center upon the four which represent stages in a continuum from immobility to mobility. For simplicity, the term "mobile" implies upward mobility, while "immobile" implies stability or downward mobility. In Figure 9.1a, if we assume

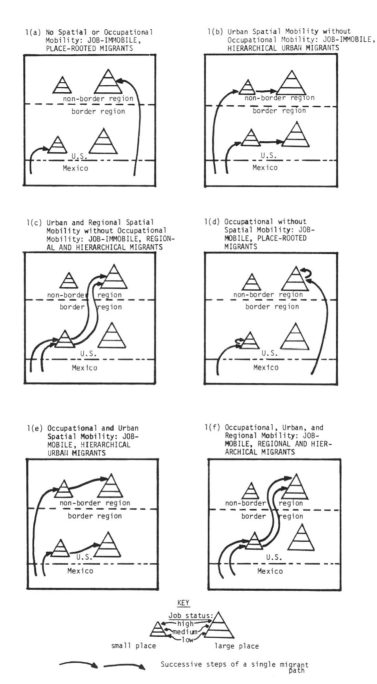

1(a) No Spatial or Occupational Mobility: JOB-IMMOBILE, PLACE-ROOTED MIGRANTS

1(b) Urban Spatial Mobility without Occupational Mobility: JOB-IMMOBILE, HIERARCHICAL URBAN MIGRANTS

1(c) Urban and Regional Spatial Mobility without Occupational Mobility: JOB-IMMOBILE, REGIONAL AND HIERARCHICAL MIGRANTS

1(d) Occupational without Spatial Mobility: JOB-MOBILE, PLACE-ROOTED MIGRANTS

1(e) Occupational and Urban Spatial Mobility: JOB-MOBILE, HIERARCHICAL URBAN MIGRANTS

1(f) Occupational, Urban, and Regional Mobility: JOB-MOBILE, REGIONAL AND HIER-ARCHICAL MIGRANTS

KEY

Job status:
high
medium
low

small place   large place

Successive steps of a single migrant path

Figure 9.1   Schema for relating undocumented occupational and spatial mobility

that the migrant to the left moved in one time period, and the one to the right in a later period, it can be seen that over time, the migrant population overall could be advancing occupationally and dispersing geographically (moving into larger urban places in non-border regions). At the individual level, though, neither occupational nor spatial mobility is taking place. Figure 9.1a represents a "commodity migrant" argument—i.e., migrant labor is passive in that it is confined to the job sector and region where it is imported. Migrant labor is viewed as a raw material without locomotion of its own, to be pressed into service and later returned to Mexico. Figures 9.1b and 9.1c each show two migration paths exhibiting spatial but not occupational mobility. In Figure 9.1b, job-immobile, hierarchical urban migrants are shown. They move from rural to urban (or from urban to larger urban) places in the United States without appreciably improving their job status. This is presumably due to a ceiling on job improvement for undocumenteds, related to their illegal status and the consequent exclusionary policies they encounter. In Figure 9.1c, job-immobile, regional and hierarchical migrants are shown; they not only move up the urban hierarchy, but from one region to another in the U.S., still without improving their job status for the reasons just cited. Figure 9.1d shows two migration paths exhibiting occupational but not spatial mobility; it represents job-mobile, place-rooted migrants. These migrants are able to break into better jobs, and to consistently improve their job status, without moving to another urban area or region. They presumably progress through a process of assimilation aided by place-specific kin and friends, and by increasing awareness of both opportunities and dangers at the destination (Derbyshire, 1969). Figure 9.1e indicates job-mobile, hierarchical urban migrants, i.e., migrants who concomitantly move into a higher status job and into a larger urban place. Finally, Figure 9.1f shows job-mobile, regional and hierarchical migrants—migrants who move into a larger city and away from the border region while increasing their job status.

Clearly, other possibilities exist; the schema given in Figure 9.1 represents only some of the most plausible alternatives, and no special argument is given here for the particular sequence displayed. These subsets of figures do represent the most likely combinations of spatial and occupational mobility—i.e., spatial without occupational mobility, occupational without spatial mobility, both types of mobility, and neither type of mobility.

Study Design and Study Population

Analysis of over 2,000 I–213 (Record of Deportable Alien) forms from the San Antonio Immigration and Naturalization Service (INS)

District indicated that over the period 1973–1981, migrants to an 88-county area of south Texas came principally from two areas—the northern Mesa Central, and the northeastern border states (Jones, 1982b). Guanajuato state led with some one-fifth of the migrants, and Dolores Hidalgo, a *municipio* with 73,400 people in 1970, had among the highest density of undocumenteds per 1,000 resident population of any *municipio* in the state. The town lies 39 miles north of Guanajuato city, and 30 miles southwest of Mexican Route 57, the major north-south trunkline in Mexico. A major explanation for the low economic status of the *municipio* is its relatively poor land—much less fertile than the lands of the Bajío farther south. Typical of many Mexican subsistence regions, a high percentage of the *municipio's* population (66 percent) is engaged in agriculture. Incomes are only about 60 percent state and national averages (*IX Censo General de Población y Vivienda*, Mexico, 1970).

On a grant from the Trull Foundation (Palacios, Texas), the authors spent five days interviewing in Dolores Hidalgo *municipio*, December 31, 1981, to January 4, 1982. With the aid of four Mexican university students and a Mexican professor, we interviewed 109 migrants who had worked in the United States in the previous five years. A small (and indeterminate) number of migrants entered legally on the latest job trip. However, the vast majority of our sample entered illegally on all trips. The *municipio* was divided into five subareas—the town itself (about one quarter of the *municipio* population), and four sectors radiating outward from it. Within each subarea, we sought out neighborhoods or hamlets identified by the parish priest and the Presidente Municipal as sending areas for emigrants to the U.S. Potential respondents were approached either in their homes or as they walked down the street, sat at the plaza, or drank beer at a corner store. The interview schedule was in a majority of cases administered by two interviewers—either two Mexican students, or a Mexican student working with one of the four professors. The schedule (14 pages) was filled in over a period of 30 minutes to an hour. First, various personal data on the respondent were requested, followed by a work-history of the respondent in Mexico and in the U.S. Finally, detailed accounts of the respondent's first and most recent jobs in the U.S. were solicited. After the formal interview, the interviewee often talked freely on other matters and frequently provided other references for us to interview. In summary, we used a combination of spatially-stratified and chain-referral sampling. The final result was 104 usable schedules, of which 37 (36 percent) were from the town, and 67 (64 percent) from the outlying sectors of the *municipio.* These percentages are reasonably close to those listed in the 1970 census for the town vs. the rest of the *municipio*, as a whole (*IX Censo*, 1970).

Table 9.1   A Profile of the Undocumented Migrant from Dolores Hidalgo Municipio, Guanajuato[a]

A.   Total Sample (N=104)

Average age of respondent at time of interview	30.6
Percentage of respondents married at time of interview	65.4
Percentage of respondents economically active in D.H., who were employed in agriculture	55.7
Average income of these respondents in D.H. (pesos per week, 1981)	1044
Average number of trips made to U.S. to work	3.7
Average number of localities worked at in the U.S.	3.0
Average number of localities worked at in Mexico (including D.H.)	1.3

B.   Migrants with Two or More Jobs in the U.S. (N=87)

Average age of respondent at time of first job in U.S.	20.8
Average age of respondent at time of latest job in U.S.	28.1
Percentage of respondents married, first job in U.S.	28.7
Percentage of respondents married, latest job in U.S.	62.1
Average years since first job in U.S.	9.4
Average years since latest job in U.S.	2.1
Average months working on first U.S. job	8.7
Average months working on latest U.S. job	9.5
Average income earned per week (current dollars): first U.S. job trip[b]	72.10
Average income earned per week (current dollars): latest U.S. job trip[c]	137.45
Average real income per week (1967 dollars): first U.S. job trip[b]	53.74
Average real income per week (1967 dollars): latest U.S. job trip[c]	62.40
Percentage charge in real income, first to latest U.S. job trip	+16.1
Percentage of income sent home, first U.S. job trip[b]	46.5
Percentage of income sent home, latest U.S. job trip[c]	40.4
Average socio-economic status of first U.S. job[d]	7.83
Average socio-economic status of latest U.S. job[d]	9.90
Percentage charge in socio-economic status, first to latest U.S. job	+26.4

Source: [a]Interview schedule administered to 104 residents of Dolores Hidalgo municipio. Guanajuato, who had been to the U.S. to work within the previous five years.

[b]Refers to income earned on the job held for the longest period during the first work trip to the U.S.

[c]Refers to income earned on the job held for the longest period during the latest work trip to the U.S.

[d]Duncan's index of socio-economic status by occupation (Reiss, Duncan, Hatt, and North, 1961).

Summary data from our sample provide a profile of the undocumented migrant from Dolores Hidalgo (Table 9.1). This profile fits those of many other village studies (Cornelius, 1976; Reichert and Massey, 1979; Wiest, 1979; Mines, 1981; Roberts, 1980), in which the migrants are found to be young, married (by the latest trip), chiefly farmers by occupation, earning below-average incomes (but not the lowest in the village), and nearly all male (all were male in our sample). Notice in the table that the average migrant made 3.7 work-trips to the U.S. over a seven-year period. Not shown in the table is the average length of time spent on a work trip to the U.S.—approximately 11 months. Assuming that the migrants returned directly to Mexico between work trips to the U.S. (which is commonly the case), this would mean 11 months in the U.S. followed by c. 16 months in Mexico, on each of the 3.7 trips. This finding indicates that our Dolores Hidalgo sample was generally of the *sojourner* type, making periodic trips to the U.S., but spending two-thirds of their time in Mexico between the first and latest trips. The lower panel of Table 9.1 focuses only on those migrants with two or more jobs in the U.S. Notice the evidence for upward occupational and income mobility in these data: average real income increased by 16.1 percent over the seven-year period separating the first and latest job. Furthermore, the socioeconomic status of this latest job averaged 26.4 percent higher than that of the first (see below for explanation of the occupational status index employed). The average weekly income for the latest job was $137.45 (in 1981 dollars), which would be just below minimum wage assuming a 40-hour week at $3.50 per hour. This wage is remarkable, because some 37 percent of the respondents worked on a farm or ranch, where wages were low. Finally, the data show a slight increase in the length of time worked on the latest job trip versus the first job trip, and a decline in the percentage of income sent home between the two trips. These statistics, in addition to the job and income mobility statistics, suggest that the undocumenteds became more integrated into U.S. society over the period. A final point of note is that approximately 80 percent of all work trips in our sample were to Texas. In subsequent discussion, "border area" and "border state" refer principally to Texas; while "nonborder state" refers principally to Oklahoma, Florida, Illinois, Arkansas, and Kansas, the chief out-of-state destinations.

Occupational Mobility

The basis for our occupational mobility measure is the Duncan socioeconomic index, developed by Otis Dudley Duncan over 20 years ago (Reiss, Duncan, Hatt, and North, 1961). This index is defined in terms of average income and educational levels of persons holding particular jobs, and it has demonstrated a high degree of stability over time, as well as a high correlation with other measures such as the NORC (National Opinion Research Center) occupational prestige scores and the U.S. Bureau of the Census's socioeconomic status scores (Miller, 1977:211–230). Almost 450 occupational types are covered by the Duncan index, which ranges from 01 for the most basic textile-mill worker, to 96 for certain categories of physicians (Robinson, Athanasiou, and Head, 1976:342–356).

There are 17 SES-levels identifiable ranging from 03 for a sawmill laborer to 27 for a bricklayer (Table 9.2). Whereas this spread is small relative to that allowed in the scale, it is significant for our migrant subpopulation, who are largely confined to the secondary labor market. Notice that the jobs in the first two categories tend to require physical strength and involve materials handling or cleaning— *i.e.,* arduous, dirty work. The craftsman and operatives positions involve some skills, but are still physically demanding jobs, often outdoors. Although movement among these SES-levels may not be of great importance to undocumenteds themselves (for whom wages, rather than job prestige, are most relevant), it is important to the host population who must compete directly with undocumenteds for jobs. One writer put it as follows:

> What I have noticed is that what may be dead-end employment . . . for an undocumented worker, could in fact be a job with mobility potential for someone who is integrated in the community. For example, washing dishes can lead to becoming a busboy; a busboy can become a waiter; and a waiter can obtain a maitre d's job. . . . We cannot look at these so-called dead-end jobs as the same for both potential occupants of the positions (George Grayson, in Brookings Institution, p. 81).

The job profiles for first versus latest job indicate a decided shift away from farm and ranch work into craftsman and operatives positions (Table 9.2). Two-thirds of the first jobs were agricultural, and 13 percent were skilled craftsman/operatives positions (chiefly lower-echelon jobs such as truck driver or roofer). By the latest job, only one-third were agricultural, and 28 percent were in the skilled category. The change in job profiles between the first urban job and the latest job indicates a pronounced shift out of construction/service jobs, and into both agricultural jobs and craftsman/operatives jobs.

The correct test of occupational mobility, however, is whether individual migrants can be traced from lower to higher status jobs— a test which is impossible with aggregated occupational profiles. For this test, we have grouped the 17 SES-levels into three occupational categories (Table 9.2):

(a) *agricultural / sawmill / outdoor laborer*—SES values from three to six;

(b) *construction / apprentice / service worker*—SES values from seven to 14; and

(c) *craftsman / operative*—SES values from 15 to 27.

Table 9.2 Numbers of Respondents by Occupation

Occupations[a]	Duncan SES index	Frequency			Percentage Distribution		
		First US job	Latest US job	First Ur-ban job in US	First US job	Latest US job	First ur-ban job in US
Sawmill laborer	03	1	4	3	1.1	3.8	7.5
(Tree trimmer)	04	0	1	0	.0	1.0	0
Sawmill operator, (hwy. constr.)	05	1	3	2	1.1	2.9	5.0
Agric., ranch worker,(ditch digger)	06	58	39	1	66.7	37.5	2.5
Total, Agriculture/Sawmill/Outdoor Laborer		60	47	6	69.0	45.2	15.0
Constr. laborer, other construc.	07	8	14	16	9.2	13.5	40.0
(Meat packing), (mechanic asst.)	08	1	4	2	1.1	3.8	5.0
Janitor	09	2	1	2	2.3	1.0	5.0
Clothes washer in laundry	10	1	1	2	1.1	1.0	5.0
Laborer in feed store	11	4	5	6	4.6	4.8	15.0
Dishwasher, busboy, gardener	12	0	1	0	0	1.0	0
(Alarm installer),(electrician asst.)	14	0	2	0	0	1.9	0
Total, Construc./Apprentice/Service Worker		16	28	28	18.4	26.9	70.0
Cook, roofer, truck/machinery driver	15	9	17	3	10.3	16.3	7.5
Painter, waiter, keymaker	16	0	4	0	0	3.8	2.5
Carpenter	19	0	2	0	0	1.9	0
Bulldozer driver, (factory clerk)	22	0	2	1	0	1.9	2.5
Welder	24	0	2	0	0	1.9	0
Bricklayer	27	2	2	1	2.3	1.9	2.5
Total, Craftsman/Operative		11	29	6	12.6	27.9	15.0
TOTAL, ALL OCCUPATIONS		87	104	40	100.0	100.0	100.0

Note: [a]Occupations in parentheses don't fit the summary category designation, but are included there on the basis of their SES scores.

Table 9.3 Occupational Mobility Frequencies Between First and Latest US Job,
Dolores Hidalgo Migrants With Two or More Jobs

Occupational category, first job	Occupational category, latest job[a]			Totals, first job
	Agricultural or sawmill	Construction or service	Craftsman or operative	
Agricultural or sawmill	29 (33.3)	15 (17.2)	16 (18.4)	60 (68.9)
Construction or service	7 (8.0)	6 (6.9)	3 (3.4)	16 (18.3)
Craftsman or operative	3 (3.4)	1 (1.1)	7 (8.0)	11 (12.5)
Totals, latest job	39 (44.7)	22 (25.2)	26 (29.8)	87 (99.7)[b]

Note: [a]Percentages of total sample are given in parentheses.

[b]Percentages do not total to 100, due to rounding errors.

These categories are not completely consistent internally, regarding the similarity of jobs included, and they hide intracategory shifts (such as from construction worker to dishwasher). However, they do identify the principal job shifts of our sample (e.g., from agricultural worker to construction worker or craftsman). In addition, they generate interjob mobility cross-tabulations suitable to the size of sample we are working with. In the tests which follow, we include only those migrants with two or more jobs in the United States in their lifetimes. This reduces the sample from 104 to 87; and still farther from 87 to 40, when we analyze migrants with at least one urban job prior to the latest job.

Occupational mobility between the first and latest jobs indicates substantial improvement in job status (Table 9.3). Upward mobility (the sum of the percentages above the diagonal in Table 9.3) characterizes 39.1 percent of the migrants with two or more jobs, while downward mobility involves only 12.6 percent. The 48.3 percent remaining were "stable," although this figure is, of course, an artifact of the grossness of the categories used. By far, the largest job shifts were out of agriculture and related work, and into both construction/ service jobs and skilled craftsman/operatives positions. Incidentally, working with the original Duncan SES scores, we find that the average within-category status change is close to zero, while the average between-category change is substantial. This tends to validate the categories used.

The conclusions on occupational mobility between the first urban and the latest jobs are quite different (Table 9.4). Downward mobility

Table 9.4   Occupational Mobility Frequencies Between First Urban and Latest US Job,
             Dolores Hidalgo Migrants With At Least One Urban Job Prior to Latest Job

Occupational category, first urban job:	Occupational category, latest job[a]			
	Agricultural or sawmill	Construc. or service	Craftsman or operative	Total, first urban job
Sawmill; outdoor construc.	4 (10.0)	1 (2.5)	1 (2.5)	6 (15.0)
Construction or service	13 (32.5)	9 (22.5)	6 (15.0)	28 (70.0)
Craftsman or operative	1 (2.5)	2 (5.0)	3 (7.5)	6 (15.0)
Totals, latest job	18 (45.0)	12 (30.0)	10 (25.0)	40 (100.0)

Note: [a]Percentages of total sample are given in parentheses.

affects 40 percent of the migrants, while only 20 percent are upwardly-mobile. Notice that the principal job movement was between construction and service jobs "back" into agricultural/sawmill jobs; almost one-third of the migrants made this move downward along the job scale. Only 15 percent moved from a construction/service job upward into the skilled category. Again, average within-category changes in the original Duncan scores were close to zero, further validating the scale.

These results refute the notion that improvement in occupational status among the undocumented population is simply the result of newer migrants taking better jobs; clearly, individual migrants move up the job ladder. But they also indicate that there is something of a job status ceiling which affects migrants after they reach the urban sector; i.e., migrants leave the urban sector—either at their discretion or under the pressures of urban living, fear of apprehension, job competition, and prejudice—to return to agricultural work, which carries low prestige even in Mexico.

Typical of many problems in the social sciences, these results raise more questions than they answer. Is this job-status ceiling in urban areas related to an income ceiling in these same areas? That is, can a migrant abandon a low-level urban job and earn almost as much (with "less hassle") as a farm worker? Another question involves the personal characteristics of migrants with different mobility experiences. What personal characteristics differentiate migrants who move up from those who move down the job ladder; or those who move up from those who move farther up the ladder? Does this suggest that some migrants are predisposed to job success in the United States and others not? Finally, to what extent are upwardly-job-mobile mi-

Table 9.5 Personal Characteristics of Dolores Hidalgo Migrants with Selected
          Job-Mobility Experiences

	First to Latest U.S. Job[a]		
	Agricultural/sawmill work to:		
Characteristic[b]	Agricultural/ sawmill (no mobility)	Construction/ service	Craftsman/ operative
Average age, latest job	29.1(29)	29.5(15)	27.4(16)
Average school years completed	2.3(29)	3.0(15)	3.5(16)
English-speaking ability (scale:4=much.....1=none)	1.55(29)	1.53(15)	2.25(16)
Percentage who can read and write	86.2(29)	93.3(15)	93.8(16)
Percentage married, latest job	75.9(29)	60.0(15)	75.0(16)
Percentage using social services in US	17.2(29)	13.3(15)	25.0(16)
Time worked on latest job (mos.)	10.6(29)	5.6(15)	16.2(16)
Weekly wages, latest job (current $)	107.14(29)	140.20(15)	166.63(16)

	First Urban to Latest U.S. Job[a]		
	Construction/service work to:		
Characteristic[b]	Agricultural/ sawmill	Construction/ service	Craftsman/ operative
Average age, latest job	28.2(13)	23.3(9)	27.3(6)
Average school years completed	3.0(13)	5.1(9)	3.7(6)
English-speaking ability	2.08(13)	1.78(9)	2.33(6)
Percentage who can read and write	84.6(13)	77.8(9)	100.0(6)
Percentage married, latest job	92.3(13)	33.3(9)	50.0(6)
Percentage using social services in US	7.7(13)	11.1(9)	33.3(6)
Time worked on latest job (mos.)	7.8(13)	4.2(9)	10.8(6)
Weekly wages, latest job (current $)	114.69(13)	138.78(9)	252.50(6)

Note: [a]Subsample size in parentheses.

      [b]Characteristics above dotted line are causally prior to the latest job.

grants also upwardly-mobile in a spatial sense—that is, to what extent
do they move up the urban hierarchy and away from the border area?
The latter question is answered in the next section.

There is conflicting evidence for the argument that undocumenteds
who take an agricultural job after having held a basic urban job, can
earn as much as migrants who remain in the urban sector. On the
one hand, migrants moving into a craftsman/operatives job earn some
$140 per week more than those moving into an agricultural job (Table
9.5, panel B). Notably, the sample size for this test is conspicuously
small ($N=6$), and it is likely that the subset of migrants able to achieve
craftsman/operatives jobs have special ambitions and characteristics
relative to those who move to agricultural jobs. On the other hand,
migrants remaining in the construction/services category averaged

only $24 more per week than migrants who entered agriculture (Table 9.5, panel B). This differential is offset by the fact that agricultural workers frequently get room and board for free. Conversely, the $25 increase in weekly income for migrants moving from agriculture to (urban) construction or services between the first and latest jobs (Table 9.5, panel A) would probably be offset by the higher costs of living in the city. In summary, net income differentials between basic urban jobs and rural or agricultural jobs may not be enough to retain migrants in the urban sector.

Further evidence suggests that migrants with different mobility experiences differ regarding other personal characteristics besides income (Table 9.5). The characteristics above the dashed line in Table 9.5 are prior in time to the latest U.S. job, and therefore may be viewed as causative in the simplest sense. Migrants who achieved a craftsman/operative job after a start in an agricultural or sawmill job tend to be younger and better-educated than migrants who either remain in agriculture, or who achieve an urban construction or services job (Table 9.5, panel A). They also tend to be more "integrated" into U.S. society, as measured by the use of social services and time worked on the latest job. Analogously, migrants who achieved a craftsman/operative job after a basic construction/service job in a town, tend to be younger and better-educated, as well as better integrated, than migrants who subsequently took an agricultural or sawmill job (Table 9.5, panel B).

Spatial Mobility

The spatial patterning of Mexican undocumenteds is a neglected area of study. Nevertheless, it has important ties to policy decisions and so is essential factor in understanding why some migrants progress occupationally while others do not. The matrices which we employ to examine spatial mobility are analogous to those for occupational mobility.

    (a) *Urban mobility* is defined in terms of movement into/out of three different urban size classes, viz., < 25,000 (town), 25-250,000 (city), and > 250,000 (metropolis).

    (b) *Regional mobility* is defined in terms of movement relative to border and nonborder regions, viz.,

        (i)   border area (south of a line connecting [but not including] these cities: Houston, Austin, Roswell, Phoenix, and Los Angeles);

        (ii) border state excluding border area; and

        (iii) nonborder state.

Table 9.6   Spatial Mobility Frequencies Between First and Latest Job, Dolores
Hidalgo Migrants With Two or More Jobs

A.   Urban Mobility

Urban size category, latest job[a]

Urban size category, first job	< 25,000	25-250,000	> 250,000	Totals, first job
< 25,000	42(48.3)	3(3.4)	21(24.1)	66(75.8)
25-250,000	3(3.4)	2(2.3)	2(2.3)	7(8.0)
> 250,000	7(8.0)	0(0.0)	7(8.0)	14(16.0)
Totals, latest job	52(5917)	5(5.7)	30(34.4)	87[d](99.8)[b]

B.   Regional Mobility

Region of latest job[a]

Region of first job	Border area	Border state, non-border area	Outside of border state	Totals, first job
Border area[c]	16(19.5)	16(19.5)	8(9.8)	40(48.8)
Border state, non-border area	3(3.7)	23(28.0)	5(6.1)	31(37.8)
Outside of border state	2(2.4)	4(4.9)	5(6.1)	11(13.4)
Totals, latest job	21(25.6)	43(52.4)	18(22.0)	82[d](100.0)

Notes: [a]Percentages of total sample are given in parentheses.

[b]Percentages do not total to 100, due to rounding errors.

[c]The area south of a line connecting (but not including) these cities:
Houston, Austin, Roswell, Phoenix, and Los Angeles.

[d]Five destinations were identifiable by size but not by region.

In the case of urban mobility, upward movement refers to progress up the urban hierarchy (thus, the term "hierarchical migrants" in Figure 9.1); while for regional mobility, upward movement refers to northward movement, crossing the regional boundaries just defined.

The results for spatial mobility between the first and latest U.S. job (Table 9.6) are analogous to those obtained for occupational mobility; i.e., there has been substantial upward movement. For urban mobility, 29.8 percent moved upward, 11.4 percent downward, and 58.6 percent were stable; while for regional mobility, 35.4 percent moved upward, 11.0 percent downward, and 53.6 percent were stable. Thus, analogous to earlier results for job mobility, approximately three times as many migrants experienced upward as downward mobility. Regarding urban mobility, almost a quarter (24.1 percent) of the migrants moved from a town to a metropolis; this was four-fifths of all migrants who moved upward in the urban hierarchy (Table 9.6A). Regarding regional mobility, one-fifth (19.5 percent) of the moves were from the border area into other parts of the state, and this constituted over one-half of the migrants who moved away from the border (Table 9.6B). Closer inspection revealed that these patterns of urban/regional mobility primarily reflect movement between first jobs in South Texas, and latest jobs in the Dallas and Houston areas (see below).

To add spatial detail to these matrices, consider Figure 9.2, which gives a conceptual mapping of migrant flows between the first and latest jobs. A South Texas agricultural and ranching zone stands out prominently; this area of small towns (with the exception of San Antonio) is the first job site for a substantial portion (43.1 percent) of all migrants with two or more jobs. Truck gardening (peaches, pecans, watermelons, peanuts, and vegetables); dairying; egg and chicken production; and cattle ranching all characterize this zone, which supplies both the San Antonio market of over one million people, and regional markets in north and east Texas. This zone may also be referred to as a "zone of transition," because it is a staging area where migrants assimilate U.S. values and learn about opportunities in urban areas. Consulting a more detailed map including only those migrants experiencing upward occupational mobility (Figure 9.3), we may note that three places in the zone were mentioned by two or more migrants: Charlotte (1980 population, 1,443, number 1 on the map), George West (population, 2,627, number 2), and Nixon (population, 2,008, number 3). All are small agricultural service centers. Migrants to these places actually worked on nearby farms and ranches, seldom getting to the towns themselves. They found jobs by asking from farm to farm, typically having walked all the way from the border. All sent a high proportion of their earnings home to Mexico. Theirs is a journey fraught with hazard and intrigue (Samora, 1971: 118–19, 124–25).

Regarding latest-job sites ("destinations") on Figures 9.2 and 9.3, several areas stand out: out-of-state sites (both agricultural and urban); a northeast Texas lumber zone; and especially, the Dallas/Fort Worth and Houston metropolitan areas. The Dallas/Fort Worth and Houston areas constitute 29.2 percent of all the latest-job sites (55.2 percent of the latest-job sites among the occupationally mobile). The out-of-state destinations include the Chicago and Pittsburgh areas, as well as agricultural communities such as Clayton and Altus, Oklahoma; Leoti, Kansas; and Immokalee, Florida.

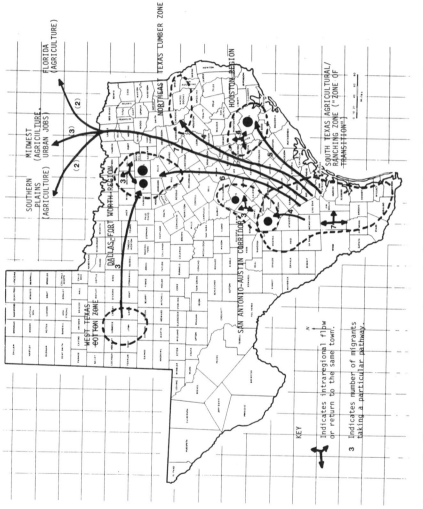

Figure 9.2 Generalized migrant pathways (≥ 3 migrants), first to latest job: Dolores Hidalgo sample

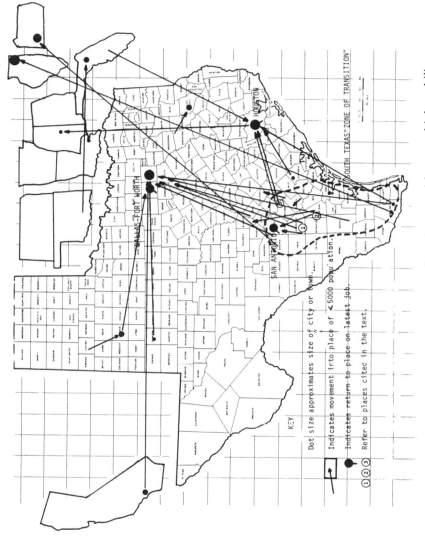

Figure 9.3 Spatial mobility, first to latest job, for migrants with upward job mobility

For sake of brevity, we will not present tabular results (analogous to Table 9.6) for spatial mobility between the first urban job and the latest job; nor will we present a breakdown of migrant personal characteristics by category of spatial mobility (as for occupational mobility in Table 9.5). Instead, the results from these analyses may be summarized as follows: (a) Between the first urban and latest jobs, about twice as many migrants moved down the urban hierarchy as up; this is largely explained by the aforementioned return to agricultural work by migrants formerly employed in metropolitan construction and service jobs. (b) Between the first urban and latest jobs, over twice as many migrants moved farther away from the border area, as moved closer. This is primarily explained by the fact that first urban jobs tended to be in Dallas or Houston, while latest jobs were found disproportionately in nonborder states. (c) Migrants who moved upward in the urban hierarchy—particularly, from small town or rural area to metropolitan area—were somewhat younger and better-educated, and tended to be better integrated into U.S. society. (d) Migrants who moved farther from the border—particularly, from the border area of Texas to elsewhere in the state—tended to have these same characteristics.

The similarity of these results to those for occupational mobility suggests that there is a strong relationship between the two. This suggestion is verified in Table 9.7, in which the definitions for upward and downward mobility and for stability are the same as we have used throughout this paper. Occupational and urban mobility are quite highly correlated; 74 percent of the migrants exhibited the same mobility category on both scales (Table 9.7A). A relatively small number of migrants (10.3 percent of the cases) advanced occupationally even though they remained in the same urban category; these migrants included both small-town agricultural workers who took skilled jobs in nearby towns, and workers remaining in Dallas and Houston, who moved into skilled from semiskilled jobs. The relationship between occupational and regional mobility is considerably lower, although still discernible; some 48 percent of the migrants exhibited the same degree of regional as of occupational mobility (Table 9.7B). A number of the migrants (18.3 percent) improved their occupational status by remaining in the same region; these include both those who remained in the same urban category, and those who moved into Dallas or Houston from smaller places in the same region. Another set of migrants (14.6 percent) moved farther away, but retained the same occupational status; these were chiefly farm workers moving from Texas to farming regions in other states.

Table 9.7   The Relationship Between Occupational and Spatial Mobility, First
To Latest US Job: Dolores Hidalgo Migrants With Two or More Jobs

A.   Urban vs. Occupational Mobility

Occupational mobility[a]

Urban mobility	Upward	Stable	Downward	Totals, urban mobility
Upward	23(26.4)	3(3.4)	1(1.1)	27(30.9)
Stable	9(10.3)	36(41.4)	5(5.7)	50(57.4)
Downward	2(2.3)	3(3.4)	5(5.7)	10(11.4)
Totals, occupational mobility	34(39.0)	42(48.2)	11(12.5)	87[c](99.7)[b]

B.   Regional vs. Occupational Mobility

Occupational mobility[a]

Regional mobility	Upward	Stable	Downward	Totals, regional mobility
Upward	13(15.9)	12(14.6)	6(7.3)	31(37.8)
Stable	15(18.3)	24(29.3)	3(3.7)	42(51.3)
Downward	4(4.9)	3(3.7)	2(2.4)	9(11.0)
Totals, occupational mobility	32(39.1)	39(47.6)	11(13.4)	82[c](100.1)[b]

Note: [a]Percentages of total sample are given in parentheses.

[b]Percentages do not total to 100.0, due to rounding errors.

[c]Five destinations were identifiable by size but not by region.

Conclusions and Discussion

Our subpopulation of Dolores Hidalgo migrants is clearly composed of sojourners rather than settlers. They stay an average of 11 months per U.S. trip, making approximately four such trips in a lifetime. They tend to be married (by the latest trip), and to maintain strong ties to family and villagers in Mexico. Over 40 percent of their earnings are repatriated there. Nevertheless, occupational and spatial mobility between the first and latest U.S. jobs are pronounced. The most significant and dominant pattern is one in which migrants begin in a South Texas "zone of transition" (south of San Antonio) where they work on a farm or ranch; and finish in a semiskilled construction, services, or skilled construction job in the Dallas or Houston areas.

Other patterns (first to latest job) include movement from South Texas agriculture in other states (with no job mobility), and movement into better jobs within the South Texas area or within the Dallas and Houston areas. Mobility between the first and latest jobs is thus best characterized as "Job-Mobile, Regional and Hierarchical Migration" (Figure 9.1F). A breakdown of the data suggests that the migrants who fit this dominant pattern are younger, better-educated, and more integrated into U.S. society, than those who do not fit this pattern.

Mobility between the first urban job and the latest job is a different matter. Downward occupational and urban mobility are the most significant patterns here. This is true even though "upward" (north-ward) movement takes place regionally. For example, many migrants who have reached the urban sector choose to leave it for an agricultural job in another state. We have noted that the reasons they may do this include the probably slight net-income differential between rural and basic urban occupations (room and board are provided on farms and ranches), and the somewhat older, less-educated, less-integrated, less "ambitious" nature of these migrants. First urban to latest job moves can thus be best characterized as "Job Immobile, Regional Migration" (a schema not indicated in Figure 9.1).

Spatial and occupational mobility are closely associated in our migrant sample, because occupational advancement is tied to movement away from rural, outdoor work and into urban, indoor work. In this sense, spatial mobility is a precursor, if not a precondition, for oc-cupational mobility.

A larger question concerns the labor-market impacts of undocu-mented workers in South Texas. It is probable that their presence somewhat depresses wages. However, our data reveal that on the latest job they average close to minimum wage ($137 per week; and $158 for urban migrants). These figures are surprisingly high for the jobs performed. The question of job displacement is also an open one. One indirect measure of displacement is the degree to which the occupational profile of undocumenteds reflects the skilled categories, vis-à-vis the profile for resident Chicanos. In our sample, the proportion of metropolitan migrants occupying latest jobs of the craftsman/operatives type is surprisingly high—43.8 percent; this compares closely to Cardenas's (1976) findings for Chicanos in San Antonio, in which 46.2 percent were engaged in craftsman/operatives and higher-status positions. We must be cautious in interpreting these figures, however. For San Antonio alone, only about one-third of our sample held craftsman/operatives positions (comparable to Cardenas's 30.6 percent among his sample of unapprehended illegals in San Antonio). Fur-thermore, within the 46.2 percent cited above, (a) San Antonio Chicanos hold higher-status jobs such as professionals and managers, as well as white-collar sales and clerical jobs, none of which our sample held; and (b) our sample held craftsman/operatives jobs which are located toward the lower-status end of the scale—e.g., truck driver, roofer, cook.

Measuring the impact of undocumented migrants on South Texas awaits more direct and accurate measures of income earned and of native workers displaced. The occupational mobility of a control group of Chicanos with analogous social and economic characteristics to undocumenteds, needs to be studied.

The value of the present study lies in its attempt to quantify occupational and spatial mobility of individual undocumented Mexican migrants to the United States. In this endeavor, we remain most indebted to the migrants who, with openness and interest, answered our questions and volunteered additional information on their experiences. Without their willing cooperation, the study could never have succeeded.

References

Baca, Reynaldo, and Dexter Bryan. 1980. "Citizenship aspirations and residency rights preferences: The Mexican undocumented worker in the binational community." Report for Sepa-Option, Los Angeles.

Briggs, Vernon M., Jr. 1975. *Mexican Migration and the U.S. Labor Market: A Mounting Issue for the Seventies.* Austin: Bureau of Business Research, University of Texas.

Brookings Institution–El Colegio de Mexico. 1978. *Structural Factors in Mexican and Caribbean Basin Migration.* Proceedings of Brookings/Colegio Symposium, The Brookings Institution, Washington, D.C.

Bustamante, Jorge. 1978. "Commodity migrants: Structural analysis of Mexican immigration to the United States." Pp. 183–203 in Stanley R. Ross, ed., *Views Across the Border: the U.S. and Mexico.* Albuquerque: University of New Mexico Press.

Cardenas, Gilberto. 1976. "Manpower Impact and Problems of Mexican Illegal Aliens in an Urban Labor Market." Ph.D. dissertation, University of Illinois.

Conway, Dennis. 1980. "Stepwise Migration: Toward a Clarification of the Mechanism." *International Migration Review* 14:3–14.

Cornelius, Wayne A. 1978. *Mexican Migration to the United States: Causes, Consequences, and U.S. Responses.* Cambridge: Center for International Studies, Massachusetts Institute of Technology.

————. 1981. *The Future of Mexican Immigrants in California: A New Perspective for Public Policy.* Program in U.S.–Mexican Studies, Working Paper #6. La Jolla: University of California.

Cross, Harry E., and James A. Sandos. 1981. *Across the Border: Rural Development in Mexico and Recent Migration to the United States.* Berkeley: University of California, Institute of Governmental Studies.

Derbyshire, Robert L. 1969. "Adaptation of adolescent Mexican-Americans to the United States Society." In Eugene B. Brody, ed., *Behavior in New Environments: Adaptation of Migrant Populations.* Beverly Hills, Calif.: Sage Publications.

Fogel, Walter A. 1978. *Mexican Illegal Alien Workers in the United States.* Los Angeles: Institute of Industrial Relations, University of California.

Guttierrez, Phillip R. 1981. "The Channelization of Mexican Nationals to the San Luis Valley of Colorado." M.A. thesis, University of Arkansas.

Jones, Richard C. 1982. "Undocumented Migration from Mexico: Some Geographical Questions." *Annals, Association of American Geographers* 72:77–87.

————. 1983. "Changing patterns of undocumented Mexican migration to South Texas." *Social Science Quarterly,* in press.

Kelley, Phillip L. 1978. "Community impact: Illegal aliens in southern Colorado's San Luis Valley." Pp. 92–128 in Kenneth F. Johnson and Nina M. Ogle, eds., *Illegal Mexican Aliens in the United States: A Teaching Manual on Impact Dimensions and Alternative Futures.* Washington, D.C.: University Press of America.

Mexico. 1970. Dirección General de Estadística. *IX Censo General de Población y Vivienda.*

Miller, Delbert C. 1977. "Social Status." Section A in his *Handbook of Research Design and Social Management.* New York: David McKay Co., pp. 211–30.

Mines, Richard. 1981. *Developing a Community Tradition of Migration: A Field Study in Rural Zacatecas, Mexico, and California Settlement Areas.* Program in U.S.–Mexican Studies, Monograph #3. La Jolla: University of California at San Diego.

North, David S., and Marion F. Houstoun. 1976. *The Characteristics and Role of Illegal Aliens in the U.S. Labor Market: An Exploratory Study.* Washington, D.C.: Linton & Co., Report prepared for the Employment and Training Administration, U.S. Department of Labor.

Portes, Alejandro. 1979. "Illegal immigration and the international system, lessons from recent legal Mexican immigrants to the United States." *Social Problems* 26:425–38.

Reichert, Josh, and Douglas S. Massey. 1979. "Patterns of U.S. migration from a Mexican sending community: A comparison of legal and illegal migrants." *International Migration Review* 13:599–623.

Reiss, Albert, Otis Duncan, Paul Hatt, and C. North. 1961. *Occupations and Social Status.* New York: The Free Press of Glencoe.

Roberts, Kenneth D. 1980. *Agrarian Structure and Labor Migration in Rural Mexico: The Case of Circular Migration of Undocumented Workers in the U.S.* Austin: Institute of Latin American Studies, University of Texas.

Robinson, John P., Robert Athanasiou, and Kendra B. Head. 1976. "Measures of occupational attitudes and occupational characteristics." Ann Arbor: Survey Research Center, Institute for Social Research, The University of Michigan.

Samora, Julian. 1971. *Los Mojados: The Wetback Story.* Notre Dame: University of Notre Dame Press.

Stoddard, Ellwyn R. 1976. "A conceptual analysis of the 'alien invasion': Institutionalized support of illegal Mexican aliens in the U.S." *International Migration Review* 10:157–89.

Wendel, B. 1953. *A Migration Schema: Theories and Observations.* Lund: Gleerup, Lund Studies in Geography, Series B, Human Geography, No. 9.

Wiest, Raymond E. 1979. "Implications of International Labor Migration for Mexican Rural Development." Pp. 85–97 in Fernando Cámara and Robert van Kemper, eds., *Migration Across Frontiers: Mexico and the U.S.* Albany: Institute for Meso-American Studies.

Wood, Charles. 1974. "Ethnic variations in the labor force." *Texas Business Review* 48:57–61.

Zarrugh, Laura H. 1974. "Gente de mi Tierra: Mexican Village Migrants in a California Community." Ph.D. dissertation, University of California.

10

The Channelization of Mexican Nationals to the San Luis Valley of Colorado

PHILLIP R. GUTTIERREZ

Historically, depressed economic conditions have inspired many migrations. People traditionally have left areas of poverty for areas of perceived economic opportunities. Recently, rural to urban migration has been a major pattern throughout the world. On an international level, millions are fleeing the less developed countries for the developed world. The massive influx of Mexican nationals to the United States is one example of this movement.

The principal purpose of this paper is to analyze the migration process of Mexican nationals to the San Luis Valley of Colorado and to identify the characteristics of the migrating individuals. Specific objectives related to the primary purpose are: (a) to describe areas of origin of this illegal migrant population; (b) to evaluate the validity of the channelization concept for the migration of undocumented Mexicans from specific areas of origin to the San Luis Valley; and (c) to identify various social, economic, and personal characteristics of this migrant population. The study demonstrates that the Mexican migration stream to the San Luis Valley of Colorado is different, possessing unique characteristics which distinguish it from streams to Texas, to the West Coast, and to the Midwest and Plains. The study hypotheses are that (a) the San Luis Valley migration stream differs from other major migration streams in the source areas and routes taken by the migrating Mexicans; and (b) information channels and communication links are the major elements involved in this channelized migration.

Current Spatial Research on Mexican Migration

Studies of illegal migration from Mexico have traditionally focused upon the positive and negative impacts upon the United States, Mexico, and specific subgroups within those countries. Authors such as Alejandro Portes (1978) and Wayne A. Cornelius (1978) have centered their attention upon the causes and consequences of this migration for various social, economic, and political groups of the United States and Mexico. Unfortunately, comprehensive descriptions of the patterns of migration, characteristics of the migrants, and the changes over time of the migration patterns do not exist.

Manuel Gamio was one of the first researchers to recognize the importance and the geographical detail of large scale migration from Mexico to the United States (Gamio, 1930). Lacking adequate census data, Gamio combined in-depth interviews of Mexican immigrants with postal data on the amounts and locations of money orders sent from the United States to Mexico. Gamio employed money orders as an index of the number and location of relatively recent immigrants from Mexico. His origin and destination data revealed that the majority were distributed throughout the United States, with the greatest number concentrated in California, Texas, and Arizona. This work on the origin and distribution of Mexican immigrants during the 1920s has formed the basis for further studies on the topic of spatial migration patterns of the Mexican migrant. Later studies employing direct interviews with Mexican undocumenteds in the U.S. include those of Samora (1971), North and Houstoun (1976), Cardenas (1976), Cardenas and Flores (1978), and Baca and Bryan (1980).

David S. North and Marion F. Houstoun (1976) considered the distribution of migrants by their mesoscale (state) origins in Mexico. They employed interviews with some 800 apprehended Mexican workers in INS offices at some 19 nonborder towns with high concentrations of illegal Mexicans. Their data revealed that the western highland states of Jalisco, Michoacán, Zacatecas, and Guanajuato, along with the border states of Chihuahua and Coahuila, were the prominent states of origin for illegal Mexican migrants.

In regard to the distribution of migrants by mesoscale destinations in the United States, a Mexican study conducted by Carlos Zazueta and Rodolfo Corona (1979) utilizing the data obtained by ENEFNEU's (Encuesta Nacional de Emigración a la Frontera Norte del País y Los Estados Unidos) interviews of some 60,000 families of Mexican workers in the United States, found a destination pattern concentrated in California (55.4 percent), Texas (23.1 percent), and Illinois (8.6 percent).

Only four other states (Colorado, Arizona, Oregon, and Florida) exhibited figures greater than 1 percent.

Richard C. Jones (1982a; 1982b) presents a geographical perspective on illegal migration from Mexico. His research, just as that of Dagodag (1975), devotes itself explicitly to spatial patterns and their changes, which are only lightly touched upon by others. He combines recent Mexican Labor Department data, INS data, and data included in the works of other researchers, to produce maps of migrant density, channelization, and change over time.

The use of the channelization concept has become important recently in explaining Mexican migration patterns. Roseman's (1971) and Jones's channelization concepts build upon concepts previously presented in sociology by George K. Zipf (1946). To Roseman, channelized migration is place-specific, occurs over relatively long distances, and is generally from a rural to a metropolitan area. Roseman further notes that "channelized migration results from strong family and friendship ties which have drawn migrants from a particular nonmetropolitan place to a metropolitan area in their search for jobs" (1971). This statement is consistent with the observation (Cornelius, 1978; 1979) that at the microscale, Mexican villages with similar economic and social characteristics may differ sharply in the number of migrants sent to the United States. It may be inferred in Cornelius's work that information channels and the historical backgrounds of migrants are important elements in the channelization process.

Evidence for channelization of migrants from specific origin areas in Mexico to specific destination areas in the United States is found in several studies. W. Tim Dagodag (1975) analyzed specific source regions for Mexican migrants to California. He utilized 3,204 Immigration and Naturalization I-213 forms (record of deportable alien), filed during the period January 1 to August 31, 1973, in the Chula Vista border patrol sector of California. He found that the western Mesa Central of Mexico (specifically the states of Jalisco and Michoacán) and the north coastal state of Baja California Norte accounted for a majority of the migrants. Richard Jones (1983), using unpublished data (N=476) from the San Antonio Immigration and Naturalization Service District 33, found a strongly channelized pattern of migration from Mexico to South Texas. The northeastern state of Coahuila and the northern Mesa Central state of Guanajuato together accounted for over 40 percent of the totals; four other states accounted for much of the rest. Finally, in work by Kenneth Johnson and Nina Ogle (1978), we find channelized migration between certain Mexican areas into the Intermontane West, Great Plains, and Midwest. For these destinations, the state of Chihuahua is the chief origin, sending migrants far inland to states such as Montana, Colorado, Kansas, Missouri, and Michigan. The San Luis Valley of Colorado is an especially important destination point for Chihuahua-origin migration. Johnson and Ogle actually interviewed apprehended Mexican nationals in the Valley, finding that nearly 50 percent were from Chihuahua, and another 12 percent from the western state of Durango.

Study Design and Study Population

Most studies of illegal migration into the United States have been based upon data obtained from apprehended migrants. This study differs in that it considers those persons who have not been apprehended. The data on undocumented Mexicans of the San Luis Valley were obtained by the author as well as by trusted friends and acquaintances. Interviews are conducted and a schedule filled out, usually in a relaxed and friendly environment. Three basic categories of interviews included: (a) unarranged direct interviews; (b) direct, previously-arranged interviews; and (c) indirect interviews, arranged and conducted by intermediaries. The short (two page) questionnaire solicited information on the personal characteristics, migration histories, and occupational status of the migrants. Eighty-five complete interviews were obtained in this way. Interviews were carried out during the summers of 1979 and 1980.

No argument can be made for a random sample of migrants from the Valley, both because of the spatial specificity of the interviews (most were in Monte Vista) and because of the chain-referral nature of sampling. Nevertheless, Monte Vista appears to be fairly typical of other towns in the San Luis Valley in its employment structure and social characteristics, and that the interviews did in fact access a cross-section of the Valley's undocumented population.

The study area, the San Luis Valley, is located in south central Colorado (Figure 10.1). The valley is a high altitude, arid area averaging less than ten inches of precipitation per year. The presence of the Rio Grande, its numerous tributaries, and an enormous supply of ground water in combination with extremely fertile soil provide a productive agricultural environment. Historically, the San Luis Valley was a part of Mexico. The area has a large Chicano population which has long provided the necessary work force for large scale agriculture and food processing. This study is concentrated in and around the town of Monte Vista (Rio Grande County). However, fringes of Alamosa, Conejos, and Saguache Counties, where the potato industry dominates, were also included.

Figure 10.1   The study area, the San Luis Valley, is in south central Colorado.

The socioeconomic characteristics of the study population are consistent with those found in other studies. The mean age is 28.4 years, and the modal age category is 21–25 (Figure 10.2). The 18 females in the sample average 24.1 years old, and the 67 males, 29.5 years. This young female population, not customarily found in such proportions in agricultural zones, may be a consequence of the employment opportunities for females in the valley. Specifically, the potato industry uses females as sorters and graders in its processing plants. During the time that the average migrant has been in the United States (3.2 years), 81 percent of the time (2.6 years) was spent

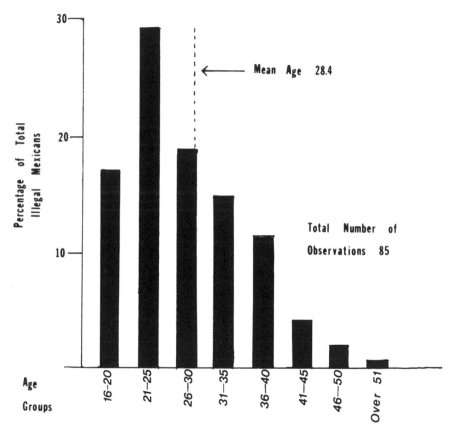

AGE   PROFILE   OF   UNAPPREHENDED   MEXICAN   NATIONALS   IN
THE   SAN   LUIS   OF   COLORADO   (1981)

Figure 10.2   Age profile of unapprehended Mexican nationals in the San Luis Valley of Colorado (1981)

in a rural area. Thus, the population is predominantly rural-based. Regarding employment, some one-half of the sample worked as agricultural laborers, while one-fifth worked in industry, chiefly potato processing (Table 10.1). A high proportion of the migrants (85.9 percent) were employed at the time of the interview, although owing to the seasonality of potato growing and processing, only 57.5 percent of the sample were employed for a full year. Apparently, the attractiveness of the Valley to migrants is the ready availability of work, rather than its quality or remuneration.

Table 10.1   Type of Job Held by Unapprehended Mexican Nationals in the San Luis Valley (1981)

Type of job	Percentage distribution
Employer or business owner	1.2
Self employed	0
Land holder	0
Landless agricultural worker	47.0
Industrial worker	21.2
Service worker	10.6
Wageless family worker	5.9
Never employed in the US	14.1
Total	100.0

Source: Survey by author.   N=85

Channelization of Migrants to the San Luis Valley

The channelization definition employed here follows that of Jones (1982b). The percentage of Valley migrants originating from a particular Mexican state is divided by the percentage of Mexican illegals to the United States as a whole which originate from that state. Thus, the measure is one of salience, or aberrance of flow from expected patterns under assumptions of stochastic independence. For the denominator of this index, I will use the percentages obtained by North and Houstoun (1976) (Table 10.2).

The resultant channelization values, theoretically varying from 0 to +∞, reflect the degree to which a particular flow exceeds that expected if Valley migrant origins mirrored those for the United States as a whole. By convention, channelized streams have values of more than one, and nonchannelized streams have values of less than or equal to one (Jones, 1982b).

Evidence for channelization in the San Luis Valley stream is apparent for only four of the nine Mexican-origin states: Chihuahua, Durango,

Table 10.2 Percentage Distributions, by Mexican Origins, of Illegal Mexican
Migrants to the US as a Whole and to the San Luis Valley of Colorado

DESTINATION

Mexican State of Origin[a]	(1) US (1975)[c]	(2) San Luis Valley (1981)[d]	(3) Channelization Values[e]
Jalisco	12.2	0	0
Chihuahua	11.8	78.0	6.67
Michoacán	10.7	0	0
Zacatecas	9.9	2.3	.23
Guanajuato	8.5	4.7	.55
Coahuila	6.7	2.3	.34
San Luis Potosí	4.8	1.2	.25
Durango	4.8	7.1	1.48
Baja California[b]	4.4	0	0
Nuevo León	3.9	0	0
Tamaulipas	3.0	0	0
Sonora	3.0	0	0
Distrito Federal	2.6	0	0
Guerrero	2.2	0	0
Sinaloa	2.2	1.2	.55
Aguascalientes	2.0	0	0
Nayarit	2.0	0	0
Colima	1.3	0	0
Vera Cruz	0.8	0	0
México	0.6	0	0
Querétaro	0.6	1.2	2.00
Hidalgo	0.6	0	0
Pueblo	0.4	0	0
Morelos	0.2	1.2	6.00
Oaxaca	0.2	0	0
Yucatán	0.2	0	0
Other States	0.4	0	0
Total	100.0	100.0	—

Note: [a]States with less than 0.2% in Column 1 are omitted from the table.

[b]Baja California Norte and Sur are combined.

[c]Source: D.S. North and M.F. Houstoun. The Characteristics and Role of
Illegal Aliens in the U.S. Labor Market: An Explanatory Study. A report prepared for the Employment and Training Administration, U.S. Dept.
of Labor (Washington, D.C.: Linton and Co., Inc., 1976).

[d]Data obtained by author.

[e]Column (2) divided by column (1).

Querétaro, and Morelos (Table 10.2). The weighted channelization value for the San Luis Valley stream (calculated by weighting state channelization values by an origin state's proportion of migrants, then summing) is 5.50. This weighted channelization value for the San Luis Valley provides a strong argument for spatially-specific flows from the central Mesa del Norte. Further proof is found in a map of points of origin in Mexico (Figure 10.3). This map indicates the strong hearth area around Chihuahua City, with outliers elsewhere in the state of Chihuahua and in Durango (around Durango City), Guanajuato (in the Leon area), Coahuila, and San Luís Potosí.

Paths of Individual Migrants

In order to further investigate migrant behavior in space, each migrant's path will be broken down into points through which he/she passed on the way to the valley. These points may be categorized as follows: (a) the point of origin or birthplace of the migrant; (b) the point of departure—i.e., the last residence in Mexico prior to arrival in the United States; and (c) the initial point of entry, or first U.S. residence— i.e., the first locality in the United States where the migrant spent a substantial amount of time prior to moving to the San Luis Valley.

POINT OF ORIGIN (MIGRANT BIRTHPLACE)

The San Luis Valley migration stream is part of the larger Intermontane West–Great Plains migration stream noted earlier. The San Luis Valley has origin profiles similar to the larger stream. Chihuahua and Durango are the major origin states for the Valley migrant stream (see Table 10.2).

The importance of Chihuahua has also been emphasized by North and Houstoun, who list it as the second-ranking origin state in the overall undocumented migration process (it had 11.8 percent of the total migrants in 1975). The importance of the Chihuahua-based migrant to the San Luis Valley is further emphasized by a 1974–76 study by Johnson and Ogle. They identified 49 percent of their apprehended Valley sample to be of Chihuahua origin (Johnson and Ogle, 1978). Nevertheless, Chihuahua does not send substantial numbers of migrants to either the California or South Texas streams.

The origin patterns for the present study reinforce the importance of the state of Chihuahua. In order to identify any random or nonrandom origin patterns within Chihuahua and adjacent states, we may locate individual villages, towns, and cities in the sending areas (Figure 10.3). Of the 67 Chihuahua-based migrants, approximately

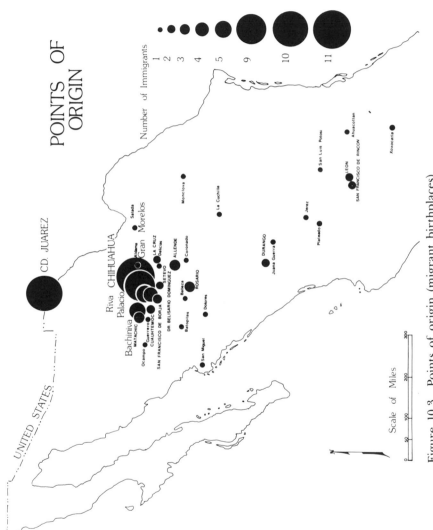

Figure 10.3 Points of origin (migrant birthplaces)

one-half were concentrated in three major cities: Chihuahua (11 migrants), Cd. Juarez (ten migrants), and Riva Palacio (nine migrants). The remaining 37 Chihuahua-based subjects came from 18 different localities, including Gran Morelos (five migrants), Bachiniva (five migrants), and Dr. Belisario Dominguez (four migrants) (see Figure 10.3). The concentration of migrants in and around the city of Chihuahua is especially interesting. Such a concentration suggests a high degree of shared knowledge about opportunities in the Valley, as well as the importance of having kin or *paisanos* to ease the settling-in process at the destination.

The migrants not based in Chihuahua may be categorized as largely urban. The majority (some three-fourths) come from the large urban centers of Leon (Guanajuato), Durango (Durango), San Luís Potosí (San Luís Potosí), and Monclova (Coahuila). In contrast to the Chihuahua-based subjects, the non-Chihuahua based migrants are dispersed. The Durango cities of Rosario and Durango together contribute about one-third of the migrants originating outside Chihuahua.

POINT OF DEPARTURE IN MEXICO (LAST RESIDENCE IN MEXICO)

The departure points in Mexico are identified in Figure 10.4. The continued importance of Chihuahua as the major point in the migration process is notable. No fewer than 82.3 percent of the respondents listed Chihuahua as their point of departure. Otherwise, the patterns are quite similar to those for points of origin. Little movement is evident in Mexico; the majority of the migrants stay only a short time in intermediate cities and do not establish residence there. Some stepwise migration is evident in the case of Ciudad Juarez. Moreover, a few migrants who listed their birthplace in the states of Morelos, Sinaloa, Zacatecas now list their last residence in Mexico as the states of Baja California Norte, Sonora, or Tamaulipas. Thus, there is some relocation to the border states by some non-Chihuahua-based subjects. Closer analysis reveals that the cities of Mexicali, Agua Prieta, and Matamoros are the specific places in the states of Baja California Norte, Sonora, and Tamaulipas, respectively.

POINTS OF ENTRY (FIRST U.S. RESIDENCE)

The entry points, or initial points of residence, for the Mexicans migrating to the San Luis Valley are defined as places where the migrants chose to remain for a period of longer than two days—generally, in order to mobilize their resources and make contacts for the trip to the Valley. A map of these entry points (Figure 10.5)

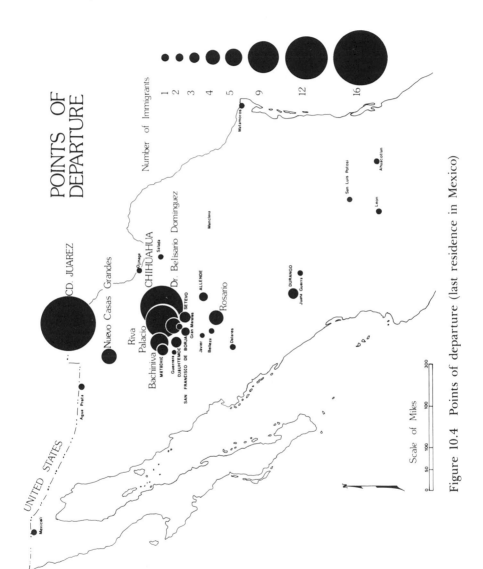

Figure 10.4 Points of departure (last residence in Mexico)

POINTS OF ENTRY

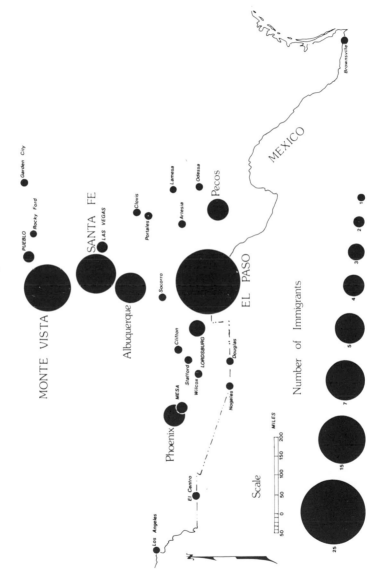

Kansas City

Fort Collins
Denver

Garden City

PUEBLO
Rocky Ford

MONTE VISTA

SANTA FE
LAS VEGAS

Clovis

Portales

Lamesa

Artesia

Odessa

Pecos

Albuquerque

Socorro

EL PASO

MEXICO

Brownsville

Phoenix
MESA

Stafford
Clifton
Wilcox
LORDSBURG

Nogales

Douglas

El Centro

Los Angeles

Scale

MILES

50   0   50   100   150   200

Number of Immigrants

1
2
3
4
5
7
15
25

Figure 10.5   Points of entry (first U.S. residence)

reveals a central corridor fringed by alternate routes to the east and west. Judging from the predominance of the central corridor, the San Luis Valley stream is obviously an entity within the larger Intermontane West–Great Plains stream. By state, Texas leads with 36.5 percent of all first-residence choices; El Paso alone is responsible for 28.2 percent of these. New Mexico accounts for 22.3 percent of the first residence choices; these are chiefly in Santa Fe and Albuquerque. Approximately 13 percent of the migrants choose Arizona as the initial residence; cities such as Phoenix and Mesa stand out as most important. Only 2.3 percent of the migrants go first to live in California, and a like percentage to Kansas and Missouri. Finally, a sizeable percentage, 15.2 percent migrate directly to the San Luis Valley, without stopping for more than two days at any intervening city.

CITIES AND TOWNS OF FINAL DESTINATION

The towns and cities denoted as the final destination in the San Luis Valley include Monte Vista (62 migrants), Center (15 migrants), Alamosa (three migrants), and Capulin (one migrant). The remaining five migrants moved to assorted places in the vicinity. These destinations reflect the chain referral method of interviewing, which was initially based upon contacts in Monte Vista.

Conclusions and Implications of the Research

In summary, migration into the San Luis Valley is highly channelized. The findings indicate a more stable and less-mobile population in the United States than is usually assumed for undocumenteds. The established agricultural subpopulation which was interviewed in this study is very different from established urban-based populations which have been studied in recent years, but in one respect they are similar— both have longer residence times than generally believed. Inasmuch as longer residence times are associated with the bringing of entire families into the U.S., and with greater use of social services, these findings may suggest certain long-run costs to the U.S.

The implications which can be drawn from this study are limited by the quality of the data set. This set is small, nonrandom, and restricted to a small geographic area. However, this data set differs from those traditionally employed in that it focuses on unapprehended as opposed to apprehended Mexicans. Thus, it taps the more established, integrated undocumenteds, as well as the more transient ones which constitute most samples taken from the apprehended subpopulation.

The data gathering techniques probably influenced and skewed the results. Nevertheless, it must be noted that all studies of undocumented workers are limited by data availability and quality. Even studies of U.S.-bound migrants in their Mexican villages suffer from the problem that they are based on data from one or a few *municipios*, and thus cannot be used to generalize about the phenomenon as a whole. Inasmuch as this study focuses on a very important (and neglected) subpopulation of undocumented Mexicans, its conclusions are valuable.

Major differences from other studies were discovered in this investigation. Contrary to other research, a significant female component was identified in the San Luis Valley sample. The undocumented migrant appears to be a more stable and better integrated component of society in the San Luis Valley than in many other areas of the United States. The identification of females may itself indicate the migration of entire family units rather than merely the married or single male. These differences from other studies are not unexpected. Unapprehended workers should have longer and more stable periods of residence in the United States than apprehended workers. Females are not detected in studies of apprehended illegal workers, chiefly because they traditionally do not appear frequently in public and thus are apprehended at much lower rates by the Immigration and Naturalization Service.

Further research on unapprehended illegals elsewhere in the United States is needed. A national survey would be a desirable goal. It would focus upon the states of California, Texas, and Illinois, where the great majority (close to 90 percent) of undocumented Mexicans probably reside (Jones, 1982a). Numerous problems would be associated with the application of a national survey. These would include (a) confidentiality; (b) when to conduct the interviews; (c) who would conduct the interviews; (d) the initial identification and contact with the prospective Mexican subjects; and (e) the numerous economic and bureaucratic obstacles. The current San Luis Valley study presents a model on which the national survey could be structured. The San Luis Valley area provided a centralized data source and a familiar environment which minimized any hostilities and problems and insured a setting in which a successful interview procedure was implemented.

References

Baca, Reynaldo, and Dexter Bryan. 1980. *Citizenship Aspirations and Residency Rights Preferences*. Report for Sepa-Option, Los Angeles, California.

Bustamante, Jorge A. 1977. "Undocumented immigration from Mexico: Research report." *International Migration Review* 11:149–77.

Cardenas, Gilberto. 1976. "Manpower Impact and Problems of Mexican Illegal Aliens in an Urban Labor Market." Ph.D. dissertation, University of Illinois.

Cardenas, Gilberto, and Ray Flores. 1978. *A Study of the Demographic and Employment Characteristics of Undocumented Aliens in San Antonio, El Paso, and McAllen.* San Antonio: Avante, Inc., for the Texas Advisory Committee, U.S. Commission of Civil Rights.

Cornelius, Wayne A. 1978. *Mexican Migration to the United States: Causes, Consequences, and U.S. Responses.* Cambridge: Center for International Studies, Massachusetts Institute of Technology.

————. 1979. "Migration to the United States: The view from rural sending communities." *Developmental Digest* 17:90–101.

Dagodag, W. Tim. 1975. "Source regions and composition of illegal Mexican immigrants to California." *International Migration Review* 9:499–511.

Gamio, Manuel. 1930. *Mexican Immigration to the United States: A Study of Human Migration and Adjustment.* Chicago: The University of Chicago Press.

Johnson, Kenneth R., and Nina M. Ogle. 1978. *Illegal Mexican Aliens in the United States: A Teaching Manual on Impact Dimensions and Alternative Futures.* Washington, D.C.: University Press of America.

Jones, Richard C. 1982a. "Undocumented migration from Mexico: Some geographical questions." *Annals, Association of American Geographers* 72:77–87.

————. 1982b. "Channelization of undocumented Mexican migrants to the U.S." *Economic Geography* 58:156–76.

————. 1983. "Changing patterns of undocumented Mexican migration to South Texas." *Social Science Quarterly*, in press.

North, David S., and Marion F. Houstoun. 1976. *The Characteristics and Role of Illegal Aliens in the U.S. Labor Market: An Exploratory Study.* A report prepared for the Employment and Training Administration, U.S. Department of Labor, Washington, D.C.: Linton & Co.

Portes, Alejandro. 1978. "Migration and underdevelopment." *Politics and Society*, August 8, pp. 1–48.

Roseman, Curtis C. 1971. "Channelization of migration flows from the rural South to the industrial Midwest." *Proceedings, Association of American Geographers* 3:140–46.

Samora, Julian. 1971. *Los Mojados: The Wetback Story.* Notre Dame: University of Notre Dame Press.

Zazueta, Carlos H., and Rodolfo Corona. 1979. *Los Trabajadores Mexicanos en Los Estados Unidos: Primeros Resultados de la Encuesta Nacional de Emigración a la Frontera Norte del País y a los Estados Unidos (ENEFNEU).* México, D.F.: Centro Nacional de Información y Estadísticas del Trabajo (CENIET).

11
Illegal Mexican Aliens in Los Angeles: Locational Characteristics

W. TIM DAGODAG

Introduction

By the 1970s, it was generally acknowledged that the Los Angeles metropolitan area had become an important destination for illegal immigrants from Mexico. Given the clandestine nature of the illegal immigration process and the alien's almost complete aversion to dealing with any agency or institution capable of gathering usable statistical information, little knowledge exists concerning the location of migrants at this destination. It is the purpose of this study to produce a much-needed estimate of the location of illegal Mexican aliens (IMAs) in metropolitan Los Angeles, thereby filling in some gaps in our knowledge of this illegal migration cycle.

Several topics will be addressed in producing this estimate and in the accompanying analysis. In order of discussion, the topics are: the general background of Hispanic population increases in Los Angeles and the implications for illegal immigration; the formulation of a methodology which approximates the location of IMAs; a cartographic display of these locations; and an analysis of the locational patterns with an emphasis on ecological factors that are associated with housing, employment and inter-racial and inter-ethnic characteristics.

Since this study involves two significant subgroups in the population, Mexican-Americans and blacks, one further point needs to be made about existing geographic literature. While the intraurban location of blacks has been studied extensively, surprisingly little work has been produced on Mexican-Americans or Mexicans in U.S. cities.

Where examined, Mexican-Americans have been treated incidentally as part of general geographic studies such as those by Nelson and Clark (1976:261–264), Palmer and Rush (1976:128–130), Rose and Christian (1982:371–374), and Steiner (1981:59–63). The conspicuous absence of empirically-based analyses of Mexican-American settlement, coupled with a similar disregard for Mexican-American/black spatial relationships, obviously complicates the formulation of useful generalizations or models of IMA settlement.

The Mexican-Origin Population in Los Angeles

Historically, Mexican-Americans or Hispanics have constituted the most numerous minority population in Los Angeles, and as such their distribution has important implications for the distribution of the IMA population.[1] It is popular belief that Mexican-American communities serve as ports of entry for newly-arrived migrants from Mexico who have legal or illegal status (Kirsch, 1977). In the last decade, however, the attractiveness of these communities (*barrios*— established neighborhoods; and *colonias*—newer migrant settlements) as a place for new migrants to settle has apparently diminished. This diminished attractiveness may be due largely to increases in population density or simply an absence of space in which to accommodate further growth. Still, the distribution of the Hispanic population carries some locational implications for IMAs who continue to settle in Los Angeles.

According to the 1970 Census, the Hispanic population was distributed chiefly in East Los Angeles (Figure 11.1), the Los Angeles County area stretching into the San Gabriel Valley, and scattered sites in the southwest and San Fernando Valley. These sites have been traditional ones of Mexican-American residence and form part of what may be considered to be a hierarchical arrangement of *barrios* that focus on East Los Angeles. In the decade 1970–80, all of the *barrios* experienced population growth and spatial expansion, some of which is attributable to the influx of IMAs (Figure 11.2).

In spite of limitations imposed by census definitions pertaining to persons of Spanish origin, Spanish language, Spanish descent, white or other, it is still possible to conclude that by 1980 the Hispanic population had experienced marked growth and exhibited new patterns of settlement. In this intervening decade, the Hispanic population in Los Angeles County increased from 1,289,399 (18.3 percent of the total population) to 2,065,727 (27.6 percent) (U.S. Census of Population and Housing, 1970; 1980). Three factors may account for this notable increase: a high birth rate among Hispanics (the highest in Los Angeles County); net-immigration of legal residents or natives; and net-im-

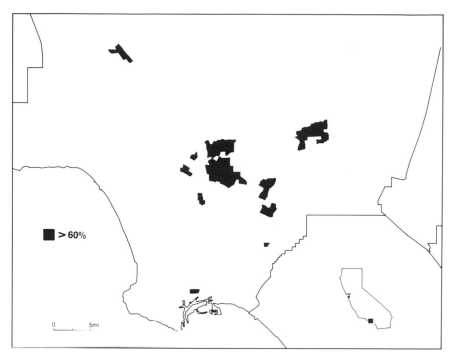

Figure 11.1   Los Angeles County: persons of Spanish language and surname by census tracts, 1970

migration of illegal aliens. It is still impossible to make any conclusions or even tenuous assumptions about the exact contribution of IMAs to the pattern on the maps. About the only valid observation is that some IMAs were counted in the census (a special effort was so made during the enumeration of the 1980 Census), but the vast majority were not, for obvious reasons. At a minimum, the maps serve to identify probable locations of IMAs based on the rationalization that kinship-friendship ties have induced settlement in proximity to Mexican American areas—a rationalization that has received support in the methodology used by the Los Angeles City Planning Department (1976) to locate illegal alien districts.

As for the numbers of IMAs involved in migration to and settlement in Los Angeles, estimates for the city and county range from several hundred thousand to over two million (Table 11.1). Here too, only the most tenuous observation can be made. The sole conclusion to be arrived at from these various estimates is that large numbers of IMAs are living in the Los Angeles area. Some inkling of the scale of this settlement can be deduced from the outward expressions of

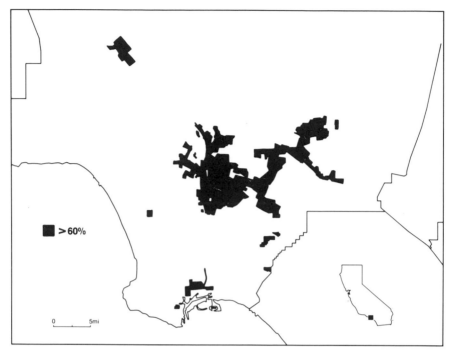

Figure 11.2   Los Angeles County: persons of Spanish language and surname
by census tracts, 1980

Mexican culture which have appeared in communities and neighborhoods during recent years. The degree of ethnic and cultural change
has been noted even in the popular periodicals, one of which referred
to the illegal alien's presence as the "Mexicanization" of Los Angeles
(*U.S. News and World Report* 1979:42). This same source goes on to
describe the observable effects of IMA settlement:

> The growing Hispanic community, swollen by illegal immigrants, has
> inherited downtown portions of this turbulent, 464-square mile me-
> tropolis and influences daily life far beyond the *barrios* of East Los
> Angeles.

Indeed, traveling through the Los Angeles metropolitan area, the
observer cannot avoid being struck by the extent of "Mexicanization"
which involves not only settlement and occupancy by Mexicans, but
the development of a sophisticated retail infrastructure to meet the
needs of the immigrant population, the dependency of industry and
various services on the IMA population for workers, and cultural
changes evident in the profusion of Spanish language media. Los
Angeles is definitely more Mexican today than it was 30, or even ten

Table 11.1   Estimates of the Illegal Mexican Alien Population in the
             Los Angeles Area

Source	Estimate	Areal unit	Date
US Immigration and Naturalization Service	2,000,000	Los Angeles County	March 1979
US Immigration and Naturalization Service	1,000,000	City of Los Angeles	March 1979
Los Angeles City Planning Department	400,000	City of Los Angeles	July 1976
Los Angeles County Board of Supervisors	1,100,000	Los Angeles County	April 1982
US News and World Report	±500,000	Los Angeles County	January 1979
US Congress, House Committee on the Judiciary, 92nd Cong.	250,000	City of Los Angeles	1971-72
Los Angeles County Grand Jury	700,000	Los Angeles County	July 1976

years ago. IMAs have contributed significantly to this ethnic and cultural transition.

If the observer is sensitive to the rapidity and magnitude of "Mexicanization," then a similar impression must be made by the extent and conditions of settlement. Entire neighborhoods and communities appear to have been occupied by IMAs, while sites as discrete as a few apartment houses or blocks have been converted to IMA use. So great is the IMA presence that specific cities and communities come to mind in connection with IMA settlement, some of which are listed (Table 11.2) as they were noted in the *Los Angeles Times* over a ten-year period. In spite of the qualitative and symptomatic nature of this listing, it is useful to the discussion since it confirms a widespread distribution of IMA activity in Los Angeles. Whether or not IMAs reside in these areas, their presence is made known in connection with employment, the use of transportation, consumption, and provision of retail services, support from public agencies and institutions, and, unfortunately, in criminal activities.

Table 11.2 Cities and Communities in Los Angeles County
          Noted in Connection With IMA Activity

Arleta	North Hollywood
Boyle Heights	Northridge
Burbank	*Norwalk
Canoga Park	Pacoima
Carson	Panorama City
*Compton	Pico-Union
Culver City	San Fernando
*El Monte	San Gabriel Valley
Highland Park	San Pedro
Hollywood	Santa Fe Springs
*Huntington Park	Santa Monica
Inglewood	South Central Los Angeles
Lincoln Heights	*South Gate
*Los Angeles	South Glendale
Los Angeles CBD	Sylmar
MacArthur Park	Van Nuys
Monterrey Park	*Venice
Mt. Washington	Watts

Source: Los Angeles Times, 1972-1982
Note: *Communities noted by Cornelius and Diez-Canedo (1976) as a
         destination of IMAs from Jalisco, Mexico.

In view of the "Mexicanization" of Los Angeles, a logical question arises concerning the kinds of areas in which IMAs are able to locate. Here a simple typology of IMA settlements produced for Southern California provides a useful framework for the eventual discussion of the school-enrollment based methodology used to estimate IMA locations. The typology takes the form of a matrix (Figure 11.3) which

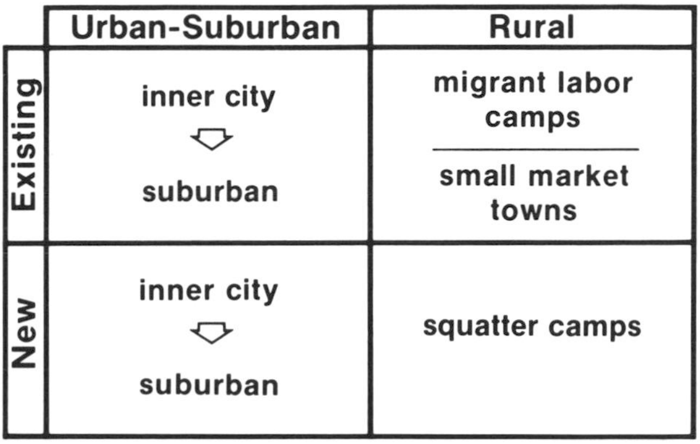

	Urban-Suburban	Rural
Existing	inner city ⇨ suburban	migrant labor camps ———————— small market towns
New	inner city ⇨ suburban	squatter camps

Figure 11.3   Typology of IMA settlements

considers both spatial and temporal characteristics. An initial distinction permits the separation of urban and rural destinations and settlements, a fact which is influenced strongly by kinship-friendship networks (Baca and Bryan 1981:738) and job preference or availability. Rural settlement takes place in farming communities, the small to moderate size market towns, formal labor camps, *de novo* squatter camps, or makeshift shelters which are located in or near to the agricultural fields. As for settlement in urban areas, IMA presence has been linked historically to *barrios* and *colonias* situated largely in the inner city, but also found at intermediate sites or out on the urban periphery. While these points about location will be elaborated on later, it should be reemphasized that the traditional *barrios* in the region are at their saturation point given the severe limitations of housing due to housing demand and redlining activities.[2] Consequently, it is not unreasonable to expect that the margins of the *barrios* have been expanded and new settlements (*colonias*), especially ones accommodating IMAs, have appeared in discontiguous areas.

What then are the major observations concerning the "Mexicanization" of Los Angeles and the role played by IMAs? First, the Hispanic population has been augmented by illegal immigration to some unknown degree—simple field observation confirms this fact. Second, in the Los Angeles metropolitan area, IMAs have settled in diverse communities, and not necessarily in ones which have required Mexican-American antecedents. As a result, there is good reason to believe that IMAs are participating in the housing market through the filtering process. Third, IMA settlement suggests the existence of spatial conflict stemming from competition for cheap and accessible housing and involving inter-racial and inter-ethnic relationships.

A Methodology for Estimating IMA Locations

Up to this point it is obvious that no precise enumeration and identification of IMA residence has been possible. The methodology offered here, however, should provide a reasonable estimate of intra-urban locations and locational attributes. Fundamentally, the methodology is based on observed changes in the racial-ethnic composition of pupil enrollments in the Los Angeles Unified School District (LAUSD, 1973, 1979). The racial and ethnic composition of this immense district (second largest in the nation), encompassing 714 square miles, changed from essentially white or Anglo to minority within the span of four to five years (Figure 11.4). This sharp increase in Hispanic enrollment, a 94 percent increase between 1966 and 1979, warranted attention and suggested some ties to increased IMA settlement in the portions of the city and county served by LAUSD.

The use of elementary school enrollment data in estimating population distributions is not a recent development (Olds, 1949; Speigleman, 1968:308). In contrast to estimates which are based on extrapolation from the U.S. Census or fluctuations in the rate of Immigration and Naturalization Service apprehensions, school enrollments present several distinct advantages: data are available on a yearly basis; the counts of pupils are reliable since they are based on the teacher's firsthand knowledge and observations about a pupil's racial and ethnic background; and, the elementary school service areas are more closely an approximation of neighborhoods than are census tracts.

Pupil enrollment data for Hispanics were used to produce an estimate of the IMA population located in the service areas of the local elementary schools. This estimate yields numbers but not locations within the LAUSD, and by extension, areas within the City of Los Angeles, other incorporated places, and county territory. It is assumed that IMA children or children of IMA parents attend elementary schools since State law does not allow citizenship status to be considered for admission purposes. Furthermore, communications with LAUSD and the Los Angeles County School District (LAUSD, Research and Evaluation; Los Angeles County Superintendent of Schools, Administrative Services; and anonymous school principals, LAUSD) at different levels, confirmed the admission of IMA pupils to elementary schools. These same sources also concurred in the view that significant increases in Hispanic enrollments were due to IMAs. For example, four principals whose schools experienced sharp increases in Hispanic enrollments admitted that 30 to 50 percent of their pupils were illegal.

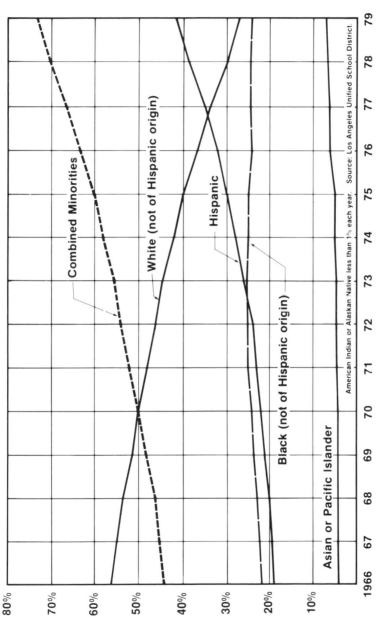

Figure 11.4 Los Angeles Unified School District: racial and ethnic percentages by year

The identification of schools associated with IMA settlement was based on two criteria: Hispanic concentrations of at least 200 pupils in 1979 and an increase in Hispanic enrollments exceeding 100 percent during the period 1973–79. This six year time period was chosen because it conforms to a period of intensive and noticeable IMA activity in Southern California. The schools meeting the criteria during these years were located and the percentage increases plotted cartographically (Figure 11.5); they are 58 in number.

Before analyzing the patterns resulting from this procedure, several points should be made to clarify methodological limitations. The data allow only inferential observations to be made, but it is believed that these inferences are basically accurate. The data pertain to the LAUSD and not the entire county, but the district includes the cities of Los Angeles, San Fernando, Vernon, Maywood, Huntington Park, Bell, South Gate, Cudahy, Carson, Gardena, and Lomita, as well as part of the county. In short, the bulk of the populated portion of the county and urban area is included in the study area. In addition, the observations are confined to the married-adults-with-children cohort of the IMA population. It can be assumed that these people are established successfully or securely enough to consider and to send their children to elementary school. On the other hand, the more transient, "sojourner" migrants, who tend to be single males, would (of course) not be represented in these data.

Resultant IMA Locations

The final map (Figure 11.5) shows the location of schools which met the two criteria, and the actual percentage increases in Hispanic enrollments for the study period. This map, along with Table 11.3, which contains selected summary characteristics for Hispanic pupils in the study schools and the school district, verifies the extent to which Hispanic increases were concentrated in a subset of schools believed to have large IMA enrollments. In a most emphatic way, the table shows that the schools experienced extraordinarily large increases in enrollments, especially when these are compared to the district-wide increase of 52.4 percent during the six years.

For the schools shown on the map, 24 experienced increases in the range of 100–200 percent, 19 showed increases ranging between 200 and 500 percent, and 15 registered increases ranging between 5,000 and 11,000 percent! These remarkable percentage increases are the cornerstone of the estimate of IMA locations, since they cannot be explained solely by the conventional population growth factors of local natural increase or net-immigration of Mexican-Americans from

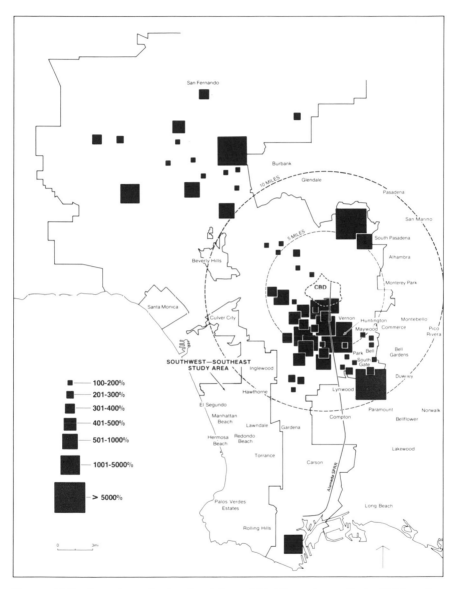

Figure 11.5 Location of schools with > 200 Hispanic pupils in 1979 and a percentage increase of > 100 for Hispanic pupils, 1973–1979

Table 11.3   Numbers of Hispanic Pupils, Los Angeles

LAUSD[a]

Year	No. of Schools	No. Hispanic Pupils	Per Cent Increase
1973	203	93,964	—
1979	203	143,186	52.4%

Schools Meeting Criteria

Year	No. of Schools	No. Hispanic Pupils	Per Cent Increase
1973	58	10,726	—
1979	58	34,640	223.0%

Note: [a]Los Angeles Unified School District

other areas. These increases, which are three, four, or five times greater than the district-wide average, must be accounted for by IMA settlement.

The location of these schools strengthens the postulated relationship between excessive increases in enrollments and illegal immigration. The majority of the schools (71 percent) are located within a ten mile radius of the Los Angeles Central Business District (CBD), while 40 percent are within a five mile radius. Of the remaining schools, 16 (28 percent) are found in the San Fernando Valley, and one is located in San Pedro near the harbor district. This distribution of schools, especially in the inner city and areas to the southwest and southeast, is understandable in the context of several ecological factors which bear on land use.

Analysis of Locational Patterns

It can be said, generally, that the location of the IMA population is responsive to two structural ecological factors and at least one be-havioral ecological factor. Addressing the structural factors first, IMA entrance into a specific neighborhood is determined by housing op-portunities. If, for example, the concentration of schools in the southwest and southeast sections of the city and county is enclosed in a wedge consisting of lines drawn at 45 degrees from the center of Los Angeles CBD, then an area of exceedingly low quality housing is delimited. A review of housing indicators at the start of the last decade supports this characterization. As expected, housing in this area was older, commanded lower values and rents, was renter occupied, and considerably substandard as indicated by the surrogate measure of overcrowding (more than 1.01 persons per room). On the whole, these housing conditions represent a marked departure from the general housing profile of Los Angeles County. Moreover, in keeping with descriptive ecological models there is a definite concentricity to the conditions observed here—the farther away from the CBD, generally the higher the relative quality of housing.

Some care, however, should be exercised in interpreting accessibility to housing based on housing quality, values, or rents. In the San Fernando Valley, for example, rents tend to be higher on average than those in the inner city. IMAs in the San Fernando Valley confront and solve this problem by doubling up, i.e., relying on several individuals to pool their financial resources and to occupy a single dwelling unit (see Dagodag, 1981). In its worst expression, "hotbedding" occurs— individuals and members of families using the same bed, sleeping in shifts.

Nevertheless, the concentration of IMAs in the southwest-southeast area is probably strongly related to housing opportunities represented by the availability of adequate low-rent housing. Over time, this availability lessens even as the quality of housing deteriorates and the rents rise; and as a result, new, adjacent areas are "invaded."

The second structural factor which is of interest is related to commercial and industrial land uses. The schools or residential neighborhoods in the delimited area are situated near to a major heavy industrial sector of the City and County. In this regard, either the Southern Pacific Railraod or Alameda Avenue can be used as a locational fix for heavy industry. Not only does this belt extend north-south through the area, but more recent additions to the industrial core now extend east into the balance of Los Angeles County. What is important to note is the proximity of IMA locations to this industrial core, as well as to the CBD core and frame. Both of these locations possess the kinds of outlets and operations requiring low skill labor, and little, if any, command of the English language. In the past, the incorporated communities of the southeast have been dormitories for workers in the industries of the area. The only difference between workers today and those 20 years ago is an ethnic one—the current labor force is of largely Mexican-American origin. Similar to housing

opportunities, the availability of jobs is a crucial and easily compre-
hended determinant of IMA locations.

These two structural factors can be summarized as follows. IMAs
are apparently exercising some, although limited, selectivity in locating
themselves in urban space. In the southwest-southeast area, for example,
housing opportunities are presented in association with sources of
employment. For IMAs, location is important because of high pe-
destrian dependency—they do not enter into the United States with
vehicles, and their acquisition and operation exposes them to the risk
of apprehension in connection with traffic violations (see U.S. Department of Transportation, 1978, for a discussion of high pedestrian-
density areas in Los Angeles). As is typical of the low income population,
IMAs cope with this problem through the use of public transportation,
reliance on limited carpooling where vehicles are accessible, or paid
private transportation in vans or trucks. Nonetheless, the proximity
of housing to places of employment is an essential locational require-
ment which has been noted not only for the southwest-southeast
example but also for the San Fernando Valley (Dagodag, 1981).

The characteristics of employment sources are of special locational
importance. Since they possess little formal training or education,
IMAs must begin in low skill jobs or those requiring marginal skills.
Industries and activities which predominate in the southwest-southeast,
as well as in the CBD frame, are services, warehousing, apparel-textiles,
food processing, furniture manufacturing, rubber, plastics, and metal
fabrication. These sources of employment include many menial, low-
pay categories. Nevertheless, these sources appear to be on the decline,
a trend which is consistent with trends in other urban areas of the
United States (Harper, 1982:88–109). In the Southeast District of the
City of Los Angeles (a formal community planning area) a net loss
of industrial firms (30 percent) was noted for the period 1971–76
(Los Angeles City Planning Department, 1977). Notwithstanding the
trend toward fewer industries, the IMA population has increased in
the area. An intriguing corollary to the pattern of IMA settlement
which has not been addressed is the possibility that inner-city sites
serve as staging areas for subsequent settlement in outlying areas such
as the San Fernando Valley. Perhaps as some industries are eliminated,
and others suburbanize, IMAs have followed them outward. Unfortunately, this form of staged intraurban migration by IMAs has not
been investigated, and cannot be with our current data set.

The final ecological factor which merits our attention is behavioral,
and it deals with residential segregation and succession of the urban
IMA population. In the IMA areas meeting the aforementioned
criteria, racial-ethnic polarization is high. Specifically, in those areas

including the bulk of the IMA population (southeast of the CBD), residential segregation between the Hispanic majority and the white and black minorities is pronounced.[3] Traditionally, the Mexican-American population has been unwilling to share its social space with the black population (Steiner, 1981:63). Some indication of this social attitude on the part of Mexican-Americans is seen in the fact that only one street gang, Watts-Vario Grape Street, in Los Angeles, has both Mexican-American and black members. It is somewhat surprising that in Los Angeles, IMAs are willing to share residential space with blacks, but less surprising when it is realized that this phenomenon is most evident in the southwest, where fewer IMAs are located and where a black majority prevails. In general, schools to the southwest and north, where black and white majorities (respectively) exist, are less segregated than those to the southeast, where a Hispanic majority prevails. This finding emphasizes the degree to which the southeast has become an entrenched Hispanic/IMA area over many decades, as opposed to the newer *barrios* where spatial expansion of Hispanics and IMAs is occurring within the larger metropolitan area.

Enrollment percentages for Hispanic, black, and white/others, for the 58 schools in 1979, may be combined and displayed graphically, as 3 variables totaling 100 percent (Figure 11.6). The inter-ethnic relationships just discussed emerge in this graph. Group I (white, with a significant Hispanic minority) includes schools in the San Fernando Valley. Group II (black, with a significant Hispanic minority) contains those schools in the southwest, all of which are west of Alameda Street (the historical racial boundary between the black ghetto to the west, and exclusively middle- and lower-class white neighborhoods to the east). Group III (dominantly Hispanic, with white and black minorities) includes schools of the Alameda Street boundary which are located in the county and the cities of South Gate, Huntington Park, Cudahy, Maywood, and Bell. The balance of the Hispanic-dominated schools having significant white minorities are found west of the CBD or are in sites elsewhere in the city and county.

A major inference to be drawn, then, is one which must be viewed against the larger background of intraregional shifts in population, housing, and employment. In keeping with current knowledge about Los Angeles, we can say that whites have moved to the suburbs of Los Angeles County, or into adjoining counties of Orange, Ventura, and San Bernardino. Housing and jobs have likewise decentralized, with the result that IMAs have been able to settle in areas abandoned by upwardly-mobile whites, and to a surprising degree by blacks who have shifted or are shifting to areas contiguous to the existing ghetto (e.g., Inglewood and Compton). Most importantly, IMAs have occupied

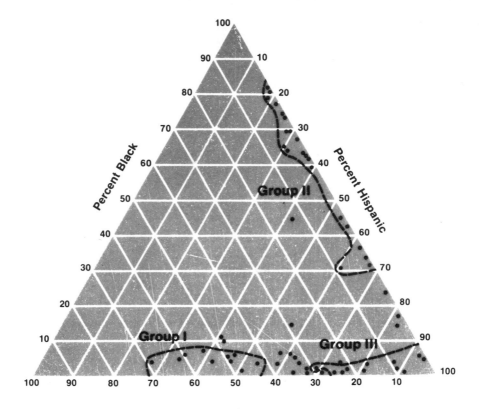

Figure 11.6   Racial-ethnic composition of 58 elementary schools, 1979

some of the worst housing in the metropolitan area—the data for 1970 were used deliberately to demonstrate the poor condition of the housing stock over ten years ago at a time when illegal immigration started to accelerate. Today, as even the most casual field observation will prove, the housing has deteriorated even more as it has aged, been over-used and under-maintained. In reference to this housing quality, the Southern California Association of Governments noted at mid-decade that between 13 and 28 percent of the units in the southwest were unsound (1979:19–22). Certainly, the continued population growth of communities in the southwest, and to a lesser extent the southeast, is maintained only by the influx of transient populations, among which IMAs are strongly represented.

Conclusions

For obvious reasons, it is important to know something about where IMAs settle once they arrive in the United States. Of course, any effort to determine these locations is plagued by the secretive nature of the migration process and a lack of statistical information. Nonetheless, this study has attempted to locate the IMA population living in the major destination of metropolitan Los Angeles. The data used were elementary school enrollments which revealed extraordinary increases in Hispanic pupil counts occurring in a relatively short period of time. These increases in Hispanic pupils, along with the LAUSD admission that IMAs contribute significantly to enrollments, provide justification for linking IMAs with specific schools and neighborhoods. The quantitative and cartographic expression of these data lead to several observations about the process of IMA intraurban location.

The pattern of IMA locations should be interpreted in the light of overall population increase and movement in metropolitan Los Angeles. Certain facts concerning such increase and movement are indisputable: whites have moved and continue to move to the suburbs and are declining in proportion to minorities, while blacks and Mexican-Americans, whose numbers are increasing in the City of Los Angeles (*Los Angeles Times*, April 13, 1980) are shifting their locations, at a more micro-scale involving areas adjacent to the CBD, within a southeast-southwest wedge. In some manner, IMAs have to be accommodated within the pattern of population dynamics exhibited by the legally resident population.

If estimates of the number of IMAs residing in metropolitan Los Angeles are correct, IMAs occupied and still do occupy a special or unique niche in the urban ecological structure of this region. The location of IMAs can be explained by the operation of several factors which focus on the availability of housing and employment. IMAs locate where housing is available to them; by definition, this means that housing is low-cost—i.e., substandard. A sufficient quantity of this type of housing exists in the inner city and in dispersed sites elsewhere in Los Angeles. The correspondence between such housing and probable IMA districts is quite close; this correspondence relates to the fact that, owing to language problems, fear of apprehension, and exploitation, IMAs have little choice but to settle in traditional zones for such migrants. This correspondence was documented clearly in the southwest-southeast area example. Analogously, IMAs will locate where there are available sources of low-skill or marginal-skill employment, and these areas tend to be close to the above. Thus, in an almost predictable fashion, IMAs are found in areas of low-quality housing which are near to industrial land use—again, this is especially evident in the inner city areas. The only departure from the linkage of housing and industry is in the situation where IMAs are employed in the services, particularly as restaurant workers, domestics, construction workers, and general day laborers.

An interesting adjunct to the locational process described here is the willingness of IMAs to take advantage of housing opportunities regardless of segregative norms which are observed in Los Angeles. Apparently, IMAs do not show any reluctance to settle on the margins of, or directly in the black ghetto as seen in sites west of Alameda Street. This type of interracial proximity is not typical of Mexican-American/black relations (Steiner, 1981) and therefore provides another argument in support of our interpretation of school enrollment data. In the inner city, IMAs have succeeded whites in the course of founding *de novo* settlements and probably as participants in the expansion of Mexican-American communities.

Notes

1. The term "Hispanic" is used here in conformance with the Los Angeles Unified School District racial-ethnic classification of pupils. It is also used synonymously with the 1970 and 1980 Census terms of Spanish surname, Spanish origin, and Spanish descent. In Los Angeles County, the vast majority of individuals classified according to the LAUSD or Census terms are Mexican-American or Mexican Nationals.

2. The State of California, Department of Savings and Loan (1977:4) noted that residential lending activity was restricted severely in both Mexican-American and black areas of Los Angeles County.

3. James A. Kushner (*Los Angeles Times*, January 19, 1981) calculated a segregation index of 91 for the City of Los Angeles in 1978.

References

Baca, Reynaldo, and Dexter Bryan. 1981. "Mexican undocumented workers in the binational community: A research note." *International Migration Review* 15:737–48.

California, Department of Savings and Loan. 1977. *Fair Lending Report, No. 1, Vol. II.*

Cornelius, Wayne A., and Juan Diez-Canedo. 1976. *Mexican Migration to the United States: The View from Rural Sending Communities.* Cambridge: Massachusetts Institute of Technology.

Dagodag, W. Tim. 1981. *A Note on the Intraurban Settlement of Illegal Mexican Aliens in the San Fernando Valley of California.* Paper, Conference of Latin Americanist Geographers, Buffalo, New York.

Harper, Robert A., 1982. "Metropolitan areas as transactional centers." Pp. 89–109 in *Modern Metropolitan Systems*, ed. Charles M. Christian and Robert A. Harper. Columbus: Charles E. Merrill Publishing Co.

Kirsch, Jonathan. 1977. "California's illegal aliens: They give more than they take." *New West* 2:26–33.

Los Angeles City Planning Department. 1976. *An Estimate of the Illegal Alien Population in Los Angeles.* Working Paper.

—————. 1977. *Environmental Impact Report for the Southeast Los Angeles District Plan.*

Los Angeles Unified School District, Research and Evaluation Branch. 1973. *Racial and Ethnic Survey*, Publication No. 332.

—————. *Racial and Ethnic Survey*, Publication No. 375.

Nelson, Howard J., and William A.V. Clark. 1976. "The Los Angeles metropolitan experience." Pp. 227–95 in *Contemporary Metropolitan American: Twentieth Century Cities*, ed. John S. Adams. Cambridge: Ballinger Publishing Co.

Olds, Edward B. 1949. "The city block as a unit for recording and analyzing urban data." *Journal of the American Statistical Association* 248:495–97.

Palmer, Martha E., and Marjorie N. Rush. 1976. "Houston." Pp. 109–49 in *Contemporary Metropolitan America: Twentieth Century Cities*, ed., John S. Adams. Cambridge: Ballinger Publishing Co.

Rose, Harold M., and Charles M. Christian. 1982. "Race and ethnicity: A competitive force in the evolution of American urban systems." Pp. 361–89 in *Modern Metropolitan Systems*, eds. Charles M. Christian and Robert A. Harper. Columbus: Charles E. Merrill Publishing Co.

Southern California Association of Governments. 1980. *Census Tract Statistics for Los Angeles County, Population and Race.*

————. 1979. *Draft Regional Housing Element.*

Spiegleman, Mortimer. 1968. *Introduction to Demography.* Cambridge: Harvard University Press.

Steiner, Rodney. 1981. *Los Angeles: The Centrifugal City.* Dubuque, Iowa: Kendall-Hunt Publishing Co.

U.S. Department of Transportation, Federal Highway Administration and California, Business and Transportation Agency, Department of Transportation. 1978. *Final Environmental Impact Statement for the Proposed Routes 1 and I-105 (El Segundo-Norwalk) Freeway Transitway.*

U.S. News and World Report. 1979. 29:42.

12
Geographical Patterns of Undocumented Mexicans and Chicanos in San Antonio, Texas: 1970 and 1980

AVELARDO VALDEZ
RICHARD C. JONES

During the 1970s there has been a marked increase in the number of undocumented Mexicans immigrating to the United States (Cornelius, 1978; Roberts, 1978; Bean et al., 1982). Studies show that these immigrants are increasingly settling in urban as opposed to rural areas as in the recent past. Concomitantly, during the 1970s a disproportionately high growth rate occurred among Chicanos in these same areas (Bean and Frisbee, 1978; U.S. Bureau of the Census, 1981). Despite the urban concentration of these groups during this decade, no research has emphasized their intraurban residential patterns.[1] This study focuses on differential patterns of Chicanos and undocumenteds in San Antonio (Bexar County), Texas in 1970–72 and in 1979–80.

Residential patterns of immigrant populations have been of consistent interest to sociologists. Much of this research is theoretically centered around the early Chicago School's concentric zone model which posits that residential patterns are a result of impersonal economic factors operating within the city (Park, Burgess, and McKenzie, 1925; Park, 1916; Hawley, 1950). This model proposes that lower-status groups are centralized near the core, whereas upper-status groups are decentralized near the periphery. Many proponents of the concentric zone model imply that newly arriving immigrants would:

(a) initially be segregated in centrally-located, lower-income ethnic areas; (b) after an extended time, improve their socioeconomic status and disperse to other subareas of the city; and (c) as a result of this redistribution, assimilate into the host society. Most studies of European ethnic immigrants have substantiated this pattern (Lieberson, 1963; Duncan, et al., 1959; Guest and Weed, 1976). This has not been the case for the residential patterns of black Americans, who continue to reside in highly segregated subareas of major cities (Duncan and Duncan, 1957; and Taeuber and Taeuber, 1965), even after experiencing social mobility (Pendelton, 1973).

Previous studies on residential patterns of Mexican-origin groups have concentrated on measuring degrees of segregation between Chicanos, blacks, and Anglos in Southwestern cities (Moore and Mittlebach, 1966; Massey, 1979; Lopez, 1981; Hwang and Murdock, 1982). These studies concur that there is a high degree of residential segregation among these groups, Chicanos tending to be less segregated from the Anglo population than are blacks. However, the degree of segregation varies greatly from city to city.

Few studies have focused on the relationship between residential patterns of Chicanos and undocumented Mexicans. Grebler, et al. (1970) measured segregation levels between Chicanos and foreign-born Mexicans. They found these two groups were residentially segregated from the dominant groups, but highly integrated among themselves. It is unknown what portion of their foreign-born Mexican sample were undocumented immigrants.

The present study is unique in that it isolates undocumented residential patterns and compares them to those of Chicanos in the early and in the late 1970s. Based on previous research of other immigrant groups, we expect that there is a residential succession process occurring among undocumenteds, Chicanos, and Anglos. That is, it is expected that undocumented Mexicans will first settle in lower-income, ethnically homogeneous Chicano neighborhoods. At the same time, Chicanos who have increased their economic status, we propose, will move into relatively higher-status adjacent subareas, displacing Anglos who move into areas of still higher status replicating the invasion-succession model. Therefore, this research attempts to determine: (a) areas of the city in which undocumenteds and Chicanos cluster; (b) the similarity and dissimilarity of residential patterns between Chicanos and undocumented Mexicans; (c) the relationship between these residential patterns and the socioeconomic status of the areas; and (d) changes in residential patterns of undocumenteds relative to Chicanos during the 1970s. The study posits that an understanding of the residential patterns of Chicanos and undocumenteds may explain how this Mexican-origin group maintains its minority status in this society.

Data and Procedures

The population of Bexar County (San Antonio), Texas grew from 830,460 in 1970 to 911,800 by 1980 (Bureau of the Census, 1974 and 1981).[2] Chicanos increased their total percentage of the population from 44 percent to 47 percent during this ten-year span. By 1980, San Antonio was the largest city in the nation whose Spanish-surnamed population comprised nearly half or more of the total. Undocumented Mexicans are estimated to comprise an additional 10 to 25 percent beyond the total Chicano population in this area (Cardenas, 1976; Bean, et al., 1982), although no precise estimate can be agreed upon. The imprecision of the estimate for San Antonio reflects the lack of solid data and unambiguous estimation techniques for undocumenteds in the United States as a whole (Sehgal and Violent, 1980; Heer, 1979). Despite inexact figures of the undocumented population for San Antonio, undocumented patterns do play an important role in the urban residential dynamics of the city.

Data on residences of undocumented Mexicans were collected from Immigration and Naturalization Service (INS) I–213 files in 1972 and 1979–80. Only records on apprehended Mexicans living in San Antonio were considered. Original samples of some 450 respondents each were taken from these files from the years 1972 and 1979–80.[3] From the I–213 form, the apprehendee's current address was assigned to a corresponding census tract. Data on census-tract location of the Chicano population were taken from the 1970 and 1980 Censuses. Thus, in this study, the census tract is the unit of analysis and pattern changes are analyzed over a ten-year period. Most studies of this nature on the Mexican-origin population have relied solely on city-wide summary measures to make inter-city comparisons. This is one of the first studies on Chicanos and undocumenteds to compare patterns by tracts for an entire city.

There may be criticism regarding the authenticity of the undocumented data, especially since the only respondents in our sample are those interviewed while detained by the INS. Nevertheless, we are reasonably confident that these respondents gave honest responses to INS inquiries. This confidence is based on the fact that the basic characteristics of our immigrant sample correspond to those of un-apprehended undocumenteds, and of immigrants in their places of origin, both studied by other researchers (Cardenas, 1976; Cardenas and Flores, 1978; Cornelius, 1978; Mines and de Janvry, 1982). In our sample, the respondents were all males. They tended to be young and in the United States less than a year during their current trip, and to have made multiple trips to and from Mexico in the last couple of years. They were mostly employed as unskilled laborers at minimal wages in the construction trades, assembly plants, light manufacturing, warehouses, and in the service sector. Although they are more transient and of a lower socioeconomic status, from a policy perspective it is this group whose impact on our nation is being debated rather than less-numerous, long-term, permanently-settled undocumented immigrants.

In order to facilitate comparisons, both undocumented and Chicano distributions are expressed as a given tract's proportion of the total individuals of this type. Furthermore, to standardize for tract population size, the resultant proportion is divided by the given tract's proportion of the total population of the city. The resultant ratio thus is a measure of the "relative density" of undocumenteds (or of Chicanos) in a given census tract (i.e., relative to the underlying population distribution). This is a more useful measure than simply the proportion alone, since it takes into consideration the relative population size of the tract. As an example, one might find 5 percent of the total undocumented sample in a partiicular tract, and 8 percent of the total population in that tract. The relative density figure for that tract would be $5/8 = 0.625$. The percentage figure alone (5 percent) would unrealistically inflate the density figure for that tract. Finally, to gauge changes in the density measure over the decade, the ratio of relative density in 1980 divided by relative density in 1970 was computed.

The economic status of census tracts was derived from Census Bureau data. Four aggregate measures were selected: median family income, median housing values, contract monthly rent, and rental units as percentage of total housing units by census tracts. These variables represent a partial measure of the socioeconomic status of the neighborhood at this subarea level. For the purpose of the study, these were used as independent variables influencing the residential patterns of both Mexican-origin groups.

Presentation of Data

Table 12.1 shows relative density ratios for undocumented Mexicans, Chicanos, and Anglos, for 1970 and 1980 (1972 and 1979–80 for undocumenteds). Those tracts with the highest density of both Mexican-origin populations are located in the central business district and on the west, south, and southwest sides of the city. Undocumenteds are, in general, much more concentrated than Chicanos. The highest

Table 12.1   Relative Density Ratios[a] For the Chicano, Undocumented Mexican, and Anglo
             Populations of San Antonio: Census Tract Series, c. 1970 and 1980

Tract series	Undocumenteds			Chicanos			Anglos		
	Rel. density:		1979/80÷	Rel. density:		1980÷	Rel. density:		1980÷
	1972	1979/80	1972	1970	1980	1970	1970	1980	1970
CBD 1100s	5.75	9.08	1.58	1.52	1.58	1.04	0.46	0.37	0.80
Northeast 1200s	0.02[b]	0.10[b]	5.00[b]	0.28	0.33	1.16	1.83	1.76	0.96
East 1300s	0.30	0.52	1.73	0.45	0.52	1.16	0.66	0.67	1.02
Southeast 1400s	0.20[b]	0.62	3.10[b]	0.72	0.98	1.36	1.38	1.07	0.78
South 1500s	0.83	0.79	0.95	1.46	1.61	1.08	0.68	0.49	0.72
Southwest 1600s	1.03	1.10	1.06	1.46	1.52	1.04	0.66	0.54	0.82
West 1700s	2.15	2.12	0.99	1.65	1.57	0.95	0.36	0.42	1.17
Northwest 1800s	0.06[b]	0.09[b]	1.50[b]	0.56	0.70	1.25	1.56	1.41	0.90
North 1900s	0.60	0.68	1.13	0.65	0.78	1.20	1.46	1.35	0.92
TOTAL POPULATION	426	403		366,504	457,659		371,787	434,247	

Notes: [a] Relative Density Ratio = the proportion of a particular group residing in a
        given tract series, divided by the proportion of the population as a whole
        residing in that series.

        [b] Based on fewer than 10 undocumenteds in census tract series.

Source: Undocumenteds: INS-213 forms from the San Antonio INS District.
        Chicanos and Anglos: US Census, 1970 and 1980.

concentration of Chicanos exhibited ratios of only approximately 1.7,
whereas undocumented ratios in the CBD were several times higher.
Chicanos and undocumenteds have lowest concentrations on the north,
east, northeast, northwest, and southeast sides of the city. It is in
these census tracts that Anglos (except for the east side which is
predominantly black) are over-represented. For instance, Anglos have
their highest ratio on the northeast side of the city where they

comprise a ratio of approximately 1.8 in both years. What emerges from this preliminary review is that the Mexican-origin population is relatively segregated from the Anglo population. Chicanos and un-documented Mexicans reach their peak concentrations in the same tract series, but undocumenteds are relatively much more clustered in a few tracts.

The third column for each group in Table 12.1 shows the changes in the relative density ratio by census tract series between 1970 and 1980. The census tract series with the greatest relative growth of undocumenteds, as well as of Chicanos, appear in the eastern and northwestern portions of the city—the areas with the lowest densities in 1970. In other words, there is apparently a dispersion of undoc-umenteds and Chicanos from their traditional areas on the west and south. Regarding the patterns of Chicano dispersion in the city, closer inspection of the high-growth tract series (the southeast, northwest, and north series) indicates two interesting patterns. In the southeast, the rapid-growth tracts are inside Interstate Loop 410 (see Figure 12.1), adjacent to tracts in which Chicanos are already concentrated. In the northwest and north, however, the rapid-growth tracts are along and outside of Loop 410. It is interesting that the "outer" of these three tract series experienced the greatest growth in a relative as well as an absolute sense. Between 1970 and 1980, between one-half and three-fourths of the growth of Chicanos in these series was in the outer tracts as opposed to tracts adjacent to the traditional Chicano core in the central city. Before drawing any inferences regarding residential shifts of this group, bear in mind that the majority of Chicanos continue to reside in central city tracts and adjacent areas. That is on an absolute level, Chicanos are only minimally located in tracts experiencing greater growth.

Regarding the Anglo population, the most notable occurrence is that between 1970 and 1980 the density ratio declined across all tract series save two—the west and the east. This stands in contrast to both undocumenteds and Chicanos, who increased their ratios all across the city. Apparently, Anglos are leaving areas in the CBD, south, and east for areas elsewhere in the city (especially, the north and far west sides). The density of Anglos drops on the north and far west sides for two reasons. First, the proportion of Chicanos has grown from 36 percent to 50 percent during this ten year span. Therefore, one would expect that Chicano residential dispersion would occur. Second, during this decade Chicanos have experienced an increase in socioeconomic status. This has resulted in their movement into higher status residential areas.

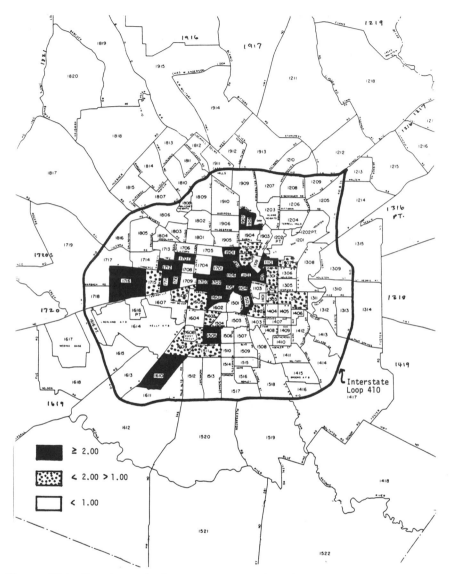

Figure 12.1   Density ratio for undocumenteds, 1972

A further graphic look at the spread of undocumenteds and Chicanos in San Antonio is gained by examination of maps at the level of census tracts (Figures 12.1–12.6). In 1972, undocumenteds were heavily concentrated (density ratio > 2.0) in 22 tracts in the CBD, west, and south sides (Figure 12.1); by 1979-80, 32 tracts in these areas exhibited heavy concentrations (Figure 12.2). Dispersion of undocumenteds into

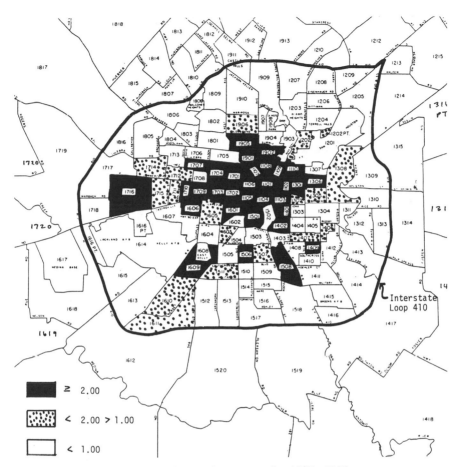

Figure 12.2   Density ratio for undocumenteds, 1979–1980

tracts adjacent to the CBD is very noticeable to the east and west; in addition, there are nonadjacent tracts to the south which show substantial growth (Figure 12.3). We are observing a phenomenon in which undocumenteds are being represented to a higher degree in the downtown and adjacent areas, as Chicanos and Anglos move outward in the city. It would be erroneous to conclude that displacement is occurring, however, because undocumented immigrants are probably still too small a population for any large scale displacement of Chicanos or any other group in this city.

The figures for Chicanos show no strong locational changes between 1970 and 1980 (Figures 12.4 and 12.5), but this is misleading in that even though relative densities remained low (less than 1.0) in both periods in peripheral areas such as the northside, southeast, and

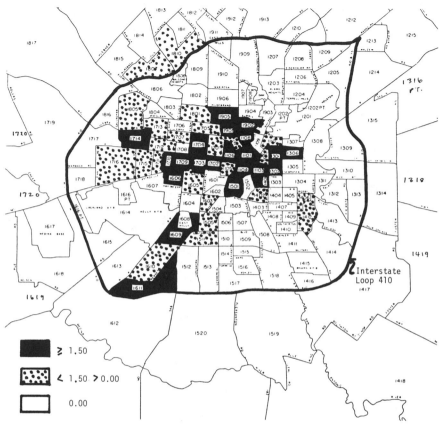

Figure 12.3   Ratio of undocumented density ratios, 1979/80 ÷ 1972.

southwest, the changes in these densities were pronounced in such areas (Figure 12.6). Chicanos are actually decentralizing faster than the population as a whole, to areas just outside Loop 410 in the northern and southwestern parts of San Antonio. Thus, Anglos are increasing most rapidly toward the margins of Bexar County, at the exurban fringe. Therefore, San Antonio represents the concentric model of residential succession at a grand (county-wide) scale.

Imbedded within the undocumented map patterns are two specific areas, encompassing 17 census tracts, which account for over half of the undocumenteds in both 1972 and in 1979-80. Their locations coincide with traditional transportation, warehousing, food processing, and manufacturing districts of the city. Ten tracts on the near-westside and CBD (1101, 1105, 1106, 1107; 1701, 1702, 1703, 1704, 1710, 1716) accounted for 50.4 percent of all undocumenteds in 1971, and 43.4 percent in 1979-80. The Southern Pacific and Missouri Pacific Railroads

Figure 12.4   Density ratio for Chicanos: 1970

meet in this area of trucking firms, cold storages, warehouses, food processing plants, and mechanical and repair shops. A second set of seven tracts on the near-southwest side (1501, 1505; 1601, 1605, 1606, 1609, 1610) accounted for 18.8 percent of all undocumented migrants in 1972, and 12.4 percent in 1979-80. This is the traditional manufacturing area of San Antonio, represented by meat packing, produce markets, stockyards, and some warehousing and transportation firms. Both areas are characterized by older dilapidated housing, small restaurants, bars, and other businesses that cater to the workers and residents living in adjacent neighborhoods. Undocumenteds are able to find ready work in enterprises located in both subareas, and it seems to be one of the major points of entry for undocumenteds arriving in the city.

We now turn to the relationship between these residential patterns and the socioeconomic status of areas of the city. Table 12.2 shows

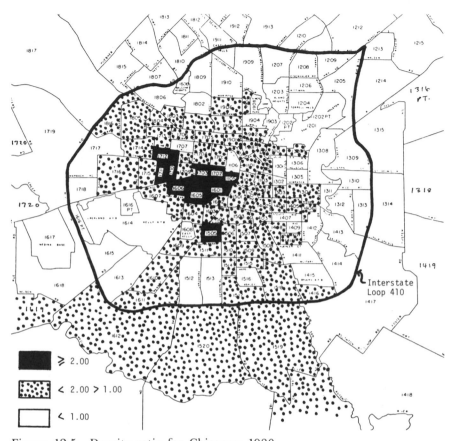

Figure 12.5   Density ratio for Chicanos: 1980

the economic status of census tract series in terms of median housing values, family income, contract monthly rent, and percent of units which were rental units, for both 1970 and 1980. The tract series with the lowest economic indicators tend to be those in the central business district and the west, south, southwest, and east sides of the city. With the exception of the east (the black area of San Antonio), these lower economic status subareas match those in which undocumented Mexicans and Chicanos are primarily concentrated (Table 12.1). Conversely, subareas with the highest economic indicators are those with the highest concentrations of Anglos. These are located on the north, northeast, and northwest sides of the city. It is worth noting that the relative status of these areas remained fairly consistent during this decade.

A more detailed analysis of these relationships may be carried out at census tract level (Table 12.3). In this analysis, we consider only

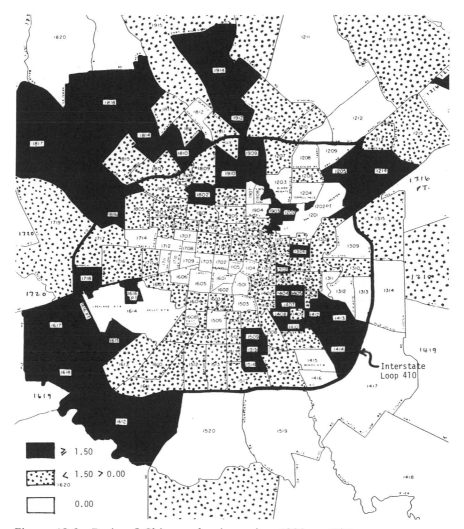

Figure 12.6   Ratio of Chicano density ratios, 1980 ÷ 1970

those tracts which had one or more sample undocumented immigrants in the given year. For 1972, there were 58 such tracts and in 1979-80, 67 tracts; these figures represent 36.5 percent and 42.1 percent, respectively, of the 159 tracts. These same tracts are employed for analyzing Chicano as well as undocumented patterns, so that the results will be comparable. In other words, we eliminate nearly 100 tracts and focus on the central, more economically-depressed area of the city where Chicanos and undocumenteds tend to coexist. The mean

Table 12.2 Economic Status Indicators of Census Tract Series, 1970 and 1980

Tract Series	Median family income		Median housing values		Median contract rent		Proportion of units which are rented	
	1970	1980	1970	1980	1970	1980	1970	1980
1100s CBD	$ 4,919	$ 8,700	$10,010	$20,750	$ 51	$ 99	.68	.69
1200s Northeast	15,972	22,669	19,688	55,700	120	264	.35	.33
1300s East	6,528	13,095	10,464	24,423	61	111	.28	.45
1400s Southeast	7,528	15,484	10,505	25,722	71	133	.29	.38
1500s South	6,348	13,352	8,836	20,379	60	116	.29	.32
1600s Southwest	6,310	13,243	8,611	20,150	64	137	.30	.36
1700s West	5,995	12,940	9,690	22,020	65	120	.28	.31
1800s Northeast	11,371	22,619	21,057	52,445	120	227	.22	.35
1900s North	12,621	22,991	23,387	55,562	128	219	.40	.44

Source: US Census, 1970 and 1980.

housing value for the 58 selected tracts in 1970 was $10,262, as opposed to a figure of $18,563 for the remaining tracts.

The results in Table 12.3 indicate, in general, that both Chicanos and undocumenteds tend to be more concentrated in those tracts with lower socioeconomic status. The only exception appears to be a low (essentially zero) correlation between the rental percentage and the relative density measure for Chicanos. This difference might be explained by the highly variable percentages of rental units among lower income areas of San Antonio compared to other large metropolitan areas; thus, this variable may not be as strong a measure of economic status here as in other cities. The signs for undocumenteds are all in the appropriate directions, with median family income and rental percentage being most closely related. The existence of undocumenteds in rental subareas of the city might be explained by the composition of the sample—single young males seeking temporary housing. It is interesting that the relationships for undocumenteds increase substantially between 1970 and 1980, indicating that they were more tied to economically disadvantaged areas in 1979-80 than in 1972. This

Table 12.3   Correlation Coefficients Between Relative Density Ratios and Socioeconomic Variables by Census Tracts, 1970 and 1980[a]

Socioeconomic variables	Undocumenteds		Chicanos	
	1970	1980	1970	1980
Median family income	-.15	-.44	-.51	-.49
Median housing values	-.07	-.21	-.56	-.59
Median contract rent	-.25	-.33	-.63	-.59
Percent of rental units	+.30	+.54	-.06	.12
N=	58	67	58	67

NOTE: [a]The socioeconomic variables for 1970 and 1980 are related to the Chicano residential densities for 1970 and 1980, and the undocumented residential densities for 1972 and 1979/80.

finding supports our earlier map analyses showing increased concentrations of undocumenteds in the downtown area as other groups move outward. For Chicanos, the relationships are generally higher (which is to be expected, given the better data base), and do not change significantly over the decade. Thus, undocumenteds have become increasingly associated with the downtown area, while Chicanos have maintained their dual association with the downtown area and with better-off sectors radiating out from there.

Discussion and Conclusions

These data indicate that undocumented immigrants have become more strongly associated with the central area of San Antonio in recent years, as the population as a whole has moved outward into higher-status areas of the city. Census tracts in the CBD and the adjacent west and southwest sides have exhibited substantial increases in relative densities of undocumenteds—particularly in the traditional industrial, transportation, and warehousing zone. Chicano patterns have been marked by movement outward in the city paralleling the general movement outward. The most pronounced Chicano percentage growth has been along Loop 410, and even absolute growth has been greater there, although the Chicano population remains strongly concentrated in areas adjacent to the traditional CBD and westside. Both undocumenteds and Chicanos continue to have their highest densities associated with the most economically-depressed areas. Although this trend is increasing for undocumenteds, it tends to be decreasing for Chicanos.

The notion of Mexican immigrants displacing Chicanos is not substantiated by these data. At the aggregate level, Chicanos continue to reside in their traditional areas in large numbers, even though undocumenteds are concentrating in these same neighborhoods. Undocumenteds probably find these areas attractive because they can find affordable housing adjacent to their principal sources of employment in the central city. On a cultural level, institutions within these areas provide greater adaptive facilitation for new residents than would other areas of the city. That is, within these neighborhoods, Mexican immigrants will find Spanish-speaking businesses and institutions such as retail stores, churches, newspapers, restaurants, and bars. In these communities the undocumented is likely to be less obvious than in other areas.

One conclusion from our correlation analysis is that the coefficients for residential patterns versus socioeconomic status are much stronger for Chicanos than undocumenteds. This is partially explained by the better data on Chicanos. However, another factor—the single status of the undocumented—may help to explain why immigrants are less tied to lower socioeconomic housing characteristics. For example, undocumenteds may live in poor rental housing in low-income neighborhoods, or in poor rental housing in more middle-income areas (often in Chicano neighborhoods), or in areas being gentrified (where housing values are in transition from low to high), or even in private homes in upper-class areas of the city. On the other hand, the Chicano data encompasses a population which is made up largely of family units. We suspect that the economic status of an area is a more important determining factor for a family, than for a single, transient individual.

Until more and better data are available, the conclusion that economic factors determine undocumented residential patterns is speculative (see also Moore and Mittlebach, 1966; Grebler, et al., 1970; and Lopez, 1981, on income as a determinant of residential location among the Mexican-origin population). Rather than these residential patterns being related to economic factors, the patterns might be a result of a selective process at the individual level. Proximity to job and particular kinship/friendship ties are two factors which would upset any interpretation strictly tied to the economic status of residential areas.

What these data do indicate is that despite pronounced decentralization of Chicanos in the city, undocumented Mexicans and Chicanos continue to reside together in segregated neighborhoods in San Antonio. A large proportion of both lower and higher status ethnics still find themselves living either in mixed Chicano/undocumented areas of the central city (near westside and southside), or in such areas adjacent to the above, largely inside Loop 410. This segregation may be actually enhanced by the constant flow of undocumented Mexicans entering this city.

The social significance of being confined to ethnically homogeneous areas is that it enhances those properties among the Mexican-origin group that socially define them as a minority group in this society (see Sumner, 1906; Wagley and Harris, 1958). For instance, being confined to these areas contributes to their unequal treatment; the maintenance of cultural characteristics that distinguish them from the larger society; low rates of intermarriage; and an awareness of their subordinate status; all of which collectively contribute to their minority status. We speculate that the continued segregation of these areas contributes to the perception of this group as a social minority by the minority group as well as by the majority group. Further research in this area might reveal how residential segregation between middle-class and lower-class Mexican origin groups contributes to the perpetuation of negative self-perceptions.

How similar are these residential patterns to those of other cities with larger undocumented populations than San Antonio—e.g., Houston, Dallas–Fort Worth, and Los Angeles? We suspect that there is more segregation of the undocumented population in these cities than in San Antonio. For example, in Los Angeles (where estimates of the undocumented population run up to one million) there have emerged specific subareas where Mexican immigrants are highly concentrated. Apparently, the larger the undocumented population in a city, the greater the tendency for emergence of specialized subareas which cater to the needs and desires of this population. The proportion of sojourners as opposed to long-term immigrants may be another distinction between San Antonio and other cities with larger undocumented populations. We suspect that cities such as San Antonio, with a greater proportion of long-term immigrant residents, are more likely to be integrated into the Chicano population, than those cities with more temporary immigrants. These are issues that are beyond data presently available to us.

Notes

1. Research on undocumented immigrants from Mexico to the U.S. has focused on: (a) push and pull factors motivating the migration; (b) regional settlement patterns; (c) impacts of the undocumenteds' migration on Mexico, on the U.S., and on the migrant population themselves; and (d) theoretical issues related to the internationalization of both economies and their mutual dependencies on this immigration process.

2. The geographic area of this study is inclusive of all Bexar County, including areas outside of incorporated San Antonio with the exception of the military bases. Hereafter, reference to San Antonio in the text will be to this larger entity.

3. The INS I-213 file records for the San Antonio District (88 counties in South Texas) only go back as far as 1972; therefore, this sample was drawn from that year instead of 1970. Also, for the 1980 files many of the forms were incomplete; thus, some of the sample had to be drawn from 1979.

References

Bean, Frank D., and W. Parker Frisbee. 1978. *The Demography of Racial and Ethnic Groups.* New York: Academic Press.

Bean, Frank D., Allan G. King, Robert D. Benford, and Laura B. Perkinson. 1982. "Estimates of number of illegal migrants in the state of Texas." Texas Population Research Center, Paper Series 4. Austin: University of Texas.

Cardenas, Gilberto. 1976. "Manpower impact and problem of Mexican illegal aliens in an urban labor market." Ph.D. dissertation, University of Illinois.

Cardenas, Gilberto, and Ray Flores. 1976. "A study of the demographic and employment characteristics of undocumented aliens in San Antonio, El Paso, and McAllen." San Antonio: Avante Systems, for the Texas Advisory Committee.

Cornelius, Wayne. 1978. *Mexican Migration to the United States: Causes, Consequences, and U.S. Responses.* Cambridge: Center for International Studies, Massachusetts Institute of Technology.

Duncan, Otis, and Beverly Duncan. 1957. *The Negro Population of Chicago.* Chicago: University of Chicago Press.

Grebler, Leo, Ralph Guzman, and Joan W. Moore. 1970. *The Mexican-American People.* New York: The Free Press.

Guest, Avery M., and James Weed. 1976. "Ethnic residential segregation: Patterns of change." *American Journal of Sociology* 81:1088–1122.

Hawley, Amos. 1950. *Human Ecology: A Theory of Community Structure.* New York: Ronald Press.

Heer, David. 1979. "What is the annual net flow of undocumented Mexican immigrants to the United States?" *Demography* 16(3):417–23.

Hwang, Sean-Shong, and Steve H. Murdock. 1982. "Residential segregation in Texas in 1980." *Social Science Quarterly* 63:737–47.

Lieberson, Stanley. 1963. *Ethnic Patterns in American Cities.* New York: The Free Press.

Lopez, Manuel M. 1981. "Patterns of interethnic residential segregation in the urban Southwest, 1960 and 1970." *Social Science Quarterly* 62 (March):50–63.

Massey, Douglas. 1979. "Residential segregation of Spanish Americans in United States urbanized areas." *Demography* 16 (November):553–63.

Mines, Richard, and Adain de Janvry. 1982. "Migration to the United States and Mexican rural development: A case study." *American Journal of Agricultural Economics* 64 (August):444–54.

Moore, Joan W., and Frank G. Mittlebach. 1966. "Residential segregation in the urban Southwest: A comparative study." Mexican American Study Project, Advanced Report 4. Los Angeles: University of California Press.

Park, Robert E. 1916. "The city: Suggestions for the investigations of human behavior in the human environment." *American Journal of Sociology* 20:577–612.

Park, Robert E., Ernest Burgess, and R.D. McKenzie, eds. 1925. *The City*. Chicago: University of Chicago Press.

Pendelton, William W. 1973. "Blacks in suburbs." In Louis Massotti and Jeffrey Hadded, eds., *The Urbanization of the Suburbs*. Beverly Hills: Sage Publications.

Roberts, Kenneth D. 1978. "Estimating the approximate size of the illegal alien population in the United States by the comparative trend analysis of age-specific death rates." *Demography* 17:159–76.

Sehgal, Ellen, and Joyce Violent. 1980. "Documenting the undocumented: Data, like aliens, are elusive." *Monthly Labor Review* 103 (October):18–21.

Sumner, William G. 1906. *Folkways*. New York: Ginn.

Taeuber, Karl, and Alma Taeuber. 1965. *Negroes in Cities*. Chicago: Aldeneum.

U.S. Bureau of the Census. 1981. *Census of Population: 1980*. Summary Tape 1B for Texas. Washington, D.C.: USGPO.

U.S. Bureau of Census. 1974. *Characteristics of the Spanish Surname Population by Census Tract, for SMSA's in Texas: 1970*. Washington, D.C.: USGPO.

Wagley, Charles, and Marvin Harris. 1958. *Minorities in the New World: Six Case Studies*. New York: Columbia University Press.

Index

The Editor and Contributors

Richard C. Jones is an Associate Professor of Geography at the University of Texas at San Antonio. He holds a Ph.D. in Geography from the Ohio State University (1973). He has published studies on undocumented migration in the *Annals, Association of American Geographers, Economic Geography, The Journal of Geography*, and *The Social Science Quarterly*. His published research also includes work on Venezuelan migration, regional development, and agricultural land use. His current research centers upon structural factors stimulating undocumented migration from sending areas in Mexico.

Jorge A. Bustamante is General Director of the Centro de Estudios Fronterizos del Norte de Mexico, in Tijuana, and one of the world's foremost specialists in border transactions and international migration. His Ph.D., in Sociology, is from Notre Dame University. He is the author of *Mexico-Estados Unidos: Bibliografía General sobre Estudios Fronterizos* (1980); of chapters in several edited volumes on U.S.-Mexican relations; of numerous articles in U.S. and Mexican journals, including the *American Journal of Sociology, The American Behavioral Scientist, The International Migration Review*, and *Fronteras;* and of a regular column in the Mexican newspaper *Uno Mas Uno*. His current research is on Americanisms in the speech of Mexicans from different regions of the country.

W. Tim Dagodag is a Professor of Geography at California State University, Northridge. He obtained his Ph.D. in Geography from the University of Oregon in 1972. His past research has emphasized migration from Mexico to the United States, Mexican-American housing patterns, and institutional discrimination in urban housing. Currently, he is researching patterns of disease among the Hispanic population of Los Angeles.

Phillip R. Guttierrez is Coordinator and Instructor of the High School Equivalency Program at Lamar Community College, Lamar, Colorado. He completed his M.A. in Geography at the University of Arkansas in 1981. Guttierrez's family has lived in the San Luis Valley of Colorado (the focus of his research) for three generations. He is interested in a number of empirical and policy aspects of undocumented migrants in the United States, particularly in the Intermontane Region. He has given several papers on his research, at national and regional meetings of geographic associations.

Richard J. Harris is an Associate Professor of Sociology at the University of Texas at San Antonio. He received his Ph.D. in Sociology from Cornell University in 1976. Previous publications include work on migration, comparative family orientations, and fertility, in such journals as *Population Review, Canadian Studies in Population,* and *The Social Science Quarterly.* He is co-editor of *The Politics of San Antonio: Community, Progress, and Power* (1983). In addition to studies of undocumented migration, he is currently working on demographic aspects of aging in the United States.

Douglas S. Massey is an Assistant Professor in the Department of Sociology, Graduate Group in Demography, The University of Pennsylvania. His Ph.D., in Sociology, is from Princeton University (1978). His research interests include international migration, residential segregation, and labor market problems of Hispanics. His publications include articles in the *American Journal of Sociology, The International Migration Review, Demography, Social Forces, The American Sociological Review,* and *Economic Geography.*

Richard Mines is a Visiting Research Economist in the Department of Agricultural Economics, The University of California at Davis, and a consultant (formerly a Visiting Research Fellow) at the Center for U.S.-Mexican Studies, The University of California at San Diego. He received his Ph.D. in Agricultural Economics from the University of California at Berkeley (1980). He has published articles and monographs concerning the impact of emigration on rural development in Mexican sending areas, and on the role of Mexican nationals in U.S. labor markets.

Joshua S. Reichert is the Inter-American Foundation representative for Mexico. He obtained his Ph.D. in Social Anthropology from Princeton University in 1979. IIe has published on a variety of topics including social change, economic development, and the impact of international labor migration on sending societies, in such journals as *The International Migration Review, Human Organization,* and *Social Problems.*

Kenneth D. Roberts is currently a Visiting Research Fellow at the Center for U.S.-Mexican Studies at the University of California at San Diego (1983-84), on leave from his teaching position at Southwestern University, Georgetown, Texas. His Ph.D. in Economics was earned from the University of Wisconsin at Madison. His major research effort has been the effects of changes in agricultural technology on the income and employment of peasant farmers in Mexico. This research has led him to the issue of outmigration factors in U.S. labor migration, and to reevaluations of studies which attempt to estimate numbers of Mexican undocumenteds in the U.S. He has published articles and monographs on each of these topics.

Avelardo Valdez is an Assistant Professor of Sociology at the University of Texas at San Antonio. His Ph.D. in Sociology is from the University of California at Los Angeles (1979). His publications focus on the assimilation of the Mexican-origin population in the U.S., on changes in intermarriage propensities of Mexican-American men in San Antonio, and on changing lifestyles and levels of life satisfaction among working-class Chicanos, in addition to his work on urban residential patterns of undocumenteds and Chicanos.

Raymond E. Wiest, Associate Professor of Anthropology at the University of Manitoba, holds a doctorate in Anthropology from the University of Oregon (1970). He has published several articles on the topics of household structure and migration, return migration and development, and conjugal roles and fertility control, all in Michoacán, Mexico. He is currently engaged in follow-up research in the Mexican community (Acuitzio del Canje, Michoacán) where he has been doing research for over ten years, and an interdisciplinary project on river bank erosion and forced relocation of people in Bangladesh.